International Economic Policies in a Globalized World

Seiichi Katayama · Heinrich W. Ursprung
Editors

International Economic Policies in a Globalized World

With 16 Figures
and 4 Tables

 Springer

Professor Seiichi Katayama

RIEB, Kobe University
Rokkodai, Nada-ku, Kobe
Japan 657-8501
Email: katayama@rieb.kobe-u.ac.jp

Professor Heinrich W. Ursprung

Department of Economics
University of Konstanz
Box D138
78457 Konstanz
Germany
Email: heinrich.ursprung@uni-konstanz.de

HF
1359
.I67
2004

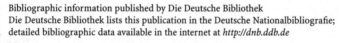

Bibliographic information published by Die Deutsche Bibliothek
Die Deutsche Bibliothek lists this publication in the Deutsche Nationalbibliografie;
detailed bibliographic data available in the internet at *http://dnb.ddb.de*

ISBN 3-540-21461-5 Springer Berlin Heidelberg New York

Springer is a part of Springer Science+Business Media
springeronline.com

© Springer-Verlag Berlin Heidelberg 2004
Printed in Germany

Cover design: Erich Kirchner, Heidelberg
Production: Helmut Petri
Printing: betz-druck

Printed on acid-free paper – 42/3130 – 5 4 3 2 1 0

Preface

In this volume we collected some of the papers that were presented at the RIEB (The Research Institute for Economics and Business Administration) International Conference at Kobe University on March 25 and 26, 2000. The contributions invited for presentation all dealt with specific aspects of the conference topic "Trade Policy: Political Economy and Dynamic Issues". In the meantime the papers collected in this volume have been revised, and some of them have been published in professional journals. This volume thus contains published as well as hitherto unpublished contributions.

We are grateful to all the authors and the conference participants, especially to those who cheerfully served as discussants and chairpersons. Our thanks also go to our colleagues at the RIEB for their encouragement, and especially to the RIEB's Director, Professor Shoji Nishijima for his support of the project. We are also grateful to Professor Arye Hillman at Bar-Ilan University, who kindly read parts of the manuscript and supplied useful comments and suggestions. In the editorial process we were fortunate to be able to rely on an excellent and able team: we are extremely grateful to Minako Okuno, Yuji Fujinaka, Tetsuya Saito for their outstanding work and to Shinya Horie who undertook the pains taking job and completed the camera-ready copy for publication. We are also grateful to Professor Charles Noussair of Emory University who kindly supplied suggestions.

Finally, we wish to gratefully acknowledge the support received from the Center of Excellence Project of the Ministry of Science and Education, the Murata Science Foundation, and the Rokkokai Foundation. Seiichi Katayama also acknowledges the Grant-in-Aid for Scientific Research of the Ministry of Education and Science.

Seiichi Katayama, Kobe University
Heinrich Ursprung, University of Konstanz

Acknowledgements to the Publishers

The editors and the publisher wish to thank Elsevier Science who has kindly given permission for the use of copyright material with regards to the following articles.

Das S (2001) Endogenous distribution and the political economy of trade policy, European Journal of Political Economy, 17 (3): 465-491

Katayama S, Ursprung H (2003) Commercial culture, political culture and the political economy of trade policy: The case of Japan, Journal of Economic Behavior and Organization, forthcoming

Epstein G, Hillman A (2002) Unemployed immigrants and voter sentiment in the welfare state, Journal of Public Economics

Bradford S (2003) Protection and jobs: explaining the structure of trade barriers across industries, Journal of International Economics

Martin R (2002) An elementary proposition concerning parallel imports, Journal of International Economics, 56 (1): 233-45

Knox D, Martin R (2003) Trade policy and parallel imports, European Journal of Political Economy, 19 (1): 133-151

Contents

Book Title:

Introduction

F13
F15

Seiichi Katayama[1] and Heinrich W. Ursprung[2]

[1] Research Institute for Economics and Business Administration, Kobe University, Rokkodai-cho, Nada-ku, Kobe 657, Japan katayama@rieb.kobe-u.ac.jp
[2] Department of Economics, University of Konstanz, Box D-138, 78457 Konstanz, Germany Heinrich.Ursprung@uni-konstanz.de

Global economic integration has taken place as the consequence of reciprocal trade liberalization, financial capital movements and international direct investment, more open immigration policies in richer countries, as well as enhanced international communication. The ten papers in this volume study political-economy aspects of policies induced by globalization: while there have been efficiency gains, the resolution of the associated domestic income-redistribution consequences of globalization has in general involved political processes. The papers are divided into two groups, with the first group being concerned with issues of trade policy and the second considering policies with regard to immigration, the environment, foreign aid, and competition.

As a group, the research papers in the first part of the volume not only cover key policy issues that are driven by the globalization process but also provide a comprehensive review of the modeling approaches of endogenous policy theory: the view of the median voter as decisive in determining policy, the view of political decision makers influenced by lobbying, the view of decision makers as choosing policy to maximize political support, the view of policy determined through electoral competition, and the view of policy as determined bye corrupt political decision makers designing policy for their own self-benefit. The traditions, respectively, of Mayer (1984) [5], Findley and Wellisz (1982) [1], Hillman (1982) [2], Young and Magee (1986) [8], Hillman and Ursprung (1988) [3], and Grossman and Helpman (1994) [4] therefore all make their appearance. This volume may therefore be valuable not only for scholars specializing in political economy and globalization but also for (graduate) teaching.

The first part of the volume is about *The political economy of trade policy*. The lead paper by Satya Das, employs the *median voter approach* in a dynamic Heckscher-Ohlin framework with overlapping generations of heterogeneous households to examine the long-run interdependence between trade policy and wealth and income distribution. Satya Das thus investigates arguably the most important feedback mechanism between the state of the economy and trade policy. The standard political economy analysis that proceeds from exogenous factor ownership is augmented by introduction of the channels that influence factor ownership. The consequent model of endogenous trade policy incorporates reverse causality that allows characterization for the first time of aspects of the long-run development of trade policy.

Chapter 2 provides an application of the *lobbying approach* to modeling endogenous protection. Since firms lobbying for a tariff provide an industry-specific public good, one would expect industry concentration to exert a positive influence on tariff protection. Most empirical investigations do however not find much support for this hypothesis suggested by Mancur Olson's analysis of collective action ([6]), Ngo Van Long attempts to uncover the source of this empirical ambiguity. Rather than using the standard setting of a Cournot oligopoly producing a homogenous product, he analyzes the case of Bertrand competition with differentiated products. This case is not only more realistic; it also permits questions to be asked that could not be investigated within the standard approach, such as for example whether an increase in substitutability among the differentiated products leads tariffs to increase or decrease? Or how does lobbying affect the average price in an industry and the variance of the distribution of product prices?

As with the lobbying approach, the *political support function approach* was introduced to endogenous trade policy in the early 1980s. In Chapter 3 Kong-Pin Chen, Cheng-Zhong Qin and Larry D. Qiu use this approach to investigate the stability of multinational trade liberalization agreements. They show, in a three-country model, how under particular circumstances circular concessions can be the only way to achieve Pareto-improving trade liberalization. The stabilizing property of multinational trade liberalization treaties derives from the fact that the opportunistic behavior of one country can be punished not only by the victim of the opportunistic behavior but also by third parties.

Chapter 4 investigates the cultural determinants of trade policy. Globalization is, after all, not only an economic phenomenon: global economic integration has significant consequences for cultural change in the long run. In our own contribution to this volume, we therefore asked how globalization influences - through cultural change - political polarization in general and trade policy in particular. Our endogenous tariff model is based on the *electoral competition approach* and captures crucial aspects of the (changes in) Japanese commercial and political culture represented through standards of fairness and trust. The complex interaction of the commercial and political culture is shown to significantly influence trade policy polarization. The stylized facts of Japanese politics suggest compatibility between the predictions of the model and the policy positions held by Japanese politicians over the last fifty years.

The last contribution in the first part of the volume is in the tradition of the *corruption approach* to portraying trade policy. Scott Bradford's model, while incorporating the crucial characteristic of the protection for sale approach, namely the explicit quid pro quo nature of the political contributions, is however not a generalization of the Grossman-Helpman model but rather is an alternative that stresses in particular the role of the labor markets in endogenous trade policy. The model is tested using US data. The empirical results provide strong evidence that protection increases with the number of workers in an industry, indicating that the standard Grossman-Helpman specification where internal characteristics of a group do not affect the endogenous policy outcome is not appropriate.

The second part of this volume is about *The political economy of international relations*. The studies here focus on other policies beyond trade policy that influence international relations. The effects of globalization through immigration and the environment have attracted the attention of policymakers, voters, and the media. In Chapter 6 Arye Hillman and Gil Epstein consider whether unemployed immigrants whose incomes are publicly financed need necessarily give rise to adverse sentiment from self-interested or non-altruistic voters. The model they formulate takes unemployment to be explained by efficiency wages, and they show that native workers can benefit from the presence of unemployed immigrants receiving tax-financed income transfers. This is because, according to the efficiency-wage hypothesis, there will exist a pool of unemployed workers acting as a labor-market disciplining mechanism; in the model immigrants disproportionately serve the function of populating the pool of the disciplining unemployed. Hillman and Epstein point out that, while their conclusions are a logical implication of the efficiency-wage hypothesis, the conclusions rely on unemployed immigrants being credibly willing or able to accept job offers that are made, and on the persistence of immigrants as disproportionately represented in the unemployment pool − and on unemployment of the immigrants indeed being explained by the efficiency-wage hypothesis.

Economists have analyzed effects of globalization on the environment and on environmental policy (a survey of the literature is provided by [7]). In Chapter 7 Kiyono and Ishikawa study global warming due to carbon leakages. Carbon leakages are defined to occur when a large country imposes an emission tax, thereby decreasing the world market price for fuel, with the consequence that global demand for fuel increases, as do then greenhouse gas emissions in other countries. Carbon leakages do not occur if decentralized environmental regulation is based on a quota system. Emission tax and quota equivalence therefore holds only in the absence of carbon leakage. Kiyono and Ishikawa examine the strategic non-equivalence between taxes and quotas by constructing a three country model with two large fuel consuming countries with mutual carbon leakages and a third fuel-exporting country that does not itself consume fuel.

Chapter 8 looks at foreign aid. Sajal Lahiri proceeds from the well-established fact that donors experience difficulties in ensuring that aid reaches the intended domestic targets. This is rather surprising since one would expect governments in the recipient countries to be obliged to honor donors' wishes as a precondition for obtaining additional future aid. To shed light on the interaction between aid donors and recipients, Lahiri develops a model in which a donor allocates a fixed amount of aid to two recipient countries. He assumes that in each recipient country an organized interest group bribes the government in order to divert some of the aid away from the intended use. The interaction between the recipient countries' governments and the lobby groups are portrayed using the corruption approach in the tradition of Grossman and Helpman. An interesting insight from the model is that countries with more corrupt governments may, ceteris paribus, receive a higher share of the total available aid.

The final two chapters relate trade policy issues to industrial organization: the topic is competition policy in open economies. Chapter 9 focuses on competition policy in a globalized world where competition policy is confronted with slicing up of the production chain. Chapter 10 considers the more specific aspect of the political choice of a parallel importing regime and tariff policy in a setting of international price discrimination by a monopolist.

Yano and Dei observe, in Chapter 9, that competition and tariff policies are substitutes, since large countries can either restrain domestic competition or impose a tariff in order to conduct a beggar-thy-neighbor policy. Since the GATT/WTO regime rules out the use of tariffs, the attention of policy makers is directed to non-tariff measures such as domestic competition policy, which is not restricted by international agreements. The objective of Yano and Dei is to characterize the national-welfare maximizing degree of market concentration. The model has the typical flavor of the industrial organization literature: in each of two countries, upstream firms use labor to produce a country-specific intermediate good. The downstream sector combines the two intermediate products to produce a single consumption good. The intermediate goods are tradable but not the consumption goods. Whereas the intermediate-good markets are perfectly competitive, the downstream sector's competitiveness is determined through welfare-maximizing competition policy.

The final chapter analyzes a special aspect of competition policy that has received a great deal of attention, especially in the context of pharmaceuticals trade: Martin Richardson's study deals with parallel imports, that is, the import of genuine goods into a country without the authorization of the intellectual property right holder in that country. The study first shows, through a model of international price discrimination by a monopolist, that parallel import regimes will always be implemented by welfare-maximizing governments if the choice set of the involved countries is restricted to either allowing parallel imports or not. Richardson then goes on to show that this result continues to hold in a model of joint choice of tariffs and the parallel import regime. The optimal tariff is actually lower in the presence of parallel imports than in its absence, which may imply that the tariff reduction is sufficiently beneficial to the monopolist that overall profitability is higher in the presence of parallel imports. Why then do we not observe all countries permitting parallel imports? Since discrimination need not be more profitable to the monopolist, admitting parallel imports may well imply an income redistribution that can

be contested through the political process. In a political-economy modification of his model, Richardson demonstrates that the prohibition of parallel
imports is more likely to emerge, the more the government cares about lobbying contributions of the global monopolist and the greater are profits from
price discrimination.

References

1. Findley R, Wellisz S (1982) Endogenous tariffs, the political economy of trade
   restrictions, and welfare, In: Bhagwati J (eds.) Import competition and response,
   Chicago, University of Chicago Press: 223-234
2. Hillman AL (1982) Declining industries and political-support protectionist motives, American Economic Review 72: 1180-1187
3. Hillman AL and Ursprung HW (1988) Domestic politics, foreign interests and
   international trade policy, American Economic Review 78: 729-745
4. Grossman G, Helpman E (1994) Protection for sale, American Economic Review
   84: 833-850
5. Mayer W (1984) Endogenous tariff formation, American Economic Review 74:
   970-985
6. Olson M (1965) The logic of collective action: Public goods and the theory of
   groups, Cambridge, MA, Harvard University Press
7. Schulze G, Ursprung H (eds.) (2001) International environmental economics: A
   survey of the issues, Oxford, Oxford University Press
8. Young L, Magee S (1986) Endogenous protection, factor returns and resource
   allocation, Review of Economic Studies 53: 407-419

The Political Economy of Trade Policy

Part I

The Political Economy of Trade Policy

Endogenous Distribution and the Political Economy of Trade Policy[*]

Satya P. Das

Indian Statistical Institute, Delhi Centre, 7 S.J.S. Sansanwal Marg, New Delhi 110016, India. das@isid.ac.in

1 Introduction

There are two discernible approaches to the political economy of trade policy. One emphasizes representative democracy. There are pressure groups for or against some form of trade protection through lobbying efforts (e.g. [8], [9], [7], [10] among many others). While Hillman and Ursrung, for example, emphasize political competition where candidates seek to win elections and are drawn by the compulsion of the desire to win political office, Grossman and Helpman portray a politician as selling protection. The other approach characterizes trade policy as emerging from direct democracy or voting. Theoretical works include [11], [12], and [13]. An empirical analysis of trade policy legislation in a direct democracy is undertaken by [18].

The underlying scenario, common to both approaches, is that a country's population is heterogeneous in terms of factor ownership. Therefore, trade policy changes have asymmetric effects on individual welfare and generate, through lobbying or voting, asymmetric pressure on policy. An equilibrium trade policy in some sense is the outcome. An implicit assumption underlying both approaches is that factor ownerships are exogenous.

In reality, however, factor ownership changes over time. For example, many developed countries have experienced a substantial increase in wealth and income inequality in recent years. It then makes sense that factor-distributional changes should be taken into account in understanding the political economy process of trade policy setting. In other words, it must be recognized

[*] Many thanks are due to a referee for comments that led to refocusing of the paper. Editorial remarks from Arye Hillman are appreciated. I also thank the participants of a trade conference, held at Kobe University in March 2000, in which a previous version of this paper was presented. Much of this paper was completed during my visit to Rutgers University and the Economic Policy Research Institute, University of Copenhagen during the summer of 1999. Warm hospitality at both institutions is appreciated. I bear solely the responsibility of remaining errors.

that trade policy as well as factor ownership distribution are endogenous and jointly dependent on other basic parameters of a market economy. The existing literature has emphasized the causal link from factor distribution to trade policy. Here, I emphasize this causal link, as well as that from trade policy to factor distribution in a simultaneous way.

The task is clearly difficult, however. First, individual heterogeneity has to be recognized at a more primitive level, which would imply unequal distribution of factor ownership. Second, in order for ownership to change, some primary factors have to be treated as tradable assets − as they are in reality. Thus, changes in commodity and asset prices, due to a change in trade policy or other basic parameters, need to be ascertained. Third, there is a built-in dynamics because of factor ownership changes. This paper sets out to make a beginning by presenting a very specific and simple version of the standard Heckscher-Ohlin economy in which there is distributional dynamics but no aggregate dynamics, and in which policy is viewed as resulting from a majority voting process. Thus, I do not deal with lobbying. The model builds upon the important work of [12].[1]

In the process, the analysis of this paper extends the existing literature on two fronts. First, from the perspective of political economy, the new element here is how long-run effects on trade policy − along with changes in distribution − may differ from short-run effects without distributional changes. Second, in comparison to the recent research on the effects of trade policy changes on personal distribution of wealth and income within a trading country, namely [5], [6], the model predicts how variations in the circumstances facing a trading economy (other than the level of protection) causes distributional changes in the long-run via politically induced changes in the level of protection.

One finding of the paper is that an increase in the international price of the labour- (capital-) intensive good facing a small open Heckscher-Ohlin economy implies a decrease (an increase) in trade protection in the short-run. The effects in the long run are similar qualitatively but greater in magnitude than the short-run effects. Moreover, the wealth-income inequality decreases or increases as the international price of the labour- or capital-intensive good rises.

Another finding is that an increase in the endowment of land (fixed capital) may, in the short-run, lead to an increase or a decrease in trade protection, depending on how the incremental land endowment is initially distributed. In the long run, however, trade protection falls unambiguously. Hence, short-

---

[1] It is noteworthy that there exists evidence to the effect that mixed asset ownerships affect votes. For instance, [17] presents an interesting empirical analysis of how portfolio diversification (i.e. mixed asset ownerships) influenced votes in the repeal of Corn Laws in the 19th century Britain. She uses the specific-factors rather than the Heckscher-Ohlin framework.

run and long-run effects may be quite opposite. Furthermore, inequality may increase or decrease.

More than the specific results, the paper demonstrates that analyzing trade protection through political economy along with endogenous distribution of factorownership is not an intractable task.

The basic model is laid out in Section 2. Section 3 examines transitional dynamics and the steady state. Effects of parametric changes are analyzed in Section 4. Section 5 considers consumption and production interventions. Section 6 concludes the paper.

2 The Model

Consider the standard 2×2 small open economy. The goods are x and y, respectively, imported and exported. To fix ideas, let the import sector be labour-intensive and let p^* denote its international price in terms of good y, the numeraire good. Assume that an import tariff/subsidy (or, equivalently, an export tariff/subsidy) is the policy instrument that is set through the political process.

The production function in each sector is Cobb-Douglas: $Q_j = A_j L_j^{\alpha_j} K^{1-\alpha_j}$, $j = x, y$, $0 < \alpha_j < 1$. The Q's, L's and K's are the respective outputs, labour and employed. Sector x being labour intensive, $\theta \equiv \alpha_x - \alpha_y > 0$. The K-input is non-reproducible and hence, called land rather than capital; K is its endowment. There are two perfectly substitutable assets: land and loans. Goods markets and trade policy relating to commodity markets being our focus, it is assumed that there is no international borrowing or lending.[2]

Each individual in the economy possesses a unit of non-tradable endowment of labour that is supplied inelastically to the market. The number of households and the total endowment of labour are normalized to one. Then K is also the mean land holding. All markets are perfectly competitive.

2.1 Household Heterogeneity

Holding of land varies across individuals, resulting from differences in preferences. This is where heterogeneity comes in. Following [5], [6] each individual lives for one period and obtains utility from own consumption and bequest passed on to the offspring ([1], [4], [16]). From now on, the terms individual, household and dynasty will be used interchangeably. The dynasty h has the utility function

$$U_{ht} = \Gamma(C_{xht}^{\gamma}, C_{yht}^{1-\gamma})^{1-\beta} \left[K_{ht+1} - \frac{D_{ht}(1+i_t)}{r_{t+1} + p_{kt+1}} - h \right]^{\beta},$$

$$\Gamma > 0, \quad h \geq 0; \quad 0 < \beta, \quad \gamma < 1, \tag{1}$$

---

[2] The complications that would arise if this were allowed will be discussed later.

where C_{xht} and C_{yht} represent consumption of the respective good at time t, γ is the share of expenditure allocated to good x, K_{kt+1} is the land bequeathed, D_{ht} the debt bequeathed, i_t is the interest rate, r_t is the land rent, p_{kt} is the land price and h is the basic preference parameter that varies across the households. We can define $B_{ht+1} \equiv K_{ht+1} - D_{ht}(1+i_t)/(r_{t+1}+p_{kt+1})$ as the net value of the bequest in terms of land. Our specification implies that land and loans are perfect substitutes. Implicitly, it assumes rational expectation with regard to land rent and land price.

Individual heterogeneity is indicated by different values of h across households. The higher h is, the greater is the marginal utility of household h from passing bequest.[3] Since it is non-negative, it means that no one would pass zero or negative bequest: at the optimum $B_{ht+1} > 0$ for all h. The parameter h has continuous and finite support, say, from 0 to 1, with density function $\phi(h) \geq 0$. Apart from $\int_0^1 \phi(h)\mathrm{d}h = 1$, no other restrictions are required, except that the median, say h_m, be less than its mean, say $\bar{h}$, i.e.

$$h_m < \bar{h}. \tag{R1}$$

This would ensure that in the steady state, the distribution of land is skewed to the right, a feature observed in most market-oriented economies (see [12]).

We would impose two more regularity conditions

$$\bar{h} < \bar{K} \tag{R2}$$

$$\omega^* > \bar{K}, \tag{R3}$$

where ω^* is the wage/rental ratio at the free trade price level. As will be seen later, the condition (R2) will imply a finite positive price of land in equilibrium. Notice that the condition (R3) is also based on the primitives facing the small open economy. It would imply that at the politically determined tariff level, $\omega > \bar{K}$, that is, the total wage bill in the economy exceeds the total earnings to land. This condition will be needed as sufficient to ensure the second-order condition in determining the optimal tariff for the median voter as well as for stability of the dynamic adjustment process. Also, it is valid from the empirical standpoint, as in most actual economies, the wage bill exceeds 50% of the total income.

While h varies across the households, it is assumed the same for any given household. Thus, a dynasty is identified with a particular h for all t. The price paid for this assumption is that the model is unable to capture social mobility. But it preserves a property that considerably aids tractability: that the median dynasty's identity is unchanged. However, its wealth holding may

---

[3] Preference heterogeneity could have been alternatively introduced in the subutility from current consumption. This would have implied that the relative risk aversion from current consumption is not equal to one and moreover, it varies across the households. Hence, our specification keeps the role played by risk aversion neutral.

vary, and exogenous shocks to the economy would change the wealth holding of the median voter and thereby, affect equilibrium trade policy in the long-run.[4]

In addition to factor earnings, the households receive a part, ϕ_{ht}, of the tariff revenues, N_t ; $N_t \gtreqless 0$ as tariff may be positive, zero or negative. A household's budget constraint can now be written as

$$p_t C_{xht} + C_{yht} + p_{kt} K_{ht+1} - D_{ht} \leq w_t + (r_t + p_{kt}) K_{ht-1} + \phi_{ht} N_t - D_{ht-1}(1 + i_{t-1})$$

where $p_t = p^*(1 + \tau_t)$ is the tariff inclusive price, τ_t being the ad valorem rate of tariff at t. Household h maximizes U_{ht} subject to its budget constraint. The choice variables are C_{xht}, C_{yht}, K_{ht+1} and D_{ht}.

In terms of sequence of things, at the beginning of each period, the political process (voting) determines the equilibrium tariff. Given this tariff, each household's choice variables are the ones indicated above.

The post-tariff optimization can be equivalently seen in two stages. In stage one, the total expenditure, $E_{ht} = p_t C_{cht} + C_{yht}$, and savings are decided, and in stage two, E_{ht} is allocated between goods x and y. The assumed form of the subutility function from bequest implies that the arbitrage condition $1 + i_t = (r_{t+1} + p_{kt+1})/p_{kt}$ holds, i.e. the returns from loan and land are equal. An individual cannot separately choose K_{ht+1} and D_{ht} but can choose B_{ht+1}, the net value of the asset. Using the arbitrage condition and the definition of E_{ht}, the budget constraint can be restated as

$$E_{ht} + p_{kt} B_{ht+1} \leq w_t + (r_t + p_{kt}) B_{ht} + \phi_{ht} N_t \qquad (2)$$

Also, using the static indirect utility expression, we have

$$U_{ht} = p^{-\gamma(1-\beta)} E_{ht}^{1-\beta} (B_{ht+1} - h)^\beta, \qquad (3)$$

where we have normalized $\Gamma[\gamma^\gamma (1 - \gamma)^{1-\gamma}]^{1-\beta}$ to one. This is maximized subject to the preceding budget constraint. The first-order condition is

$$E_{ht} = \frac{1-\beta}{\beta} p_{kt} (B_{ht+1} - h), \qquad (4)$$

and substituting this into the budget constraint gives the individual asset demand function

$$B_{ht+1} - h = \beta \left[\frac{w_t + r_t B_{ht} + \phi_{ht} N_t}{p_{kt}} + B_{ht} - h \right]. \qquad (5)$$

If we sum it up over all h and use that, for any t, $\sum_h B_{ht} = \bar{K}$ (since there is no international borrowing or lending), we get the land market clearing equation

---

[4] Moreover, knowledge of changes in wealth holding by other households is necessary in predicting the effect of exogenous shocks on indices of personal distribution of wealth and income.

$$\frac{(1-\beta)p_{kt}(\bar{K}-\bar{h})}{\beta} = w_t + r_t\bar{K} + N_t. \tag{6}$$

Note that our regularity condition (R2) ensures a finite and positive equilibrium price of land.

At this point, we follow Mayer and use the neutral assumption that tariff revenues are distributed in proportion to individual earnings in the total earnings in the economy, i.e. $\phi_{ht} = (w_t + r_t B_{ht})/(w_t + r_t\bar{K})$. Substituting this and the land market clearing equation into (5),

$$B_{ht+1} - h = (1-\beta)(\bar{K}-\bar{h})\phi_{ht} + \beta(\beta_{ht} - h). \tag{7}$$

We now begin to trace the economy from an initial steady state, along which, τ_t is given (possibly zero) and wealth holding of any household is unchanged overtime. In other words, politics is assumed to begin from a steady state situation This implies that a household's ranking in terms of h or the initial wealth is the same, hence, the median household is identified by a unique h for all t and the median-voter hypothesis holds. Formally, turning to (7), we have

$$B_h - h = (\bar{K}-\bar{h})\phi_h; \quad \text{or} \quad (\omega+\bar{h})B_h = h(\omega+\bar{K}) + (\bar{K}-\bar{h})\omega, \tag{8}$$

where ω is the wage/rental ratio. From these expressions it follows that

Result 1 *At the steady state, B_h and $B_h - h$ are increasing in h.*

That is, the household having a higher propensity to leave bequest has more wealth.[5]

Result 1 sets the stage for dynamics off the steady state as well (consequent to an exogenous shock). In view of (7), we see that, starting from the initial steady state, $B_{ht+1} - h$ in the next period is increasing in h irrespective of the tariff rate chosen in period t. Hence,

Result 2 *At any t off or along the steady state, $B_{ht} - h$, and hence, B_{ht} increase with h.*

In turn this implies that

Result 3 *The median household is the same for all t and identified with $h = h_m$.*

Assuming for now that the median voter hypothesis holds, the distributional dynamics is governed by (7) with $h = h_m$, that is,

$$B_{mt+1} - h_m = (1-\beta)(\bar{K}-\bar{h})\frac{\omega(\tau_{mt}) + B_{mt}}{\omega(\tau_{mt}) + \bar{K}} + \beta(B_{mt} - h_m). \tag{9}$$

---

[5] This is unlike the infinite horizon Ramsey model with utility from consumption of goods only, wherein, the most patient household ends up with all land or capital.

where τ_{mt} is the preferred tariff rate for the median household (and τ_{mt} would depend on B_{mt}).

In order to understand that the median voter hypothesis holds in the presence of changes in factor ownerships and how τ_{mt} is dependent on B_{mt} and other basic parameters, we need to characterize, for any given t, the tariff preference of each household type.

2.2 Tariff Preference of Household h and the Median Voter Hypothesis

If we substitute (4) and (7) into U_{ht} , we obtain

$$U_{ht} = \left[\beta^\beta (1 - \beta)^{1-\beta}\right] p_t^{-\gamma(1-\beta)} p_{kt}^{1-\beta}$$
$$\times \left[\frac{\phi_{ht}(1 - \beta)(\bar{K} - \bar{h})}{\beta} + B_{ht} - h\right] \qquad (10)$$

$$= \left[\beta^\beta (1 - \beta)^{1-\beta}\right] p_t^{-\gamma(1-\beta)} p_{kt}^{-\beta}$$
$$\times \left[p_{kt}\frac{\phi_{ht}(1 - \beta)(\bar{K} - \bar{h})}{\beta} + p_{kt}(B_{ht} - h)\right]. \qquad (11)$$

Note that the two alternative expressions (10) and (11) are a 'partially reduced form' utility function in that the price of land is an argument and at the same time, the land market clearing condition (6) is used in deriving these expressions. Individual tariff preferences will be evaluated by using (10), but expression (11) is more straightforward to interpret. Ceteris paribus, an increase in p_t reduces static welfare. An increase in p_{kt} raises the cost of passing bequest and tends to lower utility. The elasticity of this 'cost-of-living' effect on utility is the share of bequests in the "lifetime" value of wealth and income and hence, is less than one. At the same time, an increase in p_{kt} increases the current value of wealth and has a positive effect on utility (captured by the term in the square bracket). The elasticity of this effect is unity since, from the land market clearing condition, p_{kt} is proportional to aggregate income. The net impact on utility of an increase in p_{kt}, at given p_t and individual wealth, is therefore positive, that is, the wealth effect outweighs the 'cost-of-living' effect.

At any t, each household inherits B_{ht} and its most preferred tariff rate is the one that maximizes (10) at given B_{ht}. From (10) or (11), it is seen that each household's calculation of its own optimal tariff would take into account how a change in tariff would affect the land price. We analyze this next.

Notice that $N_t = p^*\tau_t(C_{xt} - Q_{xt})$, where C_{xt} and Q_{xt} are the aggregate consumption and output of good x. From Cobb-Douglas preferences, $C_{xt} = \gamma E_t/p_t$, where $E_t = \sum_h E_{ht}$ is the aggregate expenditure. However, aggregating the budget constraint of all households, it (naturally) follows that $E_t = w_t + r_t\bar{K} + N_t$. Substituting this into the demand function of good x and substituting the resulting expression into the definition of N_t,

$$N_t = \frac{\gamma \tau_t(w_t + r_t \bar{K}) - p^* \tau_t (1 + \tau_t) Q_{xt}}{1 + (1 - \gamma)\tau_t}.$$

Next, by using this expression and the national income identity $w_t + r_t \bar{K} = p_t Q_{xt} + Q_{yt}$, we can express

$$E_t = w_t + r_t \bar{K} + N_t = \frac{1 + \tau_t}{1 + (1 - \gamma)\tau_t}[p^* Q_x(p_t) + Q_y(p_t)]. \qquad (12)$$

It shows that, in the presence of tariff, total expenditure exceeds the value of national output at international prices by a factor dependent on the magnitude of tariff. Substituting (12) into (6),

$$\frac{(1 - \beta)p_{kt}(\bar{K} - \bar{h})}{\beta} = \frac{1 + \tau_t}{1 + (1 - \gamma)\tau_t}[p^* Q_x(p_t) + Q_y(p_t)]. \qquad (13)$$

Log-differentiating this expression and using $p^*(1 + \tau_t)dQ_{xt} + dQ_{yt} = 0$ along the production possibility frontier, one obtains

$$\hat{p}_{kt} = \left[\frac{\gamma}{1 + (1 - \gamma)\tau_t} - \mu_x \eta_x \tau_t\right] \widehat{(1 + \tau_t)}, \qquad (14)$$

where the 'hat' represents a proportional change and

$$\mu_x \equiv \frac{p^* Q_{xt}}{p^* Q_{xt} + Q_{yt}}$$

= share of the import sector in the national output at international prices

$$\eta_x \equiv \frac{p_t}{Q_{xt}}\frac{dQ_{xt}}{dp_t} \equiv \text{own price elasticity of the supply of the importable.}$$

Intuitively, an increase in tariff, on one hand, tends to raise tariff revenues and disposable income and increases the demand for land as an asset through an income effect. This tends to increase the price of land. On the other hand, the increase in tariff results in less production efficiency (i.e. less earnings at world prices) and thereby, lowers the demand for land. The price of land tends to decrease.

Turning now to the expression of U_{ht} and taking to account how p_{kt} is affected ht by p_t, the "price effects" in U_{ht} in expression (10) are given by

$$(1 - \beta)(\hat{p}_{kt} - \gamma \hat{p}_t) = -(1 - \beta)\left[\frac{\gamma(1 - \gamma)}{1 + (1 - \gamma)\tau_t} + \mu_x \eta_x\right]\tau_t \widehat{(1 + \tau_t)}. \qquad (15)$$

Furthermore, totally differentiating ϕ_{ht},

$$d\phi_{ht} = \frac{\omega_t(\bar{K} - B_{ht})}{(\omega_t + \bar{K})^2}\hat{\omega}_t = \frac{\omega_t(\bar{K} - B_{ht})}{\theta(\omega_t + \bar{K})^2}\widehat{(1 + \tau_t)},$$

where, recall that us $\theta = \alpha_x - \alpha_y$.

All ingredients are at hand now. Computing the change in individual utility with respect to an increase in tariff, the marginal gains and losses from an increase in tariff are given by

$$G = \frac{(1-\beta)(\bar{K}-\bar{h})(\bar{K}-B_{ht})w_t}{\theta(\omega_t + \bar{K})^2[(1-\beta)(\bar{K}-\bar{h})\phi_{ht} + \beta(B_{ht}-h)]} \tag{16}$$

$$L = (1-\beta)\left[\frac{\gamma(1-\gamma)}{1+(1-\gamma)\tau_t} + \mu_x\eta_x\right]\tau_t, \tag{17}$$

where $\widehat{U_{ht}/(1+\tau_t)} = G - L$. The terms G and L, respectively, are the personal terms of trade gain/loss and the personal deadweight loss/gain from tariff. Tariff preference would depend on how G and L change with τ_t.

To begin with, consider any household whose wealth holding is less than the average. In terms of interpersonal trade, this household is a net exporter of labour services. Thus, an increase in tariff on the labour-intensive good — which tends to increase the wage/rental ratio — bestows a personal terms-of-trade welfare gain. Hence, $G > 0$. Also, as long as $\tau_t \leq 0$, $G > 0 > L$. Hence, the household's most preferred tariff is positive. Next, Appendix A shows that if the regularity condition (R3) is met and $\tau \geq 0$, G is a declining function of τ_t. This is shown as the downward sloping G function in panel (a) of Fig. 1.

How L changes with τ_t is harder to characterize in general since $d(\eta_x\mu_x)/d\tau_t \lesseqgtr 0$. But we shall argue that the effect of this change on the magnitude of L is likely to be quite small for the following reasons. First, from the definition of L, it follows that for small values of τ_t, the marginal effect of a change in $\eta_x\mu_x$ is small also. Second, when τ_t is sufficiently high, the output of good x will be close to its specialization level and hence, $\eta_x \to 0$ (while $\mu_x \to 1$). Third, in general, as τ_t increases, Q_{xt} increases and the value of national output at international prices falls, thus, μ_x rises unambiguously. On the other hand, Appendix B shows that, given Cobb–Douglas technology, as τ_t increases, η_x changes in the opposite way: it decreases. Hence, when τ_t is not very large or small, the product $\eta_x\mu_x$ is not likely to change significantly. Appendix B also shows that the changes in p^* and $\bar{K}$ or a neutral technical progress in either sector – the parameters whose effect on tariff and distribution will be considered – have opposite effects on $\eta_x\mu_x$ too.

For these reasons, let $\eta_x\mu_x$ be treated as a constant, henceforth. It follows then that L increases with τ_t and this relationship is unaffected by relevant parametric changes.

Panel (a) of Fig. 1 depicts the G and L functions for any household with $B_{ht} < \bar{K}$. Note that, given the condition (R1), the median household falls in this category. Clearly, the optimal tariff is positive. Moreover, as a comparative statics, we see that for a higher h household and hence, with higher B_{ht} and $B_{ht} - h$, the G function is at a lower level, implying that the optimal tariff is less, as one would expect. In other words, optimal tariff is monotonically decreasing in h in the range $0 - \bar{h}$.

18   Satya P. Das

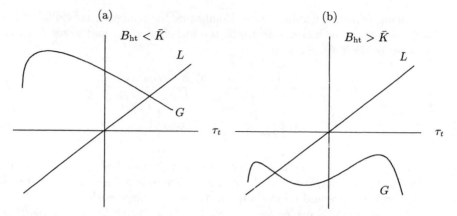

Fig. 1. Individual gains and losses from tariffs.

Turn next to a household whose wealth holding is greater than the average. The L function is the same as when $B_{ht} < \bar{K}$. Since such a household is a net importer of labour services, an increase in the wage/rental ratio leads to a personal terms-of-trade welfare loss. Hence, $G < 0$. For any $\tau_t \geq 0$, $G < 0 \leq L$ and hence, welfare is monotonically decreasing. In the range $\tau_t < 0$, the slope of the G function may be negative, zero, or even positive and greater than that of the L function; hence, the G and the L functions may intersect once or more, or may not intersect at all. It then follows that the optimal tariff is negative, but may not be monotonic with respect to h. Panel (b) of Fig. 1 exhibits this case.

Fig. 2 shows the pattern of optimal tariff across all households. Given the condition (R1), the median household's optimal tariff is positive, and, in general, we have an intuitive result

Proposition 1 *The optimal tariff is positive, zero or negative as $h \lessgtr \bar{h}$.*

In terms of Fig. 2, it is now straightforward to check that the median voter hypothesis holds. Starting with any τ less than τ_{mt}, majority will prefer a marginal increase in tariff. At any $\tau > \tau_{mt}$, a marginal reduction will be preferred by households starting from some h below h_m to $\bar{h}$ because the new tariff will be closer their optimal tariff and hence, will be welfare improving. A marginal reduction will also be preferred by those with $h > \bar{h}$ but the reasoning is slightly different. It is because their utility is monotonically decreasing over $\tau_t \geq 0$, irrespective of whether their utility function is strictly concave with respect to τ. Thus,

Proposition 2 *The median voter hypothesis holds. At t, τ_{mt} is the politically chosen tariff.*

Propositions 1 and 2 are the same as Mayer's and serve as our point of departure for dynamic analysis with endogenous distribution.

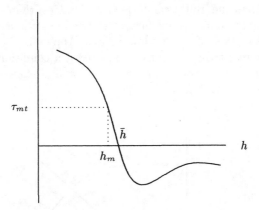

Fig. 2. Individually optimal tariff.

3 Dynamics

Given the expressions of G and L, for the median household, the first order condition is:

$$\frac{(\bar{K} - \bar{h})(\bar{K} - B_{mt})\omega(\tau_{mt})}{\theta(\omega(\tau_{mt}) + \bar{K})^2[(1 - \beta)(\bar{K} - \bar{h})\phi_{mt} + \beta(B_{mt} - h_m)]}$$
$$= \left[\frac{\gamma(1 - \gamma)}{1 + (1 - \gamma)\tau_{mt}} + \mu_x\eta_x\right]\tau_{mt}. \tag{18}$$

The l.h.s. and the r.h.s. are G_m and L_m, respectively, where both are deflated by $1 - \beta$. In terms of comparative statics later on, this equation governs the short-run effect of parametric changes without distributional changes. Equation (18) is illustrated in Fig. 3, which is, essentially, a truncated part of panel (a) of Fig. 1.

An increase in B_{mt} (at $h = h_m$) shifts the G_{mt} curve down. Thus, $\tau_{mt} = \tau(B_{mt})$ with $\partial \tau / \partial B_{mt} < 0$. Substituting this function into (9), we have

$$B_{mt+1} = (1 - \beta)h_m + (1 - \beta)(\bar{K} - \bar{h})\frac{\omega(\tau(B_{mt})) + B_{mt}}{\omega(\tau(B_{mt})) + \bar{K}} + \beta B_{mt}. \tag{19}$$

This is the basic dynamic equation.

At given τ_{mt}, an increase in B_{mt} tends to increase B_{mt+1} by a positive income effect. Indirectly however, a higher wealth position implies a lower tariff i.e. less demand for protection by the median household, a lower wage/rental ratio, a smaller share of the median household in total earnings and less accumulation of wealth. Thus, dB_{mt+1}/dB_{mt} is ambiguous in sign. Algebraically,

$$\frac{dB_{mt+1}}{dB_{mt}} = \beta + \frac{(1 - \beta)(\bar{K} - \bar{h})}{(\omega_t + \bar{K})^2}\left[\omega_t + \bar{K} + \frac{\omega_t(\bar{K} - B_{mt})}{\theta(1 + \tau_{mt})}\frac{d\tau_{mt}}{dB_{mt}}\right]. \tag{20}$$

20   Satya P. Das

Given the conditions (R2) and (R3) and that $d\tau_{mt}/dB_{mt} < 0$, the derivative is less than one. But it can be negative and less than -1. Hence, instability cannot be ruled out without further restriction. It is evident from (20) that the process is stable if β is not low enough. Appendix C proves a more general and precise result that stability is ensured if a condition stronger than (R3) holds irrespective of the magnitude of β or if β exceeds a threshold value. Hence

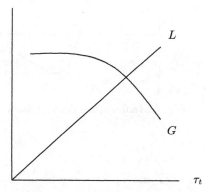

Fig. 3. The median voter.

Proposition 3 *The dynamic adjustment path of the median household's wealth is (locally) stable if*

$$\omega^* \geq \frac{2}{3}\bar{K} \quad or \ if \quad \beta \geq \frac{3\bar{K} - 2\omega^*}{2\omega^* - \bar{K}}. \tag{R4}$$

These are alternative and sufficient conditions.[6] From now on, it will be implicit that the condition (R4) is met so that the adjustment path is stable, and we will be concerned with steady state only.

Along the steady state, (19) and (18), respectively, boil down to

---

[6] Eq.(20) also indicates that if β is large enough, $-1 < dB_{mt-1}/dB_{mt} < 0$ and so that the adjustment path is monotonic. Otherwise when the dynamics would exhibit an oscillatory pattern, implying a 'political cycle of tariff and distribution'. This kind of cycle is of different nature from a standard political cycle paradigm (e.g. [2]). The latter means that decision making by politicians in pursuit of furthering their interests causes systematic changes in path of a macro economy. Here, the political process implies that, consequent to a shock, adjustment path of a macro economy may be non-monotonic. This would arise only when β is not high and the wealth of the median household is sufficiently less than the average.

$$B_m = B_m \left(\frac{\omega; \bar{K}}{+ \; +} \right) \equiv \frac{h_m \bar{K} + (\bar{K} + h_m - \bar{h})\omega}{\omega + \bar{h}} \tag{21}$$

$$\frac{(\bar{K} - \bar{h})(\bar{K} + B_m)\omega}{\theta(\omega + \bar{K}) \left[(1 - \beta)(\bar{K} - \bar{h})(\omega + B_m) + \beta(B_m - h_m)(\omega + \bar{K}) \right]}$$

$$= \left[\frac{\gamma(1 - \gamma)}{1 + (1 - \gamma)\tau_m} + \mu_x \eta_x \right] \tau_m \tag{22}$$

From (21),

$$B_m - h_m = \frac{(\bar{K} - \bar{h})(\omega + h_m)}{\omega + \bar{h}}; \quad \bar{K} - B_m = \frac{(\bar{h} - h_m)(\omega + \bar{K})}{\omega + \bar{h}}. \tag{23}$$

Using these, (22) is reduced to

$$\frac{(\bar{h} - h_m)\omega}{\theta(\omega + B_m)(\omega + \bar{h})} = \left[\frac{\gamma(1 - \gamma)}{1 + (1 - \gamma)\tau_m} + \mu_x \eta_x \right] \tau_m. \tag{24}$$

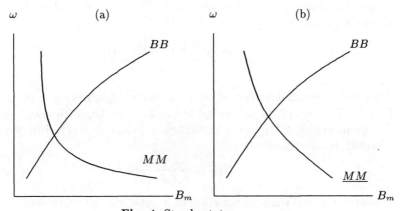

Fig. 4. Steady state.

Instead of (B_{mt}, τ_{mt}), it would be convenient to analyze steady state in the (B_m, ω) space. Eq.(21) is already expressed in this space. In (24), the function $\omega(\tau_{mt})$ can be inverted and we can write $\tau_m = g(p^*, \omega, A'_x)$, where $g_p < 0$ and $g_\omega > 0$ (< 0 if the import sector were land intensive). A'_x is inversely proportional to A_x, the technology parameter of sector x (see Appendix B). A decrease in A'_x would mean a Hicks-neutral technical progress in this sector. Thus, $\partial g / \partial A'_x > 0$. The l.h.s. of (24) can be expressed as $f(B_m, \omega)$.[7] Thus,

$$f \left(\frac{B_m, \omega}{- \; -} \right) = g \left(\frac{p^*, \omega; A'_x}{- \; + \; +} \right). \tag{25}$$

---

[7] This conditions (R1)-(R3) are used in establishing below that $\partial f / \partial \omega < 0$

Equations (21) and (25) solve the median household's wealth and the wager-rental ratio in the steady state. Graphically, this is shown in Fig. 4a. Ignore panel (b) for now. The BB and MM curves graph (21) and (25), respectively.

4 Effects of Parametric Changes

In this model economy, distribution affects trade policy and vice versa, and both are endogenous. The primitives of this economy are: (a) the external terms of trade, (b) technologies, (c) the total endowment of land, and (d) preference parameters including those of the distribution of h. Here, I analyze changes in some these primitives, namely (a), (b) and (c). Both short-run and long-run effects are examined, assuming that the economy is in the steady state initially. Short-run effect means the instant-effect on trade protection before wealth holding across households begins to change. Long-run effects compare one steady state to another. Both trade policy and distribution may change.

In what follows, we take the coefficient of variation as the measure of inequality.[8] Turning to wealth inequality first, in view of (21), observe that, along the steady state,

$$B_h = \frac{h\left(\omega + \bar{K}\right) + \left(\bar{K} - \bar{h}\right)\omega}{\omega + \bar{h}}.$$

Thus, the standard deviation of wealth holding is given by $\sigma_B = \sigma_h\left(\omega + \bar{K}\right)/\left(\omega + \bar{h}\right)$. For notational simplicity, let σ_h be normalized to one, henceforth. The mean wealth is $\bar{K}$ given to this economy. Thus, the coefficient of variation of wealth holding equals

$$\psi_B = \frac{\omega + \bar{K}}{\bar{K}\left(\omega + \bar{h}\right)}. \tag{26}$$

Similarly, the coefficient of variation of income has the expression

$$\psi_I = \frac{1}{\omega + \bar{h}} \tag{27}$$

Inequality may also be thought of in terms of utilities and

$$\psi_U = \frac{(1 - \beta)\left(\bar{K} - \bar{h}\right) + \beta\left(2\omega + \bar{K} + \bar{h}\right)}{\left(\bar{K} - \bar{h}\right)\left(\omega + \bar{h}\right)}. \tag{28}$$

Notice that the common element among all these indices is that the only endogenous variable that affects them is the wage rental ratio, and moreover, for a given set of parametric values, a higher ω implies less inequality. This

---

[8] All results also hold in terms of the proportional distance between mean and median as in [2].

is because the wage income is same for all households while asset holding and income from assets vary. Hence, an increase in the wage rate relative to the land rent implies less inequality. How parametric changes affect the wage/rental ratio is therefore critical in determining how long-run distribution is affected.

We are ready now to examine the effects of some parametric changes.

4.1 Terms of Trade and Technical Progress

The short-run effect is governed by (18). As argued earlier, the marginal loss from tariff (the r.h.s.) is unlikely to be significantly affected by these parametric changes (or by a change in the land endowment to be considered next). How the median voter's personal terms-of-trade welfare gain from tariff (the l.h.s.) is affected is then crucial. Suppose this trading country faces a decrease in the terms of trade, i.e. p^* increases. It is straightforward to obtain that, at given B_m and τ, an increase in p^* – through an increase in ω via the Stolper-Samuelson theorem – lowers G, i.e. $\partial G/\partial p^* < 0$. This implies that the equilibrium tariff falls in the short-run.

Intuitively, the median voter's personal terms-of-trade welfare gain is influenced by three factors: (a) the mean-median wealth distance, $\bar{K} - B_{mt}$, (b) the wage/rental ratio and (c) the price of land (which is implicit in the expression of G in (18). A greater mean-median wealth distance would increase the marginal terms-of-trade gain. At given factor ownership distribution, a higher wage/rental ratio would tend to increase static welfare through income wealth effect as the median household holds a higher labour endowment/wealth ratio than does the average household. This would tend to lower the marginal impact of tariff on the personal terms-of-trade welfare gain. Lastly, as discussed in Section 2, a higher land price would tend to increase static welfare and hence, would also tend to lower the terms-of-trade gain from tariff.

It is now straightforward to assess how an increase in p^* would affect G; (1) in the short-run, the mean-median wealth distance is unchanged; (2) at the original tariff level, the wage/rental ratio tends to rise via the Stolper-Samuelson theorem and this tends to lower G; (3) just as that of a change in tariff, a change in p^* has opposing effects on land price and hence, the net effect is likely to be relatively small. Thus, the overall marginal welfare gain from tariff diminishes and the median household demands less protection. This is essentially the prediction of the Mayer model (although it does not contain any asset market).

Now consider the long-run effects. How BB and MM curves may shift is crucial, as they define the steady state. As p^* increases, the BB curve is unaffected, however, while, from (25), the MM curve shifts out. Consequently, both ω and B_m rise. By the Stolper-Samuelson implications, real wage rises and the land rent falls. Also, since ω increases, the effect of distribution is clear-cut: inequality in terms of wealth, income or individual welfare falls.

As ω increases, the domestic price of the imported good must have risen. Hence, the change in equilibrium tariff is not apparent. But a related graphical technique would prove that the tariff rate falls. Instead of (25), consider

$$f\left(\frac{B_m}{-}, \frac{w}{-}\right) = \underline{g}, \tag{29}$$

where $\underline{g}$ is a constant, determining the $\underline{MM}$ curve in Fig. 4b. Let $\underline{g} = g_0$, the value of $g(\cdot)$ at the original value of p^*. Then the intersection of the same BB curve and the $\underline{MM}$ curve gives the original value of ω and B_m. Now consider an increase in p^*. We know that both ω and B_m increase and the BB curve does not shift. Hence, the $\underline{MM}$ curve must shift out. This means that $\underline{g}$ must have fallen as p^* increases. Recalling that, by definition, $\underline{g}$ is a monotonically increasing function of τ_m, it follows that τ_m must have fallen also. In summary then, the real wage increases, the land rent decreases, the tariff rate falls and distribution becomes less unequal.

Compared to the short-run effect on tariff in particular, the increase in median wealth is the new element. It reduces the mean-median wealth distance and hence, lowers the marginal personal terms-of-trade welfare gain of the median voter from tariff. Therefore, the long-run (negative) effect on tariff is greater in magnitude than the short-run effects.

It is straightforward to see that if imports were land intensive instead, the directional effects would be just the opposite. Hence,

Proposition 4 *In the short-run, an increase in the international price of the labour (land) intensive good leads to less (higher) trade protection, i.e. a lower level of import tariff (a higher level of import subsidy). In the long-run, the degree of protection also changes in the same direction but the magnitude of change is greater; moreover, the real wage increases (decreases), land rent rises (falls), wealth of the median household increases (decreases and) there is less (more) inequality.*

Now consider a neutral technical progress in the labour intensive sector. The cost parameter A'_x falls. From the zero profit condition for this sector, it follows that it is equivalent to an increase in the international price of good x. Hence, the effects are qualitatively the same as in Proposition 4.

4.2 An Increase in Land Endowment

Suppose the country's endowment of land increases. As examples, land may be reclaimed from sea, swamp or other 'unusable' areas toward productive purposes. Quality of land or land fertility may improve, which would essentially enhance the total service flow from the land input. More generally, let it represent capital accumulation.

In the short-run, the increase in $\bar{K}$ would be associated with some distribution of new land among households. Several distribution schemes may be thought of. We consider two of them. (1) Each household receives the same absolute incremental land, say, equal to $a > 0$; hence, the mean wealth changes from $\bar{K}$ to $\bar{K} + a$ and the median wealth from B_{mt} to $B_{mt} + a$. (2) Alternatively, let each household receive a proportional increase in land endowment, in which case, both $\bar{K}$ and B_{mt} increase by a factor $\lambda > 1$. As we will see, the short-run effects are just the opposite between these two schemes.

Consider case (1) first. The marginal gain expression is now

$$G = \frac{(\bar{K} + a - \bar{h})(\bar{K} - B_m)\,\omega}{\theta\,(\omega + \bar{K} + a)\,[(1 - \beta)(\bar{K} + a - \bar{h})(\omega + B_m + a) + \beta(B_m + a - h_m)(\omega + \bar{K} + a)]}.$$

The direction of change in short-run tariff is dictated by whether $\partial G / \partial a$ is positive or negative. Log-differentiating the above expression, we get

$$\left. \frac{\partial \ln G}{\partial a} \right|_{a=0} = \frac{1}{\bar{K} - \bar{h}} - \frac{1}{\omega + \bar{K}} - \frac{\omega + B_m + \bar{K} - \bar{h} + \beta\left(\bar{h} - h_m\right)}{(\bar{K} - \bar{h})(\omega + B_m)}$$

$$< \frac{1}{\bar{K} - \bar{h}} - \frac{1}{\omega + \bar{K}} - \frac{\omega + B_m + \bar{K} - \bar{h}}{(\bar{K} - \bar{h})(\omega + B_m)}$$

$$= -\frac{1}{\omega + \bar{K}} - \frac{1}{\omega + B_m} < 0.$$

In evaluating the derivative, we use (30) below, which is obtained from the steady state condition (23):

$$(1 - \beta)(\bar{K} - \bar{h})(\omega + B_m) + \beta(B_m - h_m)(\omega + \bar{K}) = (\bar{K} - \bar{h})(\omega + B_m).$$
$$(30)$$

It then follows that tariff falls in the short-run. Intuitively, as each household receives an equal initial increase in endowment, the mean-median wealth distance is unchanged. Also, there is no change in the wage/rental ratio. However, more land endowment implies a lower land price, which, as discussed earlier, would reduce G. As a consequence, the median household's demand for protection falls.

In the proportional endowment increase case (2), the marginal gain expression is

$$G = \frac{(\lambda\bar{K} - \bar{h})(\lambda\bar{K} - \lambda B_m)\,\omega}{\theta\,(\omega + \lambda\bar{K})\,[(1 - \beta)(\lambda\bar{K} - \bar{h})(\omega + \lambda\bar{K}) + \beta(\lambda B_m - h_m)(\omega + \lambda\bar{K})]},$$

log-differentiating which,

$$\left. \frac{\partial \ln G}{\partial a} \right|_{\lambda=1} = \frac{\omega}{\omega + \bar{K}} - \frac{B_m + \frac{\beta\bar{K}(\omega + \bar{h})}{\bar{K} - \bar{h}}\left(\frac{B_m}{\bar{K}} - \frac{\omega + h_m}{\omega + \bar{h}}\right)}{\omega + B_m},$$

where we have made use of (30). From (21), $B_m / \bar{K} < (\omega + h_m) / (\omega + \bar{h})$. Hence,

$$\frac{\partial \ln G}{\partial a}\bigg|_{\lambda=1} > \frac{\omega}{\omega + \bar{K}} - \frac{B_m}{\omega + B_m} = \frac{\omega^2 - \bar{K}B_m}{(\omega + \bar{K})(\omega + B_m)} > 0,$$

since, in view of the condition (R3), $\omega \geq \bar{K} > B_m$.

This would imply an increase in tariff in the short-run – just the opposite of what happens in the earlier case. Intuitively, a proportional increase in land endowment would increase the (absolute) mean-median wealth distance, which in turn, would tend to increase G. There is no effect through any change in wage/rental ratio as factor prices are unchanged. Lastly, the decrease in land price would tend to lower G. But this indirect effect is outweighed by the wealth-distance effect. The overall effect on G and hence, on equilibrium tariff is positive.

Consider now the long-run effects. An increase in $\bar{K}$ shifts the BB curve out, while the MM curve remains the same. Consequently, ω decreases and B_m increases. Given constant-returns, the decline in ω implies a decline in the real wage and an increase in the land rent. It also means – opposite to the short-run – a decrease in tariff. Intuitively, the long-run median wealth is totally independent of the initial median wealth or initial distribution of the incremental wealth. Hence, the long-run increase in B_m, which, by itself, tends to narrow the mean-median wealth distance, has a separate negative effect on G. This dominates over the short-run effects. Hence, the equilibrium tariff falls. The international price remaining unchanged, the real wage falls and land rent increases.[9]

As for inequality, an increase in $\bar{K}$ means that the average wealth rises. As w falls, the variance of wealth rises too. Thus, the effect of ψ_B is ambiguous. It is also checked that ψ_I increases, whereas, ψ_U may increase or decrease. The overall effect of land (capital) accumulation on inequality is then unclear.

Proposition 5 *In the short-run, an increase in land endowment would lead to an increase or a decrease in trade protection as households receive an equal or a proportional increase in endowment. In the long-run, however, trade protection decreases unambiguously, and moreover, (a) land rent increases and real wage falls, (b) the median voter's wealth increases and (c) inequality may increase or decrease.*

Note that this proposition holds irrespective of which sector is labour or land intensive.

5 Consumption and Production Interventions

It is assumed thus far that direct trade intervention is the only policy instrument available. This is ad hoc. [13] have examined the political- economy implications of simultaneous choice of consumption and production interventions. Their central result is that the optimal consumption tax of all

---

[9] It is apparently counter-intuitive that the land rent increases and real wage falls due to an increase in land endowment.

households is zero, irrespective of factor ownership, whereas, the pattern of optimal production subsidy is same as in case of an import tariff. Households with above-average (below-average) wealth would prefer a production tax on subsidy to the labour-intensive good. In the process, this is a more efficient outcome compared to a trade tax or subsidy.

The same result holds here together with the similar implications of changes in terms of trade, technology or land accumulation toward the type and degree of production intervention and distribution. In terms of our terminology, given production intervention (and thereby, factor rewards), there is only a price effect associated with a consumption tax and thus, the optimal consumption tax is zero for any household at each t on or off the steady state. This leaves production intervention only.

Let s_t denote production subsidy to sector x and let $S_p = p^* s_t Q_x(p_t)$ be the total cost of the subsidy program, where $p_t = p^*(1 + s_t)$ is the producer price. Analogous to (6), we have the following land market clearing condition:

$$\frac{(1 - \beta)p_{kt}\left(\bar{K} - \bar{h}\right)}{\beta} = w_t + r_t\bar{K} - S_t$$

$$= p^* Q_x(p_t) + Q_y(p_t) \equiv I^*(p^*, s_t) \qquad (6')$$

where $I^*(\cdot)$ is the total income at world prices. An increase in s_t reduces I^* and lowers land price.

Algebraically,

$$\hat{p}_{kt} = -\mu_x \eta_x s_t \left(\widehat{1 + s_t}\right) \qquad (14')$$

which can be compared to (14).

The marginal gain function for a household is same as before. The marginal loss function constitutes only the second term of L in (17) (as there is no consumption loss). Given that $\mu_x \eta_x$ changes insignificantly when s_t, p^* or $\bar{K}$ changes, the same qualitative conclusions as for tariff hold and for the same reasons.[10]

6 Conclusions

This paper extends the theory of political economy of trade protection by considering endogenous distribution of factor ownership in the standard 2×2 framework. Growth dynamics is totally suppressed in attempting to focus on distributional dynamics. The 'capital' in the Heckscher-Ohlin model distributional dynamics. The 'capital' in the Heckscher-Ohlin model is more appropriately called 'land' here. In the long run, trade policy as well as the distribution of land ownership are endogenous and they are dependent on

---

[10] Subsequent works by [14] and [15] identify situations in which tariffs may result as preferred instruments.

'more basic' primitives such as technology and preferences. Land ownership changes through participation in the market for land. In terms of the political economy, the median voter approach is used.

Terms of trade change and neutral technical progress have symmetric implication toward equilibrium trade policy (in the short-run and in the long-run) and inequality in terms of wealth, income or welfare (in the long-run). The long-run effects on trade policy are greater than the short-run effects. An increase in the endowment of land, however, may lead to an increase or a decrease in equilibrium trade protection in short-run, but in the long run, trade protection falls unambiguously. Furthermore, inequality may increase or decrease.

The economy under consideration is small and it allows trade in goods only, not in loans (so that goods trade can be focused entirely). Free mobility of loans is, in principle, straightforward to introduce but would add considerable complexity. The country's average wealth would be another variable since it can deviate from the average land holding. Moreover, with land market clearing in every period, the price of land, in the absence of trade in loans, is determined period by period, not influenced by expectation of future land prices. If loans were to move internationally, the dynamics of land price has to be considered on its own; bubbles may also rise. The dimension of the dynamics would jump from one to three: not just that of the median voter's wealth but also that of aggregate wealth and the land price.

The paper has presented an elementary, specific model of distribution-an example so to speak. However, the existing literature – perhaps the entire literature – on the political economy of trade policy assumes that factor ownerships are exogenous. Needless to say, factor ownerships evolve over time. The paper wishes to make the point that analyzing endogenous distribution – along with endogenous trade policy through the political process – is very much doable and likely to yield new insights. For example, the model illustrates a general point that the long-run effect of an exogenous shock on equilibrium protection is dependent on how the wealth holding of the median household relative to that of the average changes. After the short-run impact, the level of protection rises or falls accordingly as the median voter's wealth decreases or increases from the initial steady state. Another general point is that the commodity terms of trade effects on equilibrium trade protection and distribution depend on how the wage/rental ratio is affected. An increase in this ratio would tend to lower the demand for protection and would serve as an equalizing factor in terms of personal distribution of wealth and income. However, our result that the short-run effects of land accumulation on trade protection may be negative or positive depending on whether the initial distribution of incremental land is the same or proportional to one's initial wealth may be model-specific. But the clear-cut negative effect on protection in the long-run seems more general – and comforting in that "growth" would be accompanied by a political demand for less trade protection.

Appendix A

It is shown here that for any household with $B_{ht} < \bar{K}$, G is a negative function of τ_t, as long as the condition (R3) holds and $\tau_t \geq 0$. Given that the import sector is labour intensive, it is sufficient to show that $dG/dw_t < 0$. In the text it is already shown that

$$d\phi_{ht}/dw_{wt}. \tag{A1}$$

Next log-differentiating $w_t/\left(w_t + \bar{K}\right)^2$, we find:

$$\frac{\hat{w}_t - 2\,\widehat{\left(w_t + \bar{K}\right)}}{dw_t} = -\frac{w_t - \bar{K}}{w_t\left(w_t + \bar{K}\right)}. \tag{A2}$$

The import sector being labour intensive, the regularity condition (R3) and $\tau_t \geq 0$ imply that $w_t > w^* > \bar{K}$. Thus, the expression (A2) is negative. In view of the expressions (A1) and (A2), $dG/dw_t < 0$.

Appendix B

We show that in the marginal loss term L, μ_x and η_x change in opposite directions as p, $\bar{K}$ or A' increases.

Cobb–Douglas technologies imply that the unit cost functions are of the form, $A'_j w^{\alpha_j} r^{1-\alpha_j}$, for $j = x, y$. Thus, the zero profit conditions can be stated as

$$A'_x w^{\alpha_x} r^{1-\alpha_x} = p; \quad B_y w^{\alpha_y} r^{1-\alpha_y} = 1.$$

In log we have

$$\alpha_x \ln w + (1 - \alpha_x) \ln r = \ln p - \ln A'_x; \quad \alpha_y \ln w + (1 - \alpha_y) \ln r = -\ln B_y.$$

In this paper, we will be concerned with the effect of technical progress in a particular sector. Thus, let us, for notational simplicity, normalize B_y to one so that $\ln B_y = 0$ but keep A'_x as it is. The last two equations solve w, the wage/rental ratio.

$$\omega = (p/A'_x)^{1/(\alpha_x - \alpha_y)}.$$

Let input coefficients be denoted as usual by a_{ij}'s. Applying Shephard's lemma, we have

$$\begin{aligned}
a_{Lx} &= A'_x \alpha_x \omega^{-(1-\alpha_x)} = A'_x \alpha_x \left(p/A'_x\right)^{-(1-\alpha_x)/(\alpha_x - \alpha_y)} \\
&= A'^{(1-\alpha_y)/(\alpha_x - \alpha_y)}_x \alpha_x p^{-(1-\alpha_x)/(\alpha_x - \alpha_y)}
\end{aligned}$$

Similarly,

$$\begin{aligned}
a_{Kx} &= A'^{-\alpha_y/(\alpha_x - \alpha_y)}(1 - \alpha_x) p^{\alpha_x/(\alpha_x - \alpha_y)} \\
a_{Ly} &= A'^{(1-\alpha_y)/(\alpha_x - \alpha_y)}_x \alpha_y p^{-(1-\alpha_x)/(\alpha_x - \alpha_y)} \\
a_{Ky} &= A'^{-\alpha_y/(\alpha_x - \alpha_y)}(1 - \alpha_y) p^{\alpha_y/(\alpha_x - \alpha_y)}.
\end{aligned}$$

Next, we turn to the full employment equations

$$a_{Lx}Q_x + a_{Ly}Q_y = 1; \quad a_{Kx}Q_x + a_{Ky}Q_y = \bar{K}$$

Substituting the expression of a_{ij}'s into these,

$$\alpha_x p^{-(1-\alpha_x)/(\alpha_x-\alpha_y)}Q_x + \alpha_y p^{-(1-\alpha_y)/(\alpha_x-\alpha_y)}Q_y = A'^{-(1-\alpha_y)/(\alpha_x-\alpha_y)}$$
$$(1-\alpha_x)p^{\alpha_x/(\alpha_x-\alpha_y)}Q_x + (1-\alpha_y)p^{\alpha_y/(\alpha_x-\alpha_y)}Q_y = \bar{K}A_x'^{\alpha_y/(\alpha_x-\alpha_y)}.$$

Solving Q_x,

$$Q_x = \frac{(1-\alpha_y)p^{1/(\alpha_x-\alpha_y)} - \bar{K}\alpha_y A'^{1/(\alpha_x-\alpha_y)}}{(\alpha_x-\alpha_y)A'^{(1-\alpha_y)/(\alpha_x-\alpha_y)}p^{\alpha_x/(\alpha_x-\alpha_y)}} \Rightarrow$$

$$\frac{dQ_x}{dp} = \frac{(1-\alpha_x)(1-\alpha_y)p^{(1+\alpha_y)/(\alpha_x-\alpha_y)} + \alpha_x\alpha_y A_x'^{1/(\alpha_x-\alpha_y)}\bar{K}}{(\alpha_x-\alpha_y)^2 A_x'^{(1-\alpha_y)/(\alpha_x-\alpha_y)}p^{2\alpha_x/(\alpha_x-\alpha_y)}}.$$

Then,

$$\eta_x = \frac{p}{Q_x}\frac{dQ_x}{dp}$$

$$= \frac{(1-\alpha_x)(1-\alpha_y)p^{(1+\alpha_y)/(\alpha_x-\alpha_y)} + \alpha_x\alpha_y A_x'^{1/(\alpha_x-\alpha_y)}\bar{K}}{(\alpha_x-\alpha_y)p^{\alpha_y/(\alpha_x-\alpha_y)}\left[(1-\alpha_y)p^{1/(\alpha_x-\alpha_y)} - \bar{K}\alpha_y A_x'^{1/(\alpha_x-\alpha_y)}\right]}.$$

It is easy to see that the signs of $\partial\eta_x/\partial p$, $\partial\eta_x/\partial\bar{K}$ and $\partial\eta_x/\partial A'$ are opposite to $\partial Q_x/\partial p$, $\partial Q_x/\partial\bar{K}$ and $\partial Q_x/\partial A'_x$, while the latter set of derivatives are of the same sign as $\partial\mu_x/\partial p$, $\partial\mu_x/\partial\bar{K}$ and $\partial\mu_x/\partial A'_x$. Hence, μ_x and η_x change in opposite ways as p, $\bar{K}$ or A' changes.

Appendix C

Proposition 3 is proved here. We have $dB_{m+1}/dB_{mt} < 1$. Hence, stability is ensured if $dB_{mt+1}/dB_m > -1$. Denote the r.h.s. of (18) as $g(\tau_{mt})$ and the denominator of the l.h.s. as D. Totally differentiating the first-order condition, we then have

$$-\frac{d\tau_{mt}}{dB_{mt}}$$

$$= \frac{(\omega+\bar{K})^2\left[(1-\beta)(\bar{K}-\bar{h}) + \beta(\bar{K}-h_m)\right]}{\frac{D^2 g'(\tau_m)}{\theta\omega(\bar{K}-h)} + \frac{\bar{K}-B_m}{\theta(1+\tau_m)}\left[(1-\beta)(\bar{K}-\bar{h})(\omega^2-\bar{K}B_m) + \beta(B_m-h_m)(\omega^2-\bar{K}^2)\right]}$$

$$< \frac{\theta(1+\tau_m)(\omega+\bar{K})^2}{\bar{K}-B_m}\frac{(1-\beta)(\bar{K}-\bar{h}) + \beta(\bar{K}-h_m)}{(1-\beta)(\bar{K}-\bar{h})(\omega^2-\bar{K}B_m) + \beta(B_m-h_m)(\omega^2-\bar{K}^2)}$$

where the subscript t is ignored for notational convenience. Substituting the r.h.s. of this expression into (20), a sufficient condition for (local) stability $(dB_{mt+1}/dB_{mt} > -1)$ is

$$\frac{(1+\beta)(\omega+\bar{K})^2}{(1-\beta)(\bar{K}-\bar{h})} + \omega + \bar{K}$$

$$> A_1 \equiv \frac{\omega(\omega+\bar{K})^2\left[(1-\beta)(\bar{K}-\bar{h}) + \beta(\bar{K}-h_m)\right]}{(1-\beta)(\bar{K}-\bar{h})(\omega^2 - \bar{K}B_m) + \beta(B_m - h_m)(\omega^2 - \bar{K}^2)}$$

$$\Leftrightarrow \quad \frac{2(\omega+\bar{K})}{1-\beta} + \frac{1+\beta}{1-\beta}\frac{(\omega+\bar{K})(\omega+\bar{h})}{\bar{K}-\bar{h}} > A_1.$$

The term $\omega + \bar{K}$ cancels out from both sides. Then the above inequality is equivalent to

$$\frac{2}{1-\beta}[(1-\beta)(\bar{K}-\bar{h})(\omega^2 - \bar{K}B_m) + \beta(B_m - h_m)(\omega^2 - \bar{K}^2)]$$

$$+\frac{1+\beta}{1-\beta}\frac{\omega+\bar{h}}{\bar{K}-\bar{h}}\left[(1-\beta)(\bar{K}-\bar{h})(\omega^2 - \bar{K}B_m) + \beta(B_m - h_m)(\omega^2 - \bar{K}^2)\right]$$

$$> \omega(\omega+\bar{K})\left[(1-\beta)(\bar{K}-\bar{h}) + \beta(B_m - h_m)\right] + \beta\omega(\omega+\bar{K})(\bar{K}-B_m). \quad \text{(A3)}$$

Let the last term in the r.h.s. be expressed as

$$\frac{\beta\omega(\omega+\bar{K})(\bar{K}-B_m)}{\bar{K}-\bar{h}}(\bar{K}-\bar{h})$$

and let the coefficients of $\bar{K} - \bar{h}$ and $B_m - h_m$ be collected at one side of the inequality. The inequality (A3) is then equivalent to

$$(\bar{K}-\bar{h})A_2 + \frac{\beta(B_m - h_m)}{1-\beta}A_3 > 0, \quad \text{where} \qquad \text{(A4)}$$

$$A_2 \equiv \omega^2 - 2\bar{K}B_m - \omega\bar{K} + \beta\omega^2 + \beta\omega\bar{K} + \frac{(1+\beta)(\omega+\bar{h})(\omega^2 - \bar{K}B_m)}{\bar{K}-\bar{h}}$$

$$-\frac{\beta\omega(\omega+\bar{K})(\bar{K}-B_m)}{\bar{K}-\bar{h}}$$

$$A_3 \equiv \omega^2 - 2\bar{K}^2 - \omega\bar{K} + \beta\omega^2 + \beta\omega\bar{K} + (1+\beta)\frac{\omega+\bar{h}}{\bar{K}-\bar{h}}(\omega^2 - \bar{K}^2).$$

Consider A_2. The sixth term can be expressed as

$$\frac{(1+\beta)(\omega+\bar{h})(\omega^2 - \bar{K}B_m)}{\bar{K}-\bar{h}}$$

$$= \frac{\omega+\bar{h}}{\bar{K}-\bar{h}}(\omega^2 - \bar{K}B_m) + \frac{\beta(\omega+\bar{h})}{\bar{K}-\bar{h}}\left[\omega(\bar{K}-B_m) + (\omega-\bar{K})(\omega+B_m)\right]$$

$$= \frac{\omega+\bar{h}}{\bar{K}-\bar{h}}\left[\omega^2 - \bar{K}B_m + \beta(\omega-\bar{K})(\omega+B_m)\right] + \frac{\beta\omega(\omega+\bar{h})}{\bar{K}-\bar{h}}(\bar{K}-B_m).$$

Substituting this into A_2

$$A_2 = \omega^2 - 2\bar{K}B_m - \omega\bar{K} + \beta\omega^2 + \beta\omega\bar{K}$$

$$+ \frac{\omega + \bar{h}}{\bar{K} - \bar{h}} \left[\omega^2 - \bar{K}B_m + \beta(\omega - \bar{K})(\omega + B_m)\right] - \beta\omega(\bar{K} - \bar{h})$$

$$> \omega^2 - 2\bar{K}B_m - \omega\bar{K} + \beta\omega^2 + \beta\omega B_m \qquad (31)$$

$$+ \left[\omega^2 - \bar{K}B_m + \beta(\omega - \bar{K})(\omega + B_m)\right] \quad \text{using } \omega > \bar{K}$$

$$= 2(\omega^2 - \bar{K}B_m) - \bar{K}(\omega + B_m) + \beta\omega(\omega + B_m) + \beta(\omega - \bar{K})(\omega + B_m)$$

$$= 2(\omega^2 - \bar{K}B_m) + (\omega + B_m)\left[\beta(2\omega - \bar{K}) - \bar{K}\right]$$

$$> 2(\omega - \bar{K})(\omega + B_m) + (\omega + B_m)\left[\beta(2\omega - \bar{K}) - \bar{K}\right] \qquad (32)$$

$$\text{since } \omega^2 - \bar{K}B_m > (\omega + \bar{K})(\omega + B_m)$$

$$= (\omega + B_m)\left[\beta(2\omega - \bar{K}) - (3\bar{K} - 2\omega)\right]. \qquad (A5)$$

Similarly, using $\omega > \bar{K}$, we have

$$A_3 > \omega^2 - 2\bar{K}^2 - \omega\bar{K} + \beta\omega^2 + \beta\omega\bar{K} + (1 + \beta)(\omega^2 - \bar{K}^2)$$

$$= (2 + \beta)(\omega^2 - \bar{K}^2) - \bar{K}(\omega - \bar{K}) + \beta\omega(\omega + \bar{K})$$

$$= (\omega + \bar{K})\left[\beta(2\omega - \bar{K}) - (3\bar{K} - 2\omega)\right]. \qquad (A6)$$

Hence, as a sufficient condition, the inequality (A4) is met if the r.h.s. of (A5) and (A6) substitute A_2 and A_3, respectively in (A4) and the resulting expression is positive, that is,

$$\left[(\bar{K} - \bar{h})(\omega + B_m) + \frac{\beta(B_m - h_m)(\omega + \bar{K})}{1 - \beta}\right]$$

$$\times [\beta(2\omega - \bar{K}) - (3\bar{K} - 2\omega)] > 0, \quad \text{i.e.}$$

$$\beta(2\omega - \bar{K}) > 3\bar{K} - 2\omega \Leftrightarrow \beta > \frac{3\bar{K} - 2\omega}{2\omega - \bar{K}}. \qquad (A7)$$

But $\omega > \omega^*$, the wage/rental ratio at the free trade equilibrium. Thus, the inequality (A7) is satisfied and the dynamic path is stable if

$$\beta > \frac{3\bar{K} - 2\omega^*}{2\omega^* - \bar{K}}.$$

References

1. Aghion P, Bolton P (1997) A theory of trickle-down growth and development, Review of Economic Studies 64: 151-172
2. Alesina A, Rodrik D (1994) Distributive politics and economic growth, Quarterly Journal of Economics 109: 465-490
3. Alesina A, Roubini N, Cohen GD (1997) Political Cycles and the Macroeconomy, MIT Press, Cambridge, MA
4. Banerjee AV, Newman AF (1993) Occupational choice and the process of development, Journal of Political Economy 101: 274-298

5. Das SP (2000) Trade among similar countries and personal distribution of income and wealth, Economica 67: 265-281
6. Das SP (2001) Trade and personal distribution of wealth and income: beyond the Stolper-Samuelson theorem, Pacific Economic Review 6(1): 1-23
7. Grossman GM, Helpman E (1994) Protection for sale, American Economic Review 84: 833-850
8. Grossman GM, Helpman E (1995) The politics of free trade arrangements, American Economic Review 85: 667-690
9. Hillman AL (1982) Declining industries and political-support protectionist motives, American Economic Review 72: 1180-1187
10. Hillman AL, Ursprung HW (1988) Domestic politics, foreign interests, and international trade policy, American Economic Review 78: 719-745
11. Levy PI (1997) A political-economic analysis of free-trade agreements, American Economic Review 87: 506-519
12. Mayer W (1984) Endogenous tariff formation, American Economic Review 74: 970-985
13. Mayer W, Riezman RG (1987) Endogenous choice of trade policy instruments, Journal of International Economics 23: 377-381
14. Mayer W, Riezman RG (1989) Tariff formation in a multidimensional voting model, Economics and Politics 1: 61-79
15. Mayer W, Riezman RG (1990) Voter preferences for trade policy instruments, Economics and Politics 2: 259-273
16. Piketty T (1997) The dynamics of the wealth distribution and the interest rate with credit rationing, Review of Economic Studies 64: 173-189
17. Schonhardt-Baily C (1991) Specific factors, capital markets, portfolio diversification, and free trade: domestic determinants of the repeal of the corn laws, World Politics 43: 545-569
18. Weck-Hannemann H (1990) Protectionism in direct democracy, Journal of Institutional and Theoretical Economics 146: 389-418

Lobbying for Tariff Protection: The Case of Bertrand Rivalry

Ngo Van Long

Department of Economics, McGill University, 855 Sherbrooke Street West, Montreal, Quebec, Canada H3A 2T7. ngo.long@mcgill.ca

1 Introduction

It is generally accepted that trade policies such as tariffs and subsidies are to a large extent influenced by political considerations. Governments often respond to demands for protection that are transmitted through the political process, such as lobbying. The groups that are hurt by foreign competition make their voice heard, and their influence felt, by promising to government officials or elected representatives either rewards (for carrying out protection measures) or punishments (for failing to respond to demand for protection). Lobbying takes money and time, and often involves coordination costs. The effectiveness of lobbying by a particular interest group depends on the group's characteristics, such as group size, group cohesion, the degree of heterogeneity of group members, and so on. These may determine the extent of free riding which in turn affects the degree of success in obtaining protection.

The empirical studies on lobbying have been inconclusive. In a survey of empirical results on the deternimants of the effectiveness of lobbying, [6] (pp 417-418) reported many ambiguities:

⋯ "Most scholars indeed find an increased scope for political influence with higher degrees of concentration, but there are many that find no effect or even a negative effect. Equally ambiguous are the results of the use of numbers for the free rider effect. A large number of participants to collective action is usually hypothesized to increase the free riding problem. Sometimes indeed a negative effect of numbers on influence is reported. More often, however, a positive effect is found. Hence there appears to be relatively little direct empirical support for the [5] influential theoretical study on collective action."

Recently, [2] have attempted to consider some theoretical foundations for the source of empirical ambiguities. Their paper indicated that theoretical predictions are very sensitive to the assumptions that underline the models. The theoretical workhorse they used is the two-stage model of Cournot oligopoly with a homogenous product. Within that framework, they were able to derive a variety of results, depending on assumptions about the opportunity cost of lobbying.

The purpose of the present paper is to complement the analysis of [2] by considering lobbying within a Bertrand oligopoly with differentiated products. Using this model, we can ask certain questions that could not be asked within the HLS homogenous product model. For example, would an increase in the substitutability among the differentiated products lead to an increase or a decrease the tariff on imported goods? How does lobbying affect the average price in the industry, and the variance of the distribution of product prices? We will show that a wide variety of results emerge, depending on the assumptions about lobbying technology.

In HLS, it was assumed that entrepreneurs must divide their time between two competing activities: lobbying, and internal control. While this "time allocation model" has certain appeal, one must concede that in many real world instances, lobbying is done by professional lobbyists who have nothing to do with internal control. The alternative model, the "professional lobbyist model", has in fact been used by a number of authors, including [3]. In our present paper with differentiated products, we consider both the "professional lobbyist model" and the "time allocation model", thus we are able to compare the different predictions.

Among the interesting results that emerge from our model, we would like to draw special attention to the following propositions concerning the professional lobbyist model:

(i) If the indirect lobbying cost is linear, then only firms with the lowest production cost will lobby. This result was not reported in [3].

(ii) An increase in the substitutability among the differentiated products will lead to greater lobbying effort (Substitutability was not considered in the models cited above).

(iii) If the indirect lobbying cost is quadratic, changes in the variance of the distribution of marginal production costs have no effect on total lobbying (though lobbying levels by individual firms will be affected).

(iv) An increase in the ratio of foreign firms to domestic firms will lead to more lobbying (This was not reported in earlier models).

(v) An increase in lobbying will increase (respectively, decrease) the variance of the *distribution of prices* in the industry if the initial average foreign price exceeds (respectively, is smaller than) the initial average industry price (In the homogenous product models cited above, there is only one price, not a distribution of prices).

In the case of the time allocation model, the results include:

(vi) Firms with different marginal production costs may allocate the same amount of time to lobbying activities.

(vii) The availability of lobbying opportunities can reverse the profit ranking of firms in the oligopoly (This result is consistent with proposition 3.1 of [2]).

(viii) Assume that the number of foreign firms is small. Lobbying for tariff protection will result in an increase (respectively, decrease) in the variance of the distribution of prices in the industry if the initial average foreign price exceeds (respectively, is smaller than) the initial average industry price.

The plan of the paper is as follows: in Section 2, the basic model of Bertrand rivalry in a two-stage game is introduced. The professional lobbyist model is discussed in section 3. Section 4 examines the time allocation model. Some concluding remarks are offered in Section 5.

2 The Basic Model

We consider a domestic industry consisting of m Bertrand oligopolists producing m differentiated products, for sale only in the home country. Each firm produces only one product. The m domestic firms face competition from m^* foreign firms that export their differentiated products to the home country. The foreign firms also act as Bertrand oligopolists. The set of home firms is

$$H = \{1, 2, \cdots, m\}$$

and the set of foreign firms is

$$F = \{m + 1, m + 2, \cdots, m + m^*\}$$

Let $N = H \cup F = \{1, 2, \cdots, m + m^*\}$. By convention, firm i produces differentiated good i, where $i \in N$. Let p_i denote the price charged by firm i to the domestic consumers for a unit of its differentiated product Let t_f be the tariff per unit of output exported to the home country by foreign firm $f \in F$, and t_h be the production tax (or subsidy, if t_h is negative) per unit of output of home firm $h \in H$. The demand for firm i's product is

$$q_i = D^i(p_i, P_{-i})$$

where P_{-i} is the vector of $m + m^* - 1$ prices charged by firm i's rivals. We assume

$$D_i^i = \frac{\partial D^i(p_i, P_{-i})}{\partial p_i} < 0 \quad \text{and} \quad D_j^i = \frac{\partial D^i(p_i, P_{-i})}{\partial p_j} > 0 \text{ if } j \neq i.$$

Firm i's production cost is $C^i(q_i)$.

We consider a two-stage game. In stage 1, home firms choose lobbying levels L_h, $h \in H$, and the government announces the tariff rates t_f after the lobbying have taken place.(For simplicity, we assume that only the t_f are affected by lobbying, and that the t_h are exogenous; the details concerning stage 1 will be spelled out later.) In stage 2, all firms take tariff rates as given, and they act as Bertrand rivals.

As usual, the game is solved backward: we first characterize the equilibrium in stage 2. The profit function of firm i in stage 2 is:

$$\pi_i = (p_i - t_i)D^i(p_i, P_{-i}) - C^i(D^i(p_i, P_{-i}))$$

For simplicity, assume that $C^i(q_i) = c_i q_i$. Define $\theta_i = c_i + t_i$. Then firm i's profit function is

$$\pi_i = (p_i - \theta_i)D^i(p_i, P_{-i}) \tag{1}$$

We call θ_i the tax-inclusive marginal cost of the good produced by firm i. In general, $\theta_i \neq \theta_j$. We denote by $\theta_{\min}$ the lowest marginal cost among the home firms, and $\theta_{\max}$ the highest marginal cost among the home firms.

Profit maximization in stage 2 with respect to p_i gives the first order condition

$$p_i - \theta_i = \frac{D^i(p_i, P_{-i})}{-D_i^i} = \frac{q_i}{-D_i^i} \tag{2}$$

For tractability, in what follows we assume that the demand function for differentiated product i takes the form

$$q_i = G_i(p_N) - b_i p_i \tag{3}$$

where $0 < G_i' < b_i$ and p_N is the average price in the oligopoly:

$$p_N = \frac{1}{n} \sum_{i \in N} p_i$$

The assumption $0 < G_i' < b_i$ implies that if all firms in the oligopoly increase their price by the same amount, then the quantity demanded for good i will fall.

Substituting the demand function (3) into the first order condition (2), we obtain firm i's reaction function

$$p_i = \frac{1}{2}\left[\theta_i + \frac{G_i(p_N)}{b_i}\right] \tag{4}$$

Let the hat over p_i (respectively, q_i) denote the Nash-Bertrand equilibrium price charged by firm i (respectively, its Nash-Bertrand equilibrium output). Then, summing (4) over all i, and dividing the resulting equation by n, we obtain

$$\widehat{p}_N - \sum_{i \in N} \frac{G_i(\widehat{p}_N)}{2nb_i} = \frac{\theta_N}{2} \tag{5}$$

where θ_N is the average of the tax-inclusive marginal costs:

$$\theta_N = \frac{1}{n} \sum_{i \in N} \theta_i$$

From (5), we can write the Bertrand equilibrium average price as:

$$\widehat{p}_N = \widehat{p}_N(\theta_N) \tag{6}$$

Thus we can state a useful result:

Proposition 1 *(Stage 2 equilibrium) In a Bertrand oligopoly with differentiated products, the equilibrium average price is a function of the average of the tax-inclusive marginal costs: changes in the individual θ_i that leave θ_N unchanged have no effects on the equilibrium average price.*

Proof. See equation (5).

Remark: Proposition 1 has an important implication: If, in stage 1, the home government increases the subsidy rate for a subset of home firms, and decreases the subsidy rate for another subset of home firms, while maintaining the average subsidy rate unchanged, then the equilibrium average price in stage 2 will be unchanged. (We will see that, under certain conditions, this means that the total lobbying effort of the home oligopolists will be unchanged.)

Proposition 1 is a generalisation of the result, due to [1], that in a Cournot equilibrium with a homogenous product, the equilibrium price is independent of the distribution of marginal costs.

We now turn to Bertrand equilibrium prices of individual firms. From (4) and (6), we get

$$\widehat{p}_i = \frac{1}{2}\left[\theta_i + \frac{G_i(\widehat{p}_N(\theta_N))}{b_i}\right] = \widehat{p}_i(\theta_i, \theta_N) \tag{7}$$

Hence the Bertrand equilibrium outputs are

$$\widehat{q}_i(\theta_i, \theta_N) = G_i(\widehat{p}_N(\theta_N)) - b_i\widehat{p}_i(\theta_i, \theta_N) = \frac{1}{2}[G_i(\widehat{p}_N(\theta_N)) - b_i\theta_i] \tag{8}$$

and the Bertrand equilibrium profits are (in view of (1) and (2)):

$$\widehat{\pi}_i = [\widehat{p}_i - \theta_i]\,\widehat{q}_i = \frac{1}{b_i}\left[\widehat{q}_i(\theta_i, \theta_N)\right]^2 = \frac{1}{4b_i}\left[G_i(\widehat{p}_N(\theta_N)) - b_i\theta_i\right]^2$$

In what follows, we specialize in the case where $b_i = b$ for all i, and assume

$$G_i(P_N) = a + gP_N \tag{9}$$

where $0 < g < b_i$ and $a/b > \theta_{\max}$. Then (5) becomes

$$\widehat{p}_N = \frac{[(a/b) + \theta_N]\Omega}{2} \tag{10}$$

where

$$\Omega = \frac{1}{1 - \frac{g}{2b}} \tag{11}$$

(It is possible to obtain these equations from an underlying utility function, see the appendix). At first sight, one may think that the parameter g is a reasonable index of the substitutability among the differentiated products. Upon reflection, a more appropriate substitutablity measure should come from the underlying utility function. In the appendix, we show that an increase in the substitutability, as measured by a parameter E in the utility function, involves an increase in the ratio g/b and a decrease in a. An increase in E leads to a fall in $\widehat{p}_N$, as expected. (An increase in g while a and b are kept constant should not be interpreted as an increase in substitutability: $\widehat{p}_N$ would rise if g were to increase while a and b were to stay constant.)

In stage 1, the home government determines the tariff rates t_f on goods produced by the m^* foreign oligopolists, in response to the total lobbying pressure L exercised by the domestic firms. For simplicity, we assume $t_f = t$ for all $f \in F$. Here L is the sum of lobbying pressures, L_h, $h \in H$, by individual domestic firms:

$$L = \sum_{h \in H} L_h$$

We postulate that

$$t = t(L), \qquad t'(L) > 0, \qquad t''(L) < 0$$

The signs of these derivatives reflect the usual assumptions that the marginal effectiveness of lobbying pressure is positive and diminishing.

There are two alternative specifications of lobbying technology. In the first specification, which was adopted in [3], lobbying activities do not affect production costs, perhaps because firms hire professional lobbyists who are not in charge of the firms's production activities. In the second specification, adopted by [2], lobbying activities use up the time of entrepreneurs, who are therefore less able to concentrate on internal production matters (which may be called "monitoring activities".)

3 Specification 1: Lobbying Does not Affect Production Costs

We will consider two cases: (a) non-cooperative lobbying and (b) cooperative lobbying.

3.1 Non-Cooperative Lobbying

We now specify more precisely the two-stage game. In stage 1, each home firm $h \in H$ chooses non-cooperatively its level of lobbying pressure $L_h \geq 0$. In stage 2, after the resulting tariff rate $t(L)$ has been announced by the government, all firms, having full knowlege of t, set their prices p_i as Bertrand rivals.

Following [3], we assume that to achieve the lobbying pressure L_h, the total lobbying cost incurred by firm h is $L_h + \phi(L_h)$, where $\phi(L_h) \geq 0$ represents the associated indirect cost. (A possible interpretation is as follows: L_h is the payment made to government officials, and $\phi(L_h)$ is the cost of making such transfer payment less visible.)

In stage 1, firm h chooses $L_h \geq 0$ to maximize net profit

$$\pi_h^{net} = \frac{1}{b}[\widehat{q}_h(\theta_h, \theta_N)]^2 - L_h - \phi(L_h) \tag{12}$$

where

$$\theta_N = \frac{m\theta_H + m^*\theta_h}{n}$$

and

$$\theta_H = \frac{1}{m}\sum_{h \in H}\theta_h, \qquad \theta_h = \frac{1}{m^*}\sum_{f \in F}(\theta_f^0 + t(L)).$$

Let $\lambda_h \geq 0$ be the Kuhn-Tucker multiplier associated with the constraint $L_h \geq 0$. The first order conditions of problem (12) are:

$$\frac{2\widehat{q}_h}{b}\left[\frac{\partial\widehat{q}_h}{\partial\theta_N}\frac{\partial\theta_N}{\partial t}\right]t'(L) - 1 - \phi'(L_h) + \lambda_h = 0$$

Hence, using (8),

$$\left[\frac{1}{b}G(\widehat{p}_N(\theta_N)) - \theta_h\right]\left[\frac{\Omega gm^*}{4n}\right]t'(L) - 1 - \phi'(L_h) + \lambda_h = 0 \tag{13}$$

with

$$\lambda_h \geq 0, \qquad L_h \geq 0, \qquad \lambda_h L_h = 0 \tag{14}$$

From conditions (13) and (14), we obtain the following proposition:

Proposition 2 *If the indirect lobbying cost is linear or zero (that is, in the case $\phi'(.) = \kappa =$constant), then, in any equilibrium with $L > 0$, only those home firms with the lowest marginal cost, i.e. those with $\theta_h = \theta_{\min}$, will undertake lobbying activities. All other home firms will free ride.*

We now consider the case where the indirect lobbying cost function is strictly convex. We obtain the following result:

Proposition 3 *In the case of a strictly convex indirect lobbying cost function $\phi(\cdot)$, for any two politically active home firms, say j and k, with $\theta_j < \theta_k$, the firm with lower marginal production cost will undertake a greater level of lobbying activities, i.e., $L_j > L_k$.*

Remark 1. This proposition is in agreement with Proposition 1 in [3], for Cournot rivalry with a homogenous product.

Proof. By definition, if j and k are politically active, their lobbying pressures are positive. Hence $\lambda_k = \lambda_j = 0$ and (13) gives

$$\frac{G(\widehat{p}_N(\theta_N)) - b\theta_j}{G(\widehat{p}_N(\theta_N)) - b\theta_k} = \frac{1 + \phi'(L_j)}{1 + \phi'(L_k)}$$

Thus, $\theta_j < \theta_k$ implies $\phi'(L_j) > \phi'(L_k)$, and, since $\phi'' > 0$, we have

$$L_j > L_k.$$

We now ask the following question: if the goods become closer substitutes in the consumers' mind, will the total lobbying pressure rise? Intuitively, one would expect that the answer is "yes".

Proposition 4 *A small increase in the substitutability of the products will lead to a greater lobbying pressure for tariff protection.*

Proof. For simplicity, consider the case $m = m^* = 1$. The first order condition for stage 1's optimization problem with respect to L is

$$T(L,E) = \left[\frac{a}{b} + \frac{\Omega g}{2b}\left(\frac{a}{b} + \frac{\theta_h + (\theta_f + t(L))}{2}\right) - \theta_h\right]\left[\frac{\Omega g}{8}\right]t'(L) - 1 - \phi'(L) = 0$$

where E is the measure of substitutability (see the appendix) and $a = a(E)$, $b = b(E)$, $g = g(E)$, and $\Omega = \Omega(g)$, as specified in the appendix. The second order condition is

$$\frac{\partial T}{\partial L} < 0$$

From the standard formula for comparative statics

$$\frac{dL}{dE} = -\frac{(\partial T/\partial E)}{(\partial T/\partial L)}$$

we know that

$$\text{SIGN}\frac{dL}{dE} = \text{SIGN}\frac{\partial T}{\partial E}$$

It can be verified that the expression $\partial T/\partial E$ is positive.

□

Our next proposition concerns the invariance of total lobbying pressure:

Proposition 5 (An Invariance Theorem) *If the indirect lobbying cost function is $\phi_h(L_h) = \alpha_h + \beta_h L_h + \gamma L_h^2$, where γ is the same for all home firms, then, starting from an equilibrium where all home firms are politically active, small changes in the structure of marginal costs θ_h, $h \in H$, (so that the marginal costs of some firms increase, and other marginal costs decrease) that do not affect the mean marginal cost θ_H, will not affect the total lobbying pressure L, and hence will not affect the equilibrium tariff rate t. Thus, only the mean of the distribution of marginal costs within the domestic oligopoly matters, and the variance of that distribution has no effect on the equilibrium level of lobbying.*

Proof. With $L_h > 0$, equation (13) gives

$$\left[\frac{1}{b}G(\hat{p}_N(\theta_N)) - \theta_h\right]\left[\frac{\Omega g m^*}{4n}\right]t'(L) - 1 - \beta_h = \frac{\gamma L_h}{2} \tag{15}$$

Summing (15) over all $h \in H$, and dividing the resulting equation by m, we get

$$\left[\frac{1}{b}G(\widehat{p}_N(\theta_N)) - \theta_H\right]\left[\frac{\Omega g m^*}{4n}\right]t'(L) - 1 - \frac{1}{m}\sum \beta_h = \frac{\gamma L}{2m} \qquad (16)$$

Equation (16) uniquely determines L. Any change in the θ_h, $h \in H$, that does not affect the average θ_H, will not affect the total lobbying pressure L.

Proposition 5 is rather specific, because it relies on the assumption that $\phi_h(L_h)$ is quadratic, i.e., the marginal indirect lobbying cost, $\phi'_h(L_h)$, is a straight line $\beta_h + (\gamma/2)L_h$. What happens if the marginal indirect lobbyng cost is strictly convex? It turns out that in this case, any change in the θ_h that leaves the mean θ_H unchanged but increases the variance will reduce total lobbying L.

Proposition 6 *If the marginal indirect lobbying cost function is strictly convex (i.e. $\phi''' > 0$), then an increase in the heterogeneity of production cost (increase in the variance of the distribution of θ_h) will lead to a decrease in total lobbying.*

Proof. We offer the proof for the case where the home firms can be partitioned into two groups of equal sizes: $m/2$ firms with low marginal production cost, denoted by $\theta_{\min}$ and $m/2$ firms with high marginal production cost, denoted by $\theta_{\max}$. Assume both groups are active in lobbying. Then the first order condition for the representative low cost firm, say firm 1, is

$$\left[\frac{1}{b}G(\widehat{p}_N(\theta_N)) - \theta_{\min}\right]\left[\frac{\Omega g m^*}{4n}\right]t'(L) - 1 - \phi'(L_1) = 0$$

and, the first order condition for the representative high cost firm, say firm m, is

$$\left[\frac{1}{b}G(\widehat{p}_N(\theta_N)) - \theta_{\max}\right]\left[\frac{\Omega g m^*}{4n}\right]t'(L) - 1 - \phi'(L_m) = 0$$

Now let $\theta_{\min}$ fall by an amount $\varepsilon > 0$ and $\theta_{\max}$ increase by the same amount

$$\frac{d\theta_{\min}}{d\varepsilon} = -1 \text{ and } \frac{d\theta_{\max}}{d\varepsilon} = 1$$

Let $\rho = m/2$ and define

$$\psi_1(L_1, \varepsilon) = \left[\frac{1}{b}G(\widehat{p}_N(\theta_N)) - \theta_{\min}(\varepsilon)\right]\left[\frac{\Omega g m^*}{4n}\right]t'(\rho L_1 + \rho L_m) - 1 - \phi'(L_1) = 0$$

$$\psi_m(L_m, \varepsilon) = \left[\frac{1}{b}G(\widehat{p}_N(\theta_N)) - \theta_{\max}(\varepsilon)\right]\left[\frac{\Omega g m^*}{4n}\right]t'(\rho L_1 + \rho L_m) - 1 - \phi'(L_m) = 0$$

where

$$\frac{1}{b}G(\widehat{p}_N(\theta_N)) = \frac{a}{b} + \frac{g\Omega}{2b}\left[\frac{a}{b} + m\theta_H + m^*(\theta_h^0 + t(\rho L_1 + \rho L_m))\right]$$

Differentiating the system with respect to ε, we get

$$\begin{bmatrix} \dfrac{\partial \psi_1}{\partial L_1} & \dfrac{\partial \psi_1}{\partial L_m} \\ \dfrac{\partial \psi_m}{\partial L_1} & \dfrac{\partial \psi_m}{\partial L_m} \end{bmatrix} \begin{bmatrix} \dfrac{dL_1}{d\varepsilon} \\ \dfrac{dL_m}{d\varepsilon} \end{bmatrix} = - \begin{bmatrix} \dfrac{\partial \psi_1}{\partial \varepsilon} \\ \dfrac{\partial \psi_m}{\partial \varepsilon} \end{bmatrix}$$

where

$$\frac{\partial \psi_1}{\partial L_1} = Z_1 - \phi''(L_1), \quad \frac{\partial \psi_m}{\partial L_m} = Z_m - \phi''(L_m)$$

$$\frac{\partial \psi_m}{\partial L_1} = Z_m, \quad \frac{\partial \psi_1}{\partial L_m} = Z_1$$

$$\frac{\partial \psi_1}{\partial \varepsilon} = V = -\frac{\partial \psi_m}{\partial \varepsilon}$$

$$Z_1 = \rho \left[\frac{(\Omega gm^*)^2}{8bn} \right] [t'(L)]^2 + \rho t''(L) \left[\frac{1}{b} G(\widehat{p}_N(\theta_N)) - \theta_{\min}(\varepsilon) \right] \frac{\Omega gm^*}{4n}$$

$$Z_m = \rho \left[\frac{(\Omega gm^*)^2}{8bn} \right] [t'(L)]^2 + \rho t''(L) \left[\frac{1}{b} G(\widehat{p}_N(\theta_N)) - \theta_{\max}(\varepsilon) \right] \frac{\Omega gm^*}{4n}$$

$$V = \frac{\Omega gm^* t'(L)}{4n} > 0$$

Let

$$\Delta = \frac{\partial \psi_1}{\partial L_1} \frac{\partial \psi_m}{\partial L_m} - \frac{\partial \psi_m}{\partial L_1} \frac{\partial \psi_1}{\partial L_m}$$

Assuming the usual stability condition, we have $\Delta > 0$. Then

$$\frac{dL_1}{d\varepsilon} = \frac{1}{\Delta} [V \phi''(L_m) - V (Z_1 - Z_m)] > 0$$

$$\frac{dL_m}{d\varepsilon} = \frac{1}{\Delta} [-V \phi''(L_1) + V (Z_1 - Z_m)] < 0$$

and

$$\frac{dL}{d\varepsilon} = \frac{m}{2} \left[\frac{dL_1}{d\varepsilon} + \frac{dL_m}{d\varepsilon} \right] = \frac{mV}{2\Delta} [\phi''(L_m) - \phi''(L_1)] \tag{17}$$

Since $L_1 > L_m$ (by Proposition 3), and $\phi''' > 0$ (by hypothesis), the right-hand side of (17) is negative. This completes the proof of Proposition 6.

Finally, if the ratio of the number of foreign firms to the total number of firms (m^*/n) rises, does the total domestic lobbying increase or decrease? It turns out that the answer to this question is ambiguous. This is because the marginal gain in profit obtained by each domestic firm from a tariff increase is higher, the higher is the fraction of sellers that must pay the tariff. But, for each domestic firm, the marginal cost of obtaining a given increase in the tariff rate is also higher, if $\phi'' > 0$. Only in the special case where $\phi(.)$ is linear or zero can we be sure that an increase in the ratio m^*/n leads to a greater level lobbying L.

Proposition 7 *An increase in the ratio of the number of foreign firms to the total number of firms will lead to a greater level of lobbying if the indirect lobbying cost function is linear or zero.*

We now turn to the effect of lobbying on the variance of the distribution of prices in the industry. Define this variance as

$$V = \frac{1}{n} \sum_{i \in N} (\widehat{p}_i - \widehat{p}_N)^2$$

We can prove the following result:

Proposition 8 *An increase in lobbying will increase (respectively, decrease) the variance of the distribution of prices in the industry if the initial average foreign price exceeds (respectively, is smaller than) the initial average industry price.*

Proof: From (7), with $b_i = b$ for all i, we get

$$\widehat{p}_i - \widehat{p}_N = \frac{1}{2}(\theta_i - \theta_N) \text{for } i \in N$$

Thus, for all home firms

$$\frac{\partial}{\partial L}[\widehat{p}_h - \widehat{p}_N] = -\frac{1}{2}\left(\frac{m^*}{n}\right) t'(L) < 0$$

and for all foreign firms

$$\frac{\partial}{\partial L}[\widehat{p}_f - \widehat{p}_N] = -\frac{1}{2}\left(\frac{m^*}{n} - 1\right) t'(L) > 0$$

Thus

$$\frac{\partial V}{\partial L} = \frac{1}{n} \sum_{f \in F} (\widehat{p}_f - \widehat{p}_N) t'(L).$$

This completes the proof.

3.2 Cooperative Lobbying

Now consider the case where in stage 1 all domestic firms get together to coordinate their lobbying activities, so as to maximize the sum of their profits in stage 2, net of the total lobbying cost. We continue to assume that in stage 2, the firms are Bertrand rivals. We assume that the stage 1 cooperation is enforced by cooperative Nash bargaining with side payments.

Their collective optimization problem is

$$\max_{L^C} \sum_{h \in H} \widehat{\pi}_h(\theta_h, \theta_N(L^C)) - [L^C + \phi^C(L^C)]$$

where the superscript C denotes the cooperative choice. The first order condition is

$$\sum_{h \in H} \left[\frac{1}{b} G(\widehat{p}_N(\theta_N^C)) - \theta_h \right] \left[\frac{\Omega g m^*}{4n} \right] = 1 + \frac{d\phi^C}{dL^C}$$

which can be simplified as

$$mt'(L^C) \left[\frac{1}{b} G(\widehat{p}_N(\theta_N^C)) - \theta_H \right] \left[\frac{\Omega g m^*}{4n} \right] = 1 + \frac{d\phi^C}{dL^C} \qquad (18)$$

This equation gives the following result, which is in sharp contrast to Proposition 6:

Proposition 9 *In the case of cooperative lobbying, the level of lobbying L is dependent on the mean marginal cost θ_H and is independent of any change in the variance of the distribution of marginal costs.*

Let us compare condition (18) with the non-cooperative counterpart, which is given below:

$$mt'(L^n) \left[\frac{1}{b} G(\widehat{p}_N(\theta_N^n)) - \theta_f \right] \left[\frac{\Omega g m^*}{4n} \right] = m + \sum_{h \in H} \phi_h'(L_h^n) \qquad (19)$$

where the superscript n denotes the non-cooperative solution.(Equation (19) may be obtained from (13) on the assumption that all home firms undertake lobbying).

The difference between the two solutions L^C and L^n depends on how the aggregate indirect cost function $\phi^C(.)$ differs from the individual indirect cost functions $\phi_h(.)$. For example, it may be sensible to suppose that $\phi^C(L^C)$ as the least cost way of using the individual lobbying technologies, that is, if we define

$$\phi^C(L^C) = \min \left[\sum_{h \in H} \phi_h(L_h) \text{ suchthat } \sum_{h \in H} L_h = L^C \right] \qquad (20)$$

If (20) is assumed, then, using the envelope theorem, we get

$$\frac{d\phi^C}{dL^C} = \phi_1'(L_1^C) = \phi_2'(L_2^C) = \cdots = \phi_m'(L_m^C) \qquad (21)$$

where

$$\sum_{h \in H} L_h^C = L^C$$

The next result follows immediately:

Proposition 10 *If the aggregate indirect cost function $\phi^C(.)$ is defined by (20), then the cooperative lobbying level L^C exceeds the non-cooperative one, L^n.*

Remark 2. The above proposition is just another instance of the general conclusion that the non-cooperative supply of a public good falls short of the optimal level. But it does depends on the assumption that the aggregate indirect cost function is generated by (20). If we suppose instead that

$$\phi(L^C) = (L^C)^2 \text{ and } \phi_h(L_h) = (L_h)^2 \tag{22}$$

then (20) does not hold. In that case, it is possible that the cooperative lobbying level L^C is equal to, or even smaller than, the non-cooperative one, L^n. This is because, under (22), it is cheaper for m home firms to carry out the lobbying level L_h each, than for the coalition of m firms to carry out the aggregate lobbying level mL_h.

4 Specification 2: Lobbying Is a Detraction from Internal Control

In this section, we turn to an an alternative specification of lobbying costs. We now posit that each firm has a fixed endowment, E, of entrepreneurial time. Now we interpret L_h as the portion of entrepreneurial time that the firm h devotes to "political activities." Thus the remaining amount of time, $E - L_h$, is devoted to internal control (such as monitoring, planning, and so on). The more time the firm spends on lobbying, the less time it has for internal control. Then a firm's lobbying cost is no longer an amount of money it spends on political activities, but the increase in the marginal production cost θ_h from its "base-line level", which we denote by θ_h^0. To be concrete, let us assume that a firm's marginal production cost is the *sum* of its base-line cost and a detraction cost, $\delta(L_h)$:

$$\theta_h(L_h) = \theta_h^0 + \delta(L_h) \tag{23}$$

where $\delta(0) = 0$, $\delta'(L_h) > 0$ and $\delta''(L_h) > 0$ for $L_h \geq 0$. While L_h is determined in stage 1, the production cost in stage 2 is affected by L_h because a lower level of internal control (in the sense of planning etc.) in stage 1 implies a higher production cost in stage 2.

The firm's Bertrand equilibrium profit in stage 2 is

$$\hat{\pi}_h = [\hat{p}_h - \theta_h(L_h)]\hat{q}_h = \frac{1}{b}[\hat{q}_h(\theta_h(L_h), \theta_N)]^2 = \frac{1}{4b}[G(\hat{p}_N(\theta_N)) - b\theta_i(L_h)]^2 \tag{24}$$

where L_h is taken as given, and

$$\theta_N = \sum_{h \in H} \theta_h(L_h) + \sum_{f \in F} [\theta_f^0 + t(L)]$$

with $L = \sum_{h \in H} L_h$.

In stage 1, the firms choose L_h, $h \in H$. Again, we consider two cases: non-cooperative lobbying, and cooperative lobbying.

4.1 Case 1: Non-Cooperative Allocation of Lobbying Time

In this case, the firms choose their lobbying time in a non-cooperative fashion. The constraints are $L_h \geq 0$ and $E - L_h \geq 0$. Let the associated multipliers be λ_h and μ_h. The first order condition for firm h is

$$\frac{2\hat{q}_h}{b} \left[\frac{\partial \hat{q}_h}{\partial \theta_N} \left(\frac{\partial \theta_N}{\partial t} \frac{\partial t}{\partial L_h} + \frac{\partial \theta_N}{\partial \theta_h} \frac{\partial \theta_h}{\partial L_h} \right) + \frac{\partial \hat{q}_h}{\partial \theta_h} \frac{\partial \theta_h}{\partial L_h} \right] + \lambda_h - \mu_h = 0 \qquad (25)$$

with

$$\lambda_h \geq 0, \quad L_h \geq 0, \quad \text{and } \lambda_h L_h = 0$$

$$\mu_h \geq 0, \quad E - L_h \geq 0, \quad \text{and } \mu_h(E - L_h) = 0$$

Using the additive cost formulation in (23), we obtain from condition (25):

$$\frac{2\hat{q}_h}{b} \left[\left(\frac{\Omega g m^*}{4n} \right) t'(L) + \left(\frac{\Omega g}{4n} - \frac{b}{2} \right) \delta'(L_h) \right] + \lambda_h - \mu_h = 0 \qquad (26)$$

Since $\Omega g < 2b$, an interior solution, $0 < L_h < E$, for all domestic firms is possible, with all home firms allocating the same amount of time in lobbying:

$$\delta'(L_h) = \left(\frac{\Omega g m^*}{2bn - \Omega g} \right) t'(L) \text{ for all } h \in H \qquad (27)$$

Thus we can state:

Proposition 11 *Assume that marginal production cost is the sum of its baseline cost and a detraction cost, as in (23). Even if all firms have different baseline marginal production costs θ_h^0, there exists a non-cooperative equilibrium where they allocate the same amount of time in lobbying.*

Remark 3. This proposition is in sharp contrast to Proposition 3, where firms with lower marginal production costs undertake higher levels of lobbying activities. It should be noted that the additive form of the marginal cost function, as given in (23) is responsible for the surprising result of equal lobbying time. Let us consider an alternative formulation, where the detraction cost appears in the multiplicative fashion:

$$\theta_h(L_h) = \omega(L_h)\theta_h^0 \qquad (28)$$

where $\omega(0) = 1$, $\omega'(L_h) > 0$ and $\omega''(L_h) > 0$. In this case, using the additive cost formulation in (23), we obtain from condition (25):

$$\frac{2\hat{q}_h}{b} \left[\left(\frac{\Omega g m^*}{4n} \right) t'(L) + \left(\frac{\Omega g}{4n} - \frac{b}{2} \right) \omega'(L_h)\theta_h^0 \right] + \lambda_h - \mu_h = 0 \qquad (29)$$

In this case, it is also possible to have an interior solution for all domestic firms, but the amount of time allocated by firm h will be dependent on its base-line cost θ_h^0. Thus we can state:

Proposition 12 *Assume that marginal production cost is the product of its base-line cost and a detraction cost, as in (28). Then firms with high base-line marginal production costs θ_h^0, allocate less time in lobbying.*

A direct implication of proposition 12 is that, under the multiplicative formulation (28), lobbying opportunities can reverse the profit ranking of domestic firms. In the absence of lobbying opportunities, the marginal production cost of firm h is its base-line level θ_h^0. The higher is a firm's base-line level, the lower is its rank in terms of profit. When opportunities to lobby become available, the firms with lower base-line costs will spend more time in lobbying, and as a consequent, their marginal production costs rise, while firms with higher base-line costs do not allocate much time in lobbying, and thus their marginal production costs do not rise by much. These firms may therefore earn more profits compared with those that allocate a great deal of time in lobbying. Even though all domestic firms may earn more under the lobbying equilibrium, their profit ranking may be reversed. This reversal of profit ranking is known to occur in the Cournot case with homogenous product (see [2]). Here we establish a similar result, for Bertrand rivalry with differentiated products.

Proposition 13 *Under the multiplicative form (28) of the marginal cost function, the availability of lobbying opportunities can reverse the profit ranking of firms in the oligopoly.*

We now investigate the effect of an increase in the substitutability among the differentiated products on the equilibrium level of lobbying. From (27), we get

$$\frac{\delta'(L_h)}{t'(mL_h)} = \left(\frac{\Omega g m^*}{2bn - \Omega g} \right) \tag{30}$$

An increase in the index of substitutabilty E (see the Appendix) will lead to an increase in value of the right-hand side of equation (30). So the value of left-hand side must increase, which is possible if and only if L_h increases. Thus we have proved:

Proposition 14 *An increase in the substitutability among the differentiated products will lead to a greater lobbying effort.*

Let us turn to the effect of lobbying on the variance of the distribution of prices. Assume the additive form (23), so that all home firms undertake the same amount of lobbying. Recall that

$$\widehat{p}_i - \widehat{p}_N = \frac{1}{2}(\theta_i - \theta_N) \text{ for } i \in N$$

Thus

$$\frac{\partial}{\partial L_h}[\widehat{p}_h - \widehat{p}_N] = \frac{m^*}{2n}[\delta'(L_h) - t'(L)]$$

and

$$\frac{\partial}{\partial L_h}\left[\widehat{p}_f - \widehat{p}_N\right] = -\frac{m}{2n}\left[\delta'(L_h) - t'(L)\right]$$

Then the effect of lobbying on the variance is

$$\frac{\partial V}{\partial L_h} = (\widehat{p}_H - \widehat{p}_h)\frac{mm^*}{2n}\left[\delta'(L_h) - t'(L)\right]$$

where

$$\delta'(L_h) - t'(L) = \left[\left(\frac{2bn - \Omega g}{4n}\right)\left(\frac{\Omega gm^*}{4n}\right) - 1\right]t'(L) \tag{31}$$

The right-hand side of (31) is negative if m^*/n is sufficiently small. Thus we can state:

Proposition 15 *Assume that m^*/n is small. Lobbying for tariff protection will result in an increase (respectively, decrease) in the variance of the distribution of prices in the industry if the initial average foreign price exceeds (respectively, is smaller than) the initial average industry price.*

4.2 Cooperative Allocation of Lobbying Time

If firms can cooperate in stage 1, they will collectively solve the problem of allocation of lobbying time, $0 \leq L_h \leq E$, $h \in H$, to maximize the sum of their stage 2 profits:

$$\max J = \sum_{h \in H} \widehat{\pi}_h\left[\theta_h(L_h), \theta_N(t(L), L_1, L_2, \cdots L_m)\right] \tag{32}$$

where

$$\theta_N(t(L), L_1, L_2, \cdots L_m) = \frac{m^*\theta_h^0 + m^*t(L) + \sum_{h \in H}\left[\theta_h^0 + \delta(L_h)\right]}{n}$$

and

$$\widehat{\pi}_h\left[\theta_h(L_h), \theta_N(t(L), L_1, L_2, ..L_m)\right] = \frac{1}{b}\left[\widehat{q}_h(\theta_h, \theta_N)\right]^2$$

with

$$\widehat{q}_h(\theta_h, \theta_N) = \frac{1}{2}\left[a - b(\theta_h^0 + \delta(L_h))\right] + \frac{g\Omega}{4}\left[\frac{a}{b} + \theta_N\right]$$

Since the objective function is convex in the θ_h's (for a given θ_N), and now the firms can collectively affect the distribution of the θ_h's, there is the possibility that the solution of the joint maximization problem (32) might involve a corner solution: even if all home firms are ex-ante identical, there might be an incentive to create ex-post asymmetry so as to maximize joint profit. However, the choice variables are not the θ_h's, they are the L_h's. So, if there is sufficient concavity in the function $t(L)$, we still may have a maximum at a symmetric point.

Let λ_h and μ_h be the multipliers associated with the constraints $L_h \geq 0$ and $E - L_h \geq 0$. If there are m^* foreign firms, and $m = 2$ home firms, the first order conditions for problem (32) are:

$$\frac{\partial J}{\partial L_1} = \frac{2\widehat{q_1}}{b} \left[\frac{\Omega gmm^* t'(L_1 + L_2)}{4n} - \left(\frac{b}{2} - \frac{g\Omega}{4n} \right) \delta'(L_1) \right] +$$

$$\frac{2\widehat{q_2}}{b} \left[\frac{\Omega gmm^* t'(L_1 + L_2)}{4n} + \left(\frac{g\Omega}{4n} \right) \delta'(L_1) \right] + \lambda_1 - \mu_1 = 0 \qquad (33)$$

and

$$\frac{\partial J}{\partial L_2} = \frac{2\widehat{q_2}}{b} \left[\frac{\Omega gmm^* t'(L_1 + L_2)}{4n} - \left(\frac{b}{2} - \frac{g\Omega}{4n} \right) \delta'(L_2) \right] +$$

$$\frac{2\widehat{q_1}}{b} \left[\frac{\Omega gmm^* t'(L_1 + L_2)}{4n} + \left(\frac{g\Omega}{4n} \right) \delta'(L_2) \right] + \lambda_2 - \mu_2 = 0 \qquad (34)$$

At a symmetric solution, we have

$$\frac{\delta'(L_h)}{t'(mL_h)} = \frac{\Omega gm^*}{2b(n/m) - g\Omega} > 0 \qquad (35)$$

Comparing (35) with (30), we can state:

Proposition 16 *Under cooperative allocation of lobbying time, at a symmetric solution, the firms will use more lobbying time compared with the non-cooperative solution.*

Finally, it can be shown that the following result holds:

Proposition 17 *Under cooperative allocation of lobbying time, an increase in the substitutability of the products will lead to an increase in lobbying by home firms.*

5 Concluding Remarks

By using a model with differentiated products, we have been able to obtain additional results concerning the effects of parameter changes (such as an increase in substitutability) on the equilibrium level of lobbying, the impact of lobbying on the dispersion of prices, the possibility of reversal of profit ranking, and so on. We have found that results are very sensitive to assumptions on the mode of lobbying (e.g., whether entrepreneurial time is diverted into lobbying), on the way production costs are affected by reduced internal control (e.g., multiplicative versus additive effects), on the behavior of firms (i.e., non-cooperative versus cooperative lobbying). Our paper therefore helps explain the reported ambiguities in empirical tests on various hypotheses about the determinants of the effectiveness of lobbying.

APPENDIX : Derivation of the Demand Function from Utility Maximization.

Assume that there are two differentiated goods, q_1 and q_2, and a numeraire good x (where $p_x = 1$). Assume the quasi-linear utility function

$$U(q_1, q_2, x) = x + u(q_1, q_2)$$

where

$$u(q_1, q_2) = A(q_1 + q_2) - \frac{B}{2}(q_1^2 + q_2^2) - Eq_1q_2$$

and $0 < E < B$ to ensure strict concavity of u. Here, E is the degree of substitutablity between the two differentiated products. Maximizing U subject to the budget constraint $p_1q_1 + p_2q_2 + x = M$ yields the inverse demand functions:

$$p_i = A - Bq_i - Eq_j$$

Inverting, we get

$$q_1 = \frac{A(B - E) - Bp_1 + Ep_2}{B^2 - E^2}$$

$$= a - bp_1 + gp_N$$

where $p_N = (p_1 + p_2)/2$, and

$$a = \frac{A}{B + E}, \quad b = \frac{1}{B - E}, \quad g = \frac{2E}{(B^2 - E^2)}$$

Let

$$\Omega = (1 - \frac{g}{2b})^{-1} = \frac{B + E}{B}$$

Then

$$\widehat{p}_N = (1 - \frac{g}{2b})^{-1} \left[\frac{\theta_N + (a/b)}{2} \right] = \frac{(B + E)\theta_N + A(B - E)}{2B}$$

As E tends to zero, we have two independent monopolists and $\widehat{p}_N$ tends towards the monopoly price $(\theta_N + A)/2$.

As E tends towards B ($g/(2b)$ tends towards $1/2$) the goods become closer substitutes and the equilibrium average price falls (since $A > \theta_N$ is the restriction that ensure positive profits).

References

1. Bergstrom T, Varian H (1985) When are Nash Equilibria Independent of Agents' Characteristics?, Review of Economic Studies 52: 715-718
2. Hillman A, Long NV, Soubeyran A (2001) Protection, Lobbying, and Market Structure, Journal of International Economics 54: 383-409

3. Long NV, Soubeyran A (1996) Lobbying for Protection by Heterogenous Firms, European Journal of Political Economy 12, :19-32
4. Long NV, Soubeyran A (2001) Cost Manipulation Games in Oligopoly, with Costs of Manipulating, International Economic Review 42: 505-533
5. Olson M (1965) The Logic of Collective Action, Harvard University Press, Cambridge, MA
6. Potters J, Sloof R (1996) Interest Groups: A Survey of Empirical Models that Try to Assess Their Influence, European Journal of Political Economy 12: 403-442

The Value of Multilateral Trade Liberalization and the Need for Third-Party Sanction[*]

Kong-Pin Chen[1], Cheng-Zhong Qin[2], and Larry D. Qiu[3]

[1] Institute for Social Sciences and Philosophy, Academia Sinica, Taipei, Taiwan.
`Kongpin@gate.sinica.edu.tw`
[2] University of California, Santa Barbara, CA 93106. `qin@ust.hk`
[3] Larry D. Qiu, Department of Economics, Hong Kong University of Science and Technology, Kowloon, Hong Kong. `larryqiu@ust.hk`

1 Introduction

The GATT/WTO and preferential trade agreements help member countries to achieve further gains from trade by promoting deeper trade liberalization. In general, free trade does not automatically follow from individualistic behavior. A major reason for this has to do with the existence of monopolistic power in trade.[1] Trade liberalization requires that countries behave cooperatively and reciprocally. In certain circumstances, greater cooperation and reciprocity can only be achieved through multilateral trade agreements, as opposed to a web of bilateral trade agreements,[2] and sustained through third-party punishments.

To illustrate, consider three countries: China, Japan, and the United States. The US would be better off if Japan would open its market to US agricultural products. However, in this case, the US has few sectors with which to reciprocate because almost all US markets are already very open to Japanese products. The lack of reciprocity discourages Japan and the US from reaching a bilateral agreement for further trade liberalizations. On the other hand, China can reduce its tariffs on electrical appliances that would help Japan since Japan is a major exporter of these goods in the world, but Japan

---

[*] We benefitted from comments by Stephen Ching and participants at the International Conference on Greater China and the WTO, held in March 2001 in Hong Kong. Financial support from Hong Kong SAR Government (HKUST6214100H) is greatly acknowledged.

[1] As shown by [8], the optimal tariff for an individual country is generally not zero. Other important arguments for protection include the protection of infant industries and the political economy of trade policies.

[2] Multilateralism is not unanimously preferred to bilateralism. For example, [5] argue that it is more difficult for many countries to reach consensus on trade issues, as compared when two countries are involved. Other examples along this line include [2], [3], [6], and [9].

has few sectors with which to reciprocate. To induce China to reduce tariffs on electrical appliances, the US can phase out its Multifiber Arrangement, which sets export quotas on textile products from China and some other countries, so that China can export more textiles and clothing to the US. As a result, circular concessions may occur and, based on such concessions, a multilateral trade liberalization in three sectors would benefit all three countries.

The above illustration demonstrates an important advantage of multilateral trade agreements over bilateral ones. Such an advantage is created from bilateral imbalances of power, in the sense that one country can make more tariff concessions to another country but not conversely. Thus the former is "more powerful" because it stands to lose less from a bilateral trade war. As shown by [9], in the presence of bilateral imbalances of power, outcomes that are Pareto superior to the ones that are sustainable with bilateral trade agreements can be achieved with multilateral trade agreements and third-party punishment. The reason is simple. With bilateral agreements for deeper trade liberalization, the victim (the less powerful one) is not able to punish the defector (the more powerful one) sufficiently strongly to deter defection. However, with a multilateral trade agreement combined with third-party punishment, the joint punishment would be stronger and so deeper liberalization can be sustained. In the present paper, we explore circumstances in which *any* Pareto improvement upon the "unilateral subgame-perfect equilibrium"[3] must be supported by a multilateral trade agreement together with third-party punishment. As in [9], this paper provides a rationale for joint punishment by both the victims and nonvictims of defection. However, our paper tries to extend the work of [9] in several directions as discussed below.

We consider a three-country trade model that is shown to exhibit *triangular trade*, where a country is a net exporter to another country that in turn is a net exporter to a third country, and this third country in turn is a net exporter to the first one.[4] In [9], certain welfare improvements upon the unilateral Nash equilibrium[5] are possible via bilateral trade agreements that do not involve any thirty-party punishment. That is, only more significant improvements require multilateral trade agreements with thirty-party punishment.

---

[3] The subgame-perfect equilibrium of a two-stage game, in which the countries set their tariffs independently in the first stage and while observing these tariffs, the firms decide on their quantities independently in the second stage (see the next section). As in [9], the word "unilateral" is used to emphasize the fact that multilateral trade agreements are not yet considered.

[4] [8] (p. 236) point out that some advantageous trade deals inherently involve more than two countries since such bilateral imbalances of power link them together. In particular, they mention the following situation: "The United States sells more to Europe, Europe sells more to Saudi Arabia, Saudi Arabia sells more to Japan, and Japan sells more to the United States."

[5] In [9], only the countries behave strategically in deciding the tariffs. Both firms and consumers are competitive. Hence, the model there is basically a one-stage game.

We show, in the present paper, that there are situations in which *any* welfare improvement from the unilateral subgame-perfect equilibrium, small or large, requires a multilateral agreement with third-party punishment. This result is significant as we observe that most multilateral trade liberalizations take place in a gradual fashion.[6] Thus, our result implies that in certain circumstances third-party punishment may be required even when trade liberalization takes place gradually.

In [9], endowments are assigned to the trading countries and so supply is not affected in any way by changes in trade policies. As a result, strategic reactions by firms to changes in a country's trade policies cannot be examined in such a model. Given the trade policies of all three countries, the first welfare theorem of the general equilibrium theory implies that gains from trade are exhausted by the resulting worldwide competitive equilibrium. Gains from defecting by any country tend to be small under these assumptions. One therefore wonders whether bilateral imbalances of power become stronger or weaker without these assumptions. In the present paper, we relax these assumptions and show that bilateral imbalances of power are not as extreme as they appear to be. Hence, to realize greater gains from trade, punishment by nonvictims or third-parties should not be entirely ruled out.

There are two interesting points associated with the above-mentioned results. First, although it is generally true that collective punishment helps support Pareto-improving multilateral trade liberalizations, we show that there are situations in which the resulting trade patterns make third-party punishment *necessary* to sustain any Pareto-improving multilateral trade liberalization from the unilateral subgame-perfect equilibrium. Second, with respect to the rules and procedures governing the settlement of disputes, the WTO is clearly mute on the possibility of allowing nonvictim member countries to punish a defector.[7] An implication is that more explicit rules regarding third-party punishment may be needed in order to facilitate deeper trade liberalization in some cases.

The rest of the paper is organized as follows. In Section 2, we develop the model and analyze the value of multilateral trade liberalization. In Section 3, we examine the need for third-party punishment. Concluding remarks are in Section 4.

2 Pareto-Improving Multilateral Trade Liberalization

Consider a world in which there are three countries and three goods. We call both the countries and the goods 1, 2, and 3. Unless otherwise specified,

---

[6] For a survey of studies on gradual trade liberalization, see [10].

[7] [9] argues that nonvictim members of the WTO can punish the defecting government in some subtle ways by withdrawing some of their "goodwill" toward that government. However, this is not included as part of the WTO rules.

we distinguish the two sets of names using a superscript for countries and a subscript for goods. Each country produces two goods but consumes all three of them. Country i produces goods i and $i + 1$, for $i = 1, 2$, and 3. When $i + j > 3$, it will be understood that $i + j$ are modularized by 3. Hence, good i is produced by country i and country $i + 2$ (see Figure 1 for an illustration).

Country i's production technologies have constant marginal costs, which are denoted by c_i^i and c_{i+1}^i, respectively. Country i's demand for good j is $P_j^i(Q_j) = a_j^i - Q_j$, for $j = 1, 2, 3$. Finally, there is in each country at most one firm producing each good.

2.1 The Unilateral Subgame-Perfect Equilibrium

As the purpose of this paper is to demonstrate an advantage of multilateral trade liberalizations (over bilateral ones) and the necessity of third-party punishment, we focus on a particular trade pattern resulting from the following assumptions on the cost and demand functions:

- A1: $c_i^{i+2} > a_i^i > c_i^i$,
- A2: $a_{i+1}^i > \max\{c_{i+1}^i, c_{i+1}^{i+1}\}$,
- A3: $a_{i+2}^i > \max\{c_{i+2}^{i+1}, c_{i+2}^{i+2}\}$.

A1 implies that country i will produce good i but will not import it, because the other producer of the good (i.e., country $i + 2$) has a cost of production which is too high relative to the market demand for the good in country i. Under A2, country i will produce good $i + 1$ and will also import it from country $i + 1$. Finally, A3 implies that country i's market demand for good $i + 2$, which country i does not produce, is strong enough that it imports the good from both countries $i + 1$ and $i + 2$. Figure 1 depicts the trade flows for country 1, where the arrows indicate the directions of trade.

Given the above specifications of the cost and demand functions and hence the above pattern of trade, we can assume, without loss of generality, that country i only considers a tuple, $t^i = \left\{ t_{i+1}^i, t_{(i+1)(i+2)}^i, t_{(i+2)(i+2)}^i \right\}$, of three tariffs, where t_{i+1}^i denotes country i's tariff on good $i + 1$ (imported from country $i + 1$) and $t_{j(i+2)}^i$ is country i's tariff [8] on good $i + 2$ imported from country j for $j = i + 1, i + 2$. Let $t = \{t^1, t^2, t^3\}$ be the collection of all tariffs in the world.

We consider a *two-stage* model: Tariffs are set by the countries in the first stage and the firms observing the tariffs worldwide decide on their quantities in the second stage. We solve for a subgame-perfect equilibrium by working backwards. Due to political considerations, we assume that country i chooses its tariffs, t^i, to maximize the following weighted welfare function

---

[8] The Most Favored Nation clause of the GATT/WTO is not imposed at this point. That is, tariffs are set on a bilateral basis.

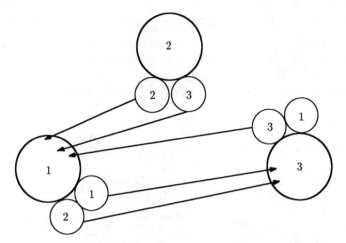

Fig. 1. The pattern of trade.
The big circles represent the countries and the small circles represent the goods.

$$W^i(t) = \sum_{h=i}^{i+1} \sum_{j=1}^{3} \Pi_{jh}^i(t) + \lambda_i \sum_{h=1}^{3} \mathrm{CS}_h^i(t) + \sum_{h=1}^{3} \mathrm{TR}_h^i(t), \tag{1}$$

where $\Pi_{jh}^i(t)$ denotes country i's profit from selling good h in country j, $\mathrm{CS}_h^i(t)$ denotes country i's consumer surplus from good h, and $\mathrm{TR}_h^i(t)$ denotes country i's tariff revenue from importing good h. They are all evaluated at the Nash equilibrium of the subgame played by the firms worldwide in the second stage led by the tariffs as embodied in t.[9] Parameter $\lambda_i > 0$ denotes the welfare weight for the total consumer surplus of country i.

Note that the functional forms of the demand functions imply that the markets are not interrelated, in the sense that a change in the price of a good in one place does not affect demand for either of the other two goods in any place. Thus, given t, the second stage Nash equilibrium quantities of the firms without subjecting to the nonnegativity constraint are given by

$$\hat{q}_{ii}^i = \frac{a_i^i - 2c_i^i}{3}, \tag{2}$$

$$\hat{q}_{i(i+1)}^i = \frac{a_{i+1}^i - 2c_{i+1}^i + c_{i+1}^{i+1} + t_{i+1}^i}{3}, \qquad \hat{q}_{i(i+1)}^{i+1} = \hat{q}_{i(i+1)}^i + c_{i+1}^i - c_{i+1}^{\prime i+1}, \tag{3}$$

$$\hat{q}_{i(i+2)}^{i+1} = \frac{a_{i+2}^i - 2c_{i+2}^{i+1} - 2t_{(i+1)(i+2)}^i + c_{i+2}^{i+2} + t_{(i+2)(i+2)}^i}{3}, \tag{4}$$

$$\hat{q}_{i(i+2)}^{i+2} = \hat{q}_{i(i+1)}^{i+1} + c_{i+2}^{\prime i+1} - c_{i+2}^{\prime i+2},$$

[9] The Nash equilibrium in each stage is unique under our specifications of the demand and cost functions.

where $c'^{i+2}_i = c^{i+2}_i + t^i_{i+1}$, $c'^{i+1}_{i+1} = c^{i+1}_{i+1} + t^i_{i+1}$, $c'^{i+1}_{i+2} = c^{i+1}_{i+2} + t^i_{(i+1)(i+2)}$, $c'^{i+2}_{i+2} = c^{i+2}_{i+2} + t^i_{(i+2)(i+2)}$, where $\hat{q}^i_{jk}$ denotes the quantity of good k produced by country i and sold in country j. Thus, by substituting (2)-(4) into the weighted welfare functions in (1), simple calculation shows that the subgame-perfect equilibrium tariffs without subjecting to the nonnegativity constraint are given by

$$\hat{t}^i_{i+1} = \frac{(5 - 2\lambda_i)a^i_{i+1} + (\lambda_i - 1)c^i_{i+1} + (\lambda_i - 4)c^{i+1}_{i+1}}{10 - \lambda_i}, \tag{5}$$

$$\hat{t}^i_{(i+1)(i+2)} = \frac{2(3 - 2\lambda_i)a^i_{i+2} + (3\lambda_i - 6)c^{i+1}_{i+2} + \lambda_i c^{i+2}_{i+2}}{4(3 - \lambda_i)}, \tag{6}$$

$$\hat{t}^i_{(i+2)(i+2)} = \frac{2(3 - 2\lambda_i)a^i_{i+2} + (3\lambda_i - 6)c^{i+2}_{i+2} + \lambda_i c^{i+1}_{i+2}}{4(3 - \lambda_i)}. \tag{7}$$

When $1.5 < \lambda_i < 3$, A3 and Eq.s (6) and (7) imply $\hat{t}^i_{(i+1)(i+2)} < 0$ and $\hat{t}^i_{(i+2)(i+2)} < 0$. When $\lambda_i < 2.5$, A2 and equation (5) imply that good $i+1$ will be produced in both country i and country $i + 1$ and it will also be imported by country i from country $i + 1$. Hence, as shown in Proposition 1 below, country i imposes a positive tariff only on good $i + 1$ that it imports from country $i+1$ when $1.5 < \lambda_i < 2.5$. The *unilateral subgame-perfect equilibrium* refers to the subgame-perfect equilibrium of the above two-stage model with the quantities and the tariffs all subject to the nonnegativity constraint.

Proposition 1. *Assume A1 − A3 hold and $1.5 < \lambda_i < 2.5$. Assume that further negative quantities and tariffs are not feasible. Then $t^{*i}_{(i+1)(i+2)} = t^{*i}_{(i+2)(i+2)} = 0$ and $t^{*i}_{i+1} > 0$ in the unilateral subgame-perfect equilibrium.*

Proof. Note first that the separability of the objective function implies that, in the unilateral subgame-perfect equilibrium, the tariff t^{*i}_{i+1} is determined by maximizing $\Pi^i_{i(i+1)}(t) + \lambda_i CS^i_{i+1}(t) + TR^i_{i+1}(t)$, subject to the nonnegativity constraint. By (5), $\hat{t}^i_{i+1} > 0$ when $1.5 < \lambda_i < 2.5$. We thus have $t^{*i}_{i+1} > 0$.

Observe next that $t^i_{(i+1)(i+2)}$ and $t^i_{(i+2)(i+2)}$ only appear in consumer surplus, CS^i_{i+2}, and tariff revenue, TR^i_{i+2}. Furthermore, both CS^i_{i+2} and TR^i_{i+2} are functions of only these two tariffs. Consequently, in the unilateral subgame-perfect equilibrium, the tariffs $t^{*i}_{(i+1)(i+2)}$ and $t^{*i}_{(i+2)(i+2)}$ are determined by maximizing $\lambda_i CS^i_{i+2}\left(t^i_{(i+1)(i+2)}, t^i_{(i+2)(i+2)}\right) + TR^i_{i+2}\left(t^i_{(i+1)(i+2)}, t^i_{(i+2)(i+2)}\right)$, subject to the nonnegativity constraint. By (4), this sum is concave.[10] Hence, it is also concave in any one of the two tariffs holding the other one constant. By (6) and (7), both $\hat{t}^i_{(i+1)(i+2)}$ and $\hat{t}^i_{(i+2)(i+2)}$ are negative when $1.5 < \lambda_i < 2.5$. Thus, by the concavity of $\lambda_i CS^i_{i+2} + TR^i_{i+2}$, $t^{*i}_{(i+1)(i+2)} = t^{*i}_{(i+2)(i+2)} = 0$.

---

[10] Recall that in calculating subgame-perfect equilibrium, firms' quantities must be as in (2)-(4), given any tariff collection t.

□

Eqs. (5)-(7) imply that for free trade to be a unilateral subgame-perfect equilibrium outcome, we must have $a^i_{i+1} = c^i_{i+1} = c^{i+1}_{i+1}$ and $a^i_{i+2} = c^{i+1}_{i+2} = c^{i+2}_{i+2}$. These conditions in turn imply that country i only produces good i and there is no trade. What this shows is simply that in the static two-stage model, it is impossible to support free trade as a unilateral subgame-perfect equilibrium outcome.

2.2 Pareto-Improving Trade Liberalization

When $t^{*i}_{(i+1)(i+2)} = t^{*i}_{(i+2)(i+2)} = 0$ and $t^{*i}_{i+1} > 0$, which is the unilateral subgame-perfect equilibrium as shown in Proposition 1, we say that the three countries make "circular concessions ." Building upon Proposition 1, we show in this section that any Pareto-improving trade liberalization agreement from the unilateral subgame-perfect equilibrium would require countries to make "circular concessions." This in turn implies that no Pareto-improving bilateral trade liberalization agreement is possible in the static two-stage model.

Proposition 2. *With the same assumptions as in Proposition 1, a Pareto improvement from the unilateral subgame-perfect equilibrium is possible through and only through a multilateral trade agreement that involves circular concessions in tariff reductions, such that country i reduces its tariffs, t^{*i}_{i+1}, on good $i + 1$, $i = 1, 2, 3$.*

Proof. From Proposition 1, the only possible trade liberalization from the unilateral subgame-perfect equilibrium in country i is to reduce its tariff on good $i + 1$, for $i = 1, 2, 3$. Denote by $w^i(t)$ the part of country i's weighted welfare function that will be affected by such trade liberalization in all countries. Then[11]

$$w^i(t) = \Pi^i_{(i+2)i}(t^{i+2}_i) + w^i_{i+1}(t^i_{i+1}) \tag{8}$$

where $w^i_{i+1}(t^i_{i+1}) = \Pi^i_{i(i+1)}(t^i_{i+1}) + \lambda_i CS^i_{i+1}(t^i_{i+1}) + TR^i_{i+1}(t^i_{i+1})$.

Let country i reduce its tariff from t^{*i}_{i+1} by an amount ϵ^i with $0 < \epsilon^i \le t^{*i}_{i+1}$. By (8), such a trade liberalization in country i causes a reduction in country i's own welfare by the amount $\Delta w^i_{i+1}(\epsilon^i) = w^i_{i+1}(t^{*i}_{i+1}) - w^i_{i+1}(t^{*i}_{i+1} - \epsilon^i)$[12] and an increment in country $i + 1$'s welfare by the amount $\Delta \Pi^{i+1}_{i(i+1)}(\epsilon^i) =$

---

[11] As noticed before, linearity in cost and demand functions implies that country i's profit from selling good i to country $i + 2$ does not depend on tariff levels other than t^{i+2}_i. Similarly, a country's consumer surplus and tariff revenue associated with good $i + 1$ do not depend on tariffs other than t^i_{i+1}.

[12] Since the tariff levels before trade liberalization agreements are taken to be those in the unilateral tariff Nash equilibrium, we can write such welfare changes simply as functions of the tariff reductions only.

$\Pi^{i+1}_{i(i+1)}(t^{*i}_{i+1} - \epsilon^i) - \Pi^{i+1}_{i(i+1)}(t^{*i}_{i+1})$. Thus, country i only gains from trade liberalization in country $i+2$ and it becomes better off only when this gain exceeds its loss resulting from its own trade liberalizations. This shows that Pareto-improving trade liberalizations must be all of the sort "country i reduces its tariff on good $i+1$ imported from country $i+1$." Such trade liberalizations involve all three countries and, therefore, Pareto-improving trade liberalization agreements are all necessarily multilateral. To complete the rest of the proof, it suffices to show the existence of tariff reductions, $\epsilon^1, \epsilon^2, \epsilon^3$, such that

$$\Delta\Pi^i_{(i+2)i}(\epsilon^{i+2}) \geq \Delta w^i_{i+1}(\epsilon^i), \quad i = 1, 2, 3,$$

with strict inequality for at least one country.

Note first that $\Delta w^i_{i+1}(\epsilon^i)$ and $\Delta\Pi^i_{(i+2)i}(\epsilon^{i+2})$ are both continuous, monotonically increasing functions of ϵ^i and ϵ^{i+2}, respectively. Furthermore, both terms are zero when $\epsilon^i = \epsilon^{i+2} = 0$. Thus, by choosing ϵ^1 to be sufficiently small, the Intermediate Value Theorem would imply that there are $\epsilon^2 < t^{*2}_3$ and $\epsilon^3 < t^{*3}_1$ such that

$$\Delta\Pi^i_{(i+2)i}(\epsilon^{i+2}) = \Delta w^i_{i+1}(\epsilon^i), \quad i = 2, 3. \tag{9}$$

Note also that by assumptions $A1 - A2$,

$$\frac{\partial[w^i_{i+1} + \Pi^{i+1}_{i(i+1)}]}{\partial t^i_{i+1}}$$
$$= \frac{1}{9}[(1 - 2\lambda_i)a^i_{i+2} - (5 - \lambda_i)c^i_{i+1} + (4 + \lambda_i)(c^{i+1}_{i+1} + t^i_{i+1}) - 6t^i_{i+1}] < 0$$

holds for $\lambda_i \geq 1$ and $t^i_{i+1} > 0$. Thus, it follows that when ϵ^i is small enough,[13]

$$\Delta\Pi^{i+1}_{i(i+1)}(\epsilon^i) > \Delta w^i_{i+1}(\epsilon^i), \quad i = 1, 2, 3. \tag{10}$$

That is, the total net gain from country i's trade liberalization is positive. Together (9) and (10) imply $\Delta\Pi^1_{31}(\epsilon^3) > \Delta w^3_1(\epsilon^3)$, $\Delta w^3_1(\epsilon^3) = \Delta\Pi^3_{23}(\epsilon^2) > \Delta w^2_3(\epsilon^2)$, and $\Delta w^2_3(\epsilon^2) = \Delta\Pi^2_{12}(\epsilon^1) > \Delta w^1_2(\epsilon^1)$. This shows $\Delta\Pi^1_{31}(\epsilon^3) > \Delta w^1_2(\epsilon^1)$. We have therefore shown the existence of tariff reductions of all three countries that make country 1 better off without making countries 2 and 3 worse off. □

The circular nature of the concessions as established in Proposition 2 implies that when a country, say country 1, revokes its concession to country 2, country 2 can do no better than to revoke its concession to country 3 in order

---

[13] Our choice of ϵ^2 depends on ϵ^1 via functions $\Delta\Pi^2_{12}(\epsilon^1)$ and $\Delta w^2_3(\epsilon^2)$ together with the Intermediate Value Theorem. Since these functions are continuous and monotonically increasing and since they are both zero when $\epsilon^1 = \epsilon^2 = 0$, ϵ^2 is small whenever ϵ^1 is small. Similarly, ϵ^3 is small whenever ϵ^2 is small. Hence, both ϵ^2 and ϵ^3 are small enough whenever ϵ^1 is small enough.

to avoid double losses.This action inflicts no punishment upon country 1. This means that country 3's punishment, a third-party punishment, has to be in place in order to deter country 1 from defecting. The possibility of sustaining Pareto-improving trade liberalizations from the unilateral subgame-perfect equilibrium via third-party punishment is studied in the next section.

3 Sustaining Multilateral Trade Liberalization via Third-Party Punishment

As a direct implication of Proposition 2, country $i + 1$ does not have any leverage to inflict damage upon country i for defecting on any given Pareto-improving trade liberalization agreement. Thus, country $i + 1$, the victim of country i's defection, must rely on country $i + 2$ to carry out the needed punishment for deterring country i from defecting on the given agreement. This confirms our early point that in circumstances where trading partners have to make circular concessions, the victimized partner may have to rely on a third-party to punish the defector in order to make the circular concessions self-enforcing.

When trade is infinitely repeated and punishment by third-parties is permissible, a trade liberalization agreement can be sustained by the following strategy of the trading countries, provided that the agreement is Pareto superior to the unilateral subgame-perfect equilibrium and that future payoffs are not heavily discounted:

Stick to the agreement in the first period and continue to do so for as long as no country defects. If, however, one country defects by raising its tariffs, set the tariff as in the unilateral subgame-perfect equilibrium.

The above strategy is the trigger strategy which is commonly used in the standard proof of the classic Folk theorem, according to which the strategies are self-enforcing (i.e. they form a subgame-perfect equilibrium of the corresponding infinitely repeated game) for large enough discount factors. The reader is referred to [6] (pp. 128-129) as an example. Note also that by reverting to their unilateral subgame-perfect equilibrium tariffs, one country provides a third-party punishment by forcing the defector to pay a higher tariff. In addition, as explained above, a Pareto improvement from the unilateral subgame-perfect equilibrium is not sustainable without third-party punishment.[14] We have thus shown

---

[14] [4] have shown that in a game with symmetric and separable payoff functions (which our model fits), any subgame-perfect equilibrium in which players play symmetric strategies can be sustained by a subgame-perfect equilibrium in which third-party sanction is not used; i.e., third-party sanction is of no use. Their result does not contrast our result because the players play asymmetric strategies in Proposition 3.

Proposition 3. *Suppose trade is infinitely repeated. Then, under the same conditions as in Proposition 1, every Pareto-improving trade liberalization agreement from the unilateral subgame-perfect equilibrium can be sustained via strategies that necessarily involve third-party punishment, provided that the discount factor is large enough for each country.*

As shown by Proposition 2, circular concessions in terms of trade liberalizations (tariff reductions) are necessary for any Pareto improvement from the unilateral subgame-perfect equilibrium, small or large, so that country i's gain from country $i + 2$'s concession outweighs the loss of its own concession to country $i+1$, for $i=1, 2, 3$. Thus, in our setting, Proposition 3 implies that gains from trade are sustainable when and only when third-party punishment is permitted and the trading countries do not heavily discount their future payoffs.

4 Conclusion

We build a simple model with three countries to show that circular concessions may sometimes be the only way to achieve Pareto-improving trade liberalization. The circular nature of the concessions implies in particular that Pareto-improving trade liberalization must be multilateral. It also implies the necessity for third-party punishment in sustaining Pareto-improving trade liberalization agreements. An implication of the results here is that more explicit rules than those currently governing the settlement of disputes under WTO regarding third-party punishment may sometimes be needed.

The results of this paper are driven by some very specific assumptions. For example, the model is constructed in such a way that the resulting optimal tariffs are negative for two out of three goods in every country. Moreover, different countries impose positive tariffs on different goods. Relaxation of these assumptions will certainly affect our results. However, the basic spirit survives. What we have argued essentially is that in order to realize gains from trade, sometimes what we call "circular concessions" are required in which each country grants concession to one other country but in turn is (more than) compensated by a third country. This type of gain from trade will require third-party punishment for enforcement. Consequently, a multilateral trade relation can realize certain gains from trade that are not achievable through bilateral trade agreements.

This idea of synergy creation through multilateral trade agreements does not depend on the assumptions discussed above. These assumptions are only used to greatly simplify our technical argument. Our argument is also different from the argument presented by [9], which stresses the improvement of third-party sanctions in enforcing multilateral trade agreement. We are more concerned with the creation of surplus through circular concessions. Although different in spirit, we believe our insight to be a useful complementary argument in favor of multilateral trade relations.

References

1. Bagwell K, Staiger RW (1990) A Theory of Managed Trade, American Economic Review 84(4): 779-95
2. Bagwell K, Staiger, RW (1999) An Economic Theory of GATT, American Economic Review, 89(1): 215-248
3. Bhagwati J, Panagariya A (1996) The Theory of Preferential Trade Agreements: Historical Evolution and Current Trends, American Economic Review Papers and Proceedings 86(2): 82-87
4. Bendor J, Mookherjee D (1990) Norms, Third-Party Sanction, and Cooperation, Journal of Law, Economics and Organization 6: 33-63
5. Deardorff AV, Stern RM (1997) Multilateral Trade Negotiations and Preferential Trading Agreements, In: Deardorff AV and Stern RM (eds.) Analytical and Negotiating Issues in the Global Trading System, Ann Arbor: The University of Michigan Press
6. Gintis H (2000) Game Theory Evolving: A Problem-Centered Introduction to Modeling Strategic Behavior. Princeton University Press
7. Johnson HG (1953-1954) Optimal Tariffs and Retaliation, Review of Economic Studies 21: 142-53
8. Krugman PR, Obstfeld M (2000) International Economics: Theory and Policy. Addison-Wesley, Fifth Edition
9. Maggi G (1999) The Role of Multilateral Institutions in International Trade Cooperation, American Economic Review 89(1): 190-214
10. Staiger R (1995) International Rules and Institutions for Trade Policy, Chapter 29, In: Grossman GM and Rogoff K (eds.), Handbook of International Economics, Volume III, North-Holland

Commercial Culture, Political Culture and the Political Economy of Trade Policy: The Case of Japan*

Seiichi Katayama[1] and Heinrich W. Ursprung[2]

[1] Research Institute for Economics and Business Administration, Kobe University, Rokkodai-cho, Nada-ku, Kobe 657, Japan katayama@rieb.kobe-u.ac.jp
[2] Department of Economics, University of Konstanz, Box D-138, 78457 Konstanz, Germany Heinrich.Ursprung@uni-konstanz.de

1 Introduction

Social interactions are shaped both by formal institutions and prevailing cultural norms. The formal institutions place external constraints on individual behavior while the cultural norms are personally internalized to become components of an individual's preferences or belief system.

Although constraints, preferences, and beliefs are all constituent parts of the economic model of behavior, economic theory has largely neglected the influence of specific institutional characteristics, and more so of specific cultural traits, on social interaction — whether the interaction be commercial or political.[1] We focus in this paper on consequences of cultural idiosyncrasies from both of these perspectives. We adopt a long-term view in which the commercial and political culture is liable to change, and trace the consequences of this cultural drift for political-economic interaction. There is no generally ac-

---

* This paper was written during the second author's visit at the Research Institute for Economics and Business Administration, Kobe University. He wishes to thank this institution for its warm hospitality. Helpful comments by Fumio Dei, Arye Hillman, Junko Kato, Nobeoka Kentaro, and Ikuo Kume are gratefully acknowledged. Kotaro Suzumura gave us very useful comments at the 2003 spring meeting of Japanese Economic Association. We are also grateful to seminar participants at the City University of Hong Kong, Emory University, Florida International University, MacGill University, Southern Illiois University and the University of Chile.

[1] The neglect of institutional considerations is more evident in traditional welfare-theoretic policy studies than in political-economic investigations. Nevertheless, many authors have noticed an unfortunate disregard for institutional details also in political-economic studies. For a discussion of this issue in the context of modeling endogenous trade policy, see [26].

cepted, precise, definition of the concept of culture,[2] and we apply the term to describe norms of social interaction that have evolved over time without any formal institutional backup. Such behavioral norms belong in Hayek's ([11], chapter 2) terminology in the realm of "cosmos" and are characterized by conservatism, conformity, tacit knowledge, emotional encoding, and mutual reinforcement. Most importantly, culturally based social norms imply entitlements and obligations that are often encoded as standards of appropriate behavior such as fairness, and are enforced through reputation effects (cf. [31], chapters 1 and 2).

We shall not be concerned here with the determinants and evolution of culture; we take cultural traits as given and investigate their influence on endogenous policy formation in the specific cultural setting of contemporary Japan.[3] The focus of the investigation is on political polarization, one of the key aspects of political-economic interaction. Since cultural traits are of especially great consequence when different cultures clash in the course of political-economic interactions, we have chosen Japan as an example. Japan, after all, is endowed with a very specific culture that contrasts significantly with the culture of her main trading partners and the political-economic positioning of the country vis-à-vis the rest of the world has always played a major role in Japanese politics.

Given the fact that delineating the political-economic relationship with her main allies and trading partners has always been an issue of utmost importance in Japan's political discourse and debate, we portray the political process with the help of an endogenous trade policy model. This model, on the one hand, is designed to capture a major aspect of Japanese economic policy. On the other hand, the model's implications are supposed to transcend the important but nevertheless specific trade-policy field and to provide an overall picture of the observed policy positions held by the principal players acting in the Japanese political landscape.

The paper is organized as follows. Section 2 provides some information about the cultural traits that distinguish Japan from the United States and describes the modeling approaches employed to portray these cultural traits. In section 3 we set up an endogenous trade policy model and analyze the influence of Japanese commercial culture on policy formation in a given environment of political culture. The influence of the political culture on policy polarization is analyzed in section 4. In the concluding section 5 we compare the predictions of our model with the long-term changes in policy polarization observed in post-WWII Japan.

---

[2] [15], [19] and [27] are three contributors in a special twin-issue of the European Journal of Political Economy that studies the concept of political culture.

[3] For a model which endogenizes commercial culture in an international trade context, see [18].

2 Commercial and Political Culture in Japan

2.1 Commercial Culture

The key distinguishing feature of the post-WWII Japanese commercial environment, as compared to the commercial environment in the United States, is the inter-firm specialization in tightly integrated production networks known as *Keiretsu* . Relationship-specific investments are the source of relational quasi rents (cf. [1]) that, ceteris paribus, increase the productivity of an entire network. Since sufficiently complete contracts protecting relationship-specific investments from opportunistic behavior of the investor's business partners are extremely costly or may even be unavailable, relationship-specific investments can only expected to be undertaken in a commercial environment in which business partners behave according to high standards of fairness and are, furthermore, trusted to do so. The notion that incomplete incentive contracts that are doomed to fail in an environment of selfish agents can become superior in an environment fostering fairness and trust is theoretically confirmed and supported by a series of experiments in a recent paper by [7].[4] *Fairness* and its counterpart *trust* thus represent the backbone of productivity-enhancing commercial networks.

It is generally believed that the commercial environment in Japan is characterized by a high degree of fairness and trust. Empirical studies of the automotive industry support this impression. [5], for example, define trust *as one party's confidence that the other party in the exchange relationship will not exploit its vulnerabilities* and document that supplier trust is significantly higher in Japan than in Korea or the United States. [30] also conclude that Japanese suppliers tend to confront a higher level of trust and a lower level of opportunism than U.S. suppliers. They point out that, in contrast to U.S. suppliers, Japanese suppliers distinguish between different types of trust – customer opportunism, competence trust and goodwill trust. Most importantly, however, reciprocity is more embedded in the Japanese conceptualization of trust than in the U.S. counterpart.

These findings are complemented by comparative studies of supplier involvement in the automotive industry. In the mid-1980s the major Japanese companies manufactured less than 30% of their component parts in-house compared to 70% at General Motors ([1]). In product development, the authoritative study by [2] reports that Japanese suppliers do four times more engineering work for a typical project than U.S. suppliers (p.136). The representative Japanese project, as a consequence, relies heavily on *black box parts* (designed by the supplier according to cost/performance requirements specified by the assembler) while the average U.S. project relies on *detail-controlled*

---

[4] For the measurement of trust (social capital), see [27]. An econometric study investigating the influence of trust on economic performance is to be found in [21].

parts for which most engineering work, including parts drawing, is done by the assembler (p.144). European suppliers lie somewhere in between.

Such observations substantiate the view that because it is endowed with a large stock of goodwill, the Japanes business environment sustains a higher level of asset specificity, which, in turn, can explain performance differences (see, for example, [4], and [5]).

The identification of the origin and determinants of trust is more controversial. There are two schools of thought. In his popular treatise on trust, [9] endorses and propagates the *culturist* view that fairness and trust between business partners is an externality deriving from general norms of reciprocity of the surrounding societal network. In this view, trust cannot be cultivated intentionally. It rather represents a cultural trait that individual business organizations accept as given. In the Japanese context, [13] traces the contemporary commercial culture back to the neo-Confucian ethical tradition that reached its greatest refinement during the 250 years of the Tokugawa shogunate (1603–1868). This tradition emphasized values such as group identification, collective responsibility, loyalty, reciprocal obligations, harmony, honesty and individual performance (see also [19]).

On the other hand, several studies on the determinants of trust (see, for example, [5], and [30]) support the *nurturist* view that which maintains that it is possible to intentionally cultivate and develop trust in a dyadic commercial relationship. Partnering is thus seen as a culturally neutral capability that can be developed over time by a strategic management decision to build up the required reputation. An interesting case study presented by [3] documents that since 1989, Chrysler Corporation has made a conscious attempt to move away from the traditional arms-length relationship in supplier management and has been able to duplicate some key aspects of the Japanese Keiretsu system within a relatively short period of time. In 1989, for example, 95% of Chrysler's suppliers were chosen through competitive biding, whereas six years later 95% of components were "re-sourced" to partner suppliers, and between 1990 and 1994 the total number of suppliers decreased from 2500 to 1387. It appears that Chrysler has been able to overcome the two fundamental problems associated with moving from arms-length relationships to supplier partnerships, namely, to compensate suppliers fairly and to provide them with adequate incentives to undertake relationship-specific efforts and investments. Chrysler's success offers evidence that the Keiretsu system is not culturally bound and is applicable outside Japan.

We do not intend to take a position in this controversy on the origins of fairness and trust. We rather proceed from the observation that the level of fairness and trust varies considerably across business communities and that this attribute is characterized by considerable persistence. Whether it is a country's culture that largely determines the level of fairness and trust in business partners or a costly build-up of reputation in dyadic business relationships (which, of course, may be facilitated by an accommodating cultural background) is not material for our argument. In any case, we treat fairness and trust in business partners as an exogenous phenomenon that changes only slowly over time, and we refer to such standards of fairness and trust as a given aspect of the commercial culture.

Our model contrasts a domestic economy in which economic relationships are strongly influenced by fairness and trust with a foreign economy where these features are absent or less significant, and we consider the endogenous formation of a policy that dominates the international economic relations between the two countries. The analysis stresses the long-term relationship between local suppliers of intermediate goods and downstream firms producing a final product for the world market. To portray this relationship we exemplarily employ the vertical Keiretsu relationship within a Japanese corporate group that has market and political interactions with a foreign industry where the vertical relationships are at arms length.

In portraying the economic relationships we make use of the Keiretsu representation developed by [32]. We are well aware that this representation does not do justice to all facets of the complex Keiretsu relationships.[5] Nevertheless we use this model as a handy and neat building block which captures one key aspect of the Japanese commercial system. The key idea of this Keiretsu representation is that fairness and trust promote suppliers' willingness to invest in customer-specific assets because the suppliers have good reason to trust that these investments will be honored in the future in fair price-negotiations. The relationship-specific long-term investments reduce the cost of the down-stream producer, the so-called (Japanese) J-maker. The price-setting mechanism is portrayed through a standard Nash bargaining solution.

The parameter measuring the relative bargaining power of the monopsonistic J-maker vis-à-vis his Keiretsu supplier is a convenient indicator of the fairness standards in the domestic economy (Japan). We use this parameter to summarize the commercial culture. In the competing foreign (U.S.) industry, the commercial culture does not support long-term relationships based solely on trust, and we model this commercial environment as a perfectly competitive market for component parts. In this competitive environment, suppliers have no reason to trust that an investment in customer-specific assets not enforced through formal contracts will be profitable in the future. Specialized assets rather expose a naive supplier to the uncovered risk of opportunistic exploitation since his business "partner" benefits from the investment. The out-sourced component parts of the (American) A-maker, as a consequence, do not incorporate (non-contractable) relationship-specific investments. The two scenarios coalesce in the limit if all bargaining power is with the J-maker. We can thus interpret the American market environment as one extreme on a continuum that ranges from environments in which agents behave in a completely fair and trustworthy manner to environments populated by completely opportunistic agents.

---

[5] For a lucid description of the complex real-life Keiretsu relationships, see, for example, [25].

2.2 Political Culture

Culturally transmitted norms of social interaction also shape the behavior of persons in political life. We acknowledge the influence of political culture by specifying policy-makers' preferences in a manner that allows various social norms to be accommodated. We model the domestic (Japanese) political process using the electoral competition approach (cf.[34] and [16]). We believe that the scope of this approach is sufficiently wide to portray changes in political culture that have taken place in modern (i.e. post WWII) Japan. The electoral competition approach does, however, exclude some institutional and cultural settings, since it emphasizes the influence of interest groups and thus principal-agent problems between government and voters at large. Our picture of the political process rules out the traditional view that maintains that politicians act like benevolent dictators; we rather describe politicians as rational utility maximizers who face election constraints. The electoral competition approach also recognizes that the Japanese political system is embedded in a cultural setting in which wholesale corruption or crony-capitalism is absent. We do not interpret the long and rather troubling history of monumental political scandals permeating the highest levels of Japanese politics as a sign of cultural deterioration.[6] We rather concur with [15], who see merit when voters can still be scandalized by disclosures that political discretion has been used in illegal ways. Scandals are, in this view, an indicator of a culture that values political integrity. As we see the political culture in Japan, "official corruption," which implies an explicit interaction between politicians and donors of campaign contributions, does, in the usual course of events, not take place. Policies are not corruptly "for sale" (to use the terminology of [10]), nor does the political culture allow politicians to convert political support into personal income (cf. [33]) − at least not on an overwhelming scale.

Our model portrays a political culture in which policies are designed with a view to electoral success. The policy platforms of the political parties competing for electoral success respond to the anticipated reaction of clientele interest groups who support election campaigns. The political culture is thus such that politicians are to some degree "personally corrupted", because they deviate from ideological policy stances to enhance election prospects. The degree to which the politicians are personally corrupted, or alternatively, the

---

[6] In the long reign of the Liberal Democratic Party (LDP), major scandals broke at least every five or six years, the most notorious being Showa Denko (1948), the black Mist (1966), Lockheed (1976), Recruit (1988-89), and Sagawa Kyubin (1993). The Sagawa Kyubin scandal undeniably proved − just as the Lockheed scandal before − that politicians and bureaucrats had systematically accepted bribes in exchange for making exceptions to Japan's nominally rigid regulatory rules. Japanese citizens, however, did not simply accept these scandals with a cynical tolerance of "politics as usual". Following each scandal, there was media-led public outcry and the party's popularity would plummet (see [28], p.5, 140, and 202).

degree to which politicians feel an obligation towards the policy interest of their clientele (which the politicians may have internalized in the form of ideological motives), is a characterizing attribute of the political culture. We describe changes in Japanese political culture through a parameter measuring the relative weight of the ideological and electoral motives in political preferences. The parameter describing the prevailing political culture thus plays a similar role to the parameter describing the prevailing commercial culture: both measure the prevalence of internalized obligations or standards of fairness vis-à-vis close associates in the respective social network.[7]

In the next section we analyze the influence of Japanese *commercial* culture on trade policy formation by assuming that policy-makers have not been captured by particular special interests. That is, competing political parties do not subscribe to political ideologies accommodating particular economic interests; they exhibit perfect personal corruption and choose the trade policies that maximize electoral prospects. In section 4 we then relax this assumption to investigate the influence of changes in the prevailing *political* culture on political polarization.

3 Commercial Culture and Endogenous Policy

A combination of the basic idea of the Keiretsu representation by [32] and the standard form of the electoral competition model results in a two-county (partial equilibrium) model in which five players strategically interact with each other: (1) the domestic (Japanese) producer of the final good (i.e. the J-maker), (2) the domestic Keiretsu supplier S, (3) the foreign (American) producer of the final good (i.e. the A-maker), (4) the domestic political party P_L that advocates a relatively liberal trade policy, and (5) the domestic political party P_P that advocates a more protectionist trade policy. This set-up gives rise to the following natural sequencing of strategic moves summarized in Figure 1. The least reversible move is the long-term investment in relationship-specific assets undertaken by the Keiretsu supplier S.[8] The supplier S thus moves first by deciding on the value k of his Keiretsu investment.[9] Then the policy regime is decided upon: the two competing political parties P_L and P_P simultaneously announce their policy platforms t_L and t_P designated in terms of a tariff on imported intermediate goods. The three players who are

---

[7] For an alternative but in principle similar way of portraying political culture, see [6].

[8] We simplify the [32] representation by assuming that the J-maker needs only one input. We thereby relegate the problems associated with the public good character of the suppliers' campaign expenditures to the background. For an analysis of the easy-riding effects occurring in this context, see [33].

[9] In the paper by [32] the suppliers' investment decisions and the production decisions by the final-goods producers are made at the same time. Our sequencing, however, seems to be more in line with the underlying idea.

directly affected by the trade policy outcome, the two producers of the final good and the Keiretsu supplier S, observe these policy pronouncements and simultaneously decide on how much they will support the competing political parties. Notice that we assume here with [16] that the foreign interest, the American A-maker, can, in principle, interfere in the domestic (i.e. Japanese) political process. The political support takes the form of campaign expenditures (denoted by L_J, L_A, and L_S, respectively) that, via a contest success function, determine the election outcome and thereby the implemented trade policy t. In Figure 1 the stochastic designation of the winner of the political contest is represented as a fictitious move by "nature" N. After the trade policy regime t is revealed, the two final—goods producers, the J—maker and the A-maker, simultaneously determine their respective output y_J and y_A. In the final move, the J-maker negotiates the price p for the intermediate good with the Keiretsu supplier S.

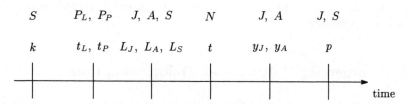

Fig. 1. The sequencing of moves.

The following equations portray the economic relationships:

$$\pi_J = y_J \left(A - Y - p - w_0 + \theta w_0 \sqrt{k} \right) \tag{1}$$

$$\varphi = y_J(p - c) - k \tag{2}$$

$$\pi_A = y_A \left(A - Y - c^* - w_0 \right) \tag{3}$$

Equation (1) defines the profit π_J of the J-maker. The J-maker and the A-maker are Cournot competitors. Y denotes total output ($Y = y_A + y_J$) and the market demand function is $P = A - Y$. The variable p denotes the price (cost) of the input per unit of output, and w_0 the per unit assembly cost if the input is bought from a domestic or foreign outside supplier who has not made any relationship-specific investments. The last term in the bracket therefore denotes the reduction in assembly cost due to the Keiretsu investment k (θ is a parameter). In (2), the (domestic) Keiretsu supplier produces the intermediate good under constant average cost c; his profit is denoted by φ. The A-maker's profit π_A is defined in (3). The A-maker's supplier sells under perfect competition, so the input price equals his constant average cost of production c^*. In accordance with [32] we shall maintain the assumption that the cost of producing the basic intermediate good is lower in country A than in country J: that is, $c^* < c$. The A-maker thus buys his input at the price c^*. The basic assembly costs w_0 are assumed to be the same in the two countries.

We solve the model by backward induction. The price of the input is determined as a Nash bargaining solution. The J-maker's bargaining objective is to maximize his per-unit cost-reduction $[(1 + t)c^* + w_0] - \left[p + w_0 - \theta w_0 \sqrt{k}\right] = (1 + t)c^* - p + \theta w_0 \sqrt{k}$, where $(1 + t)c^*$ is the tariff-inclusive cost of the imported input. The Keiretsu supplier's bargaining objective is to maximize his per unit profit $p - c$. Denoting the J-maker's bargaining power by α and the Keiretsu -supplier's by $1 - \alpha$, the Nash product is: [10]

$$G = \left[(1 + t)c^* - p + \theta w_0 \sqrt{k}\right]^\alpha [p - c]^{1-\alpha} . \tag{4}$$

The resulting Nash bargaining price that maximizes G is

$$p = (1 - \alpha) \left(\theta w_0 \sqrt{k} - \delta\right) + c, \tag{5}$$

where δ denotes the input price difference $c - (1 + t)c^*$ in country J. Notice, that for $\alpha = 1$, the price p equals the average cost c.

The parameter α is our measure for the prevailing commercial culture. If $\alpha = 1$, the supplier has no bargaining power and will thus not be treated in a "fair" manner: his relationship-specific investment will not be honored. On the other hand, if $\alpha = 0.5$, both negotiating parties enjoy the same bargaining power, which implies that suppliers' relationship-specific investments will be honored in a perfectly fair manner.

Preceding the bargaining stage, the J-maker and the A-maker simultaneously determine their outputs y_J and y_A. Maximizing π_J and π_A as given in (1) and (3) and taking into account the bargaining price in (5) yields

$$y_J = \frac{1}{3}[A + c^* - 2c - w_0 + 2(1 - \alpha)\delta + 2\alpha\theta w_0 \sqrt{k}] \quad \text{and} \tag{6}$$

$$y_A = \frac{1}{3}[A + c - 2c^* - w_0 - (1 - \alpha)\delta - \alpha\theta w_0 \sqrt{k}]. \tag{7}$$

The corresponding profits are $\pi_J = y_J^2$, $\pi_A = y_A^2$ and

$$\varphi = y_J(1 - \alpha) \left[w_0\theta\sqrt{k} - \delta\right] - k. \tag{8}$$

The J-maker's profit function $\pi_J(\delta) = y_J^2$ is increasing and convex, the A-maker's profit function $\pi_A(\delta) = y_A^2$ is decreasing and convex, and the Keiretsu

---

[10] The Nash bargaining solution is a normative concept. It can be shown that if a bargaining solution satisfies the three axioms *invariance to equivalent utility representations*, *independence of irrelevant alternatives*, and *Pareto efficiency*, then it is characterized by the maximum of the *generalized* Nash product $(U_1 - d_1)^\alpha (U_2 - d_2)^{1-\alpha}$, where (U_1, U_2) denote feasible payoff pairs, (d_1, d_2) the consequences of disagreement, and $\alpha \in [0, 1]$. If the symmetry axiom is added one arrives at the *regular* Nash bargaining solution with $\alpha = 1/2$.

-supplier's profit function $\varphi(\delta)$ is decreasing and concave:[11]

$$\frac{\partial \pi_J}{\partial \delta} = \frac{4}{3}(1-\alpha)y_J \geq 0, \quad \frac{\partial^2 \pi_J}{\partial \delta^2} = \frac{8}{9}(1-\alpha)^2 \geq 0, \quad \frac{\partial \pi_A}{\partial \delta} = -\frac{2}{3}(1-\alpha)y_A \leq 0,$$

$$\frac{\partial^2 \pi_A}{\partial \delta^2} = \frac{2}{9}(1-\alpha)^2 \leq 0, \quad \frac{\partial \varphi}{\partial \delta} \leq 0, \quad \frac{\partial^2 \varphi}{\partial \delta^2} = -\frac{4}{3}(1-\alpha)^2 \leq 0.$$

In the campaign-contribution or lobbying stage of the game that precedes the production-decision stage, the J-maker has an evident incentive to support the liberal trade policy party. The Keiretsu -supplier and the foreign interest, the A-maker, on the other hand, have an incentive to support the protectionist party. Since campaign contributions are a pure public good for the protectionist interests, only the interest with the higher stake will actively support the protectionist party.[12] It turns out that the Keiretsu supplier's stake is always larger than the A-maker's stake.[13] We thus have

Lemma 1. *Only the Keiretsu supplier actively supports the protectionist party in the election campaign. The A-maker, who is also in favor of the protectionist party, remains passive ($L_A = 0$).*

In deciding on their respective political contributions L_J and L_S, the J-maker and his Keiretsu supplier S maximize their respective expected profits $E\Pi$ taking into account how the trade policy stances of the competing political parties affect their profits. Following the electoral competition approach, we assume that the political parties are able to commit to their respective policy platforms. We thus arrive at the following maximization calculus:

$$\max_{L_J} E\Pi_J = w\pi_J(\delta_P) + (1-w)\pi_J(\delta_L) - L_J \tag{9}$$

$$\max_{L_S} E\Pi_S = w\varphi(\delta_P) + (1-w)\varphi(\delta_L) - L_S \tag{10}$$

The variable w denotes the probability of the protectionist party's winning the election, L_J (L_S) the J-maker's (the Keiretsu supplier's) lobbying outlays, and

---

[11] In order to establish that φ varies negatively with δ we assume that the J-maker would be able to stay in business if he had to buy basic domestic inputs: $y_J(K = \delta = 0) = A + c^* - 2c - w_0 > 0$.

[12] For a formal proof of this general result and an application in a related context (ecological protectionism), see [16].

[13] Using the ((6) through (8)), we compute the difference of the stakes of the supplier and the foreign producer as

$$D \equiv \Delta\Phi - \Delta\pi_A$$

$$= \frac{1-\alpha}{3}(\delta_L - \delta_P)\left[\frac{1}{3}\Omega + \left(\frac{14}{3}\alpha - 2\right)w_0\theta\sqrt{k} + \frac{7}{3}(1-\alpha)(\delta_L - \delta_P)\right],$$

where $\Omega = A - w_0 - 7c^* + 8c > 0$ (see note 10). For $\alpha \in (1/2, 1)$, D is thus positive.

δ_L (δ_P) the liberal (protectionist) party's trade policy pronouncement. The probability w is determined via a standard Tullock contest success function:

$$w = \frac{\xi L_S}{\xi L_S + L_J}, \quad \text{for } L_S + L_J > 0 \quad \text{and} \quad w = \frac{1}{2}, \quad \text{for } \xi L_S + L_J = 0 \quad (11)$$

The parameter ξ measures the relative lobbying efficiency of the supplier. We assume that $\xi > 1$, i.e. the supplier is more efficient in lobbying than the J-maker. The rationale behind this assumption is that protecting the supplier from import competition is seen, at least in the political arena, as the protection of the whole work force of the supplier, whereas trade liberalization is not believed to have a significant positive impact on employment in the final goods sector. It will turn out that to arrive at an interior equiliburium the supplier indeed needs to be more officient in lobbying than the J-maker.

It is worthwhile to point out in this context that all models of endogenous protectionist trade policies assume some kind of asymmetry such as $\xi > 1$; in other words, independent of the chosen approach to modeling the political economic interaction, one always needs some kind of bias in favor of the import-competing sector to arrive at a *protectionist* equilibrium.[14] In the median-voter type models pioneered by [22] this bias is concealed in the (asymmetric) distribution of stakes or political participation costs, in the regulation models in the tradition of [14] in the specification of the political support function, in the corruption models in the sense of [10] in the ability to form interest groups. In the lobbying models pioneered by [8] the required asymmetry is introduced either by assuming different lobbying productivities or by restricting the feasible set of policies to the use of protectionist instruments. This is the route we have chosen in our electoral competition model as well. As a matter of fact, we use both types of asymmetries: a higher lobbying productivity of the import-competing sector vis-à-vis the export sector and a non-negative tariff on imported inputs. The fact that both ingredients are necessary in our model is due to the weak position of the Keiretsu supplier in the final negotiation stage of the game. If the political position of the Keiretsu supplier is not strong enough, he cannot sustain a positive profit because of his weak economic position vis-à-vis his foreign low-cost competitors (remember, $c < c^*$), and the whole set-up collapses.

The above mentioned considerations reflect, of course, simply an artifact of the specification of our model. The assumption of a higher lobbying productivity on the part of the import-competing sector might, however, be questioned on the grounds that the export sector appears to have relatively more political clout in Japan than the export sectors in other developed democracies because of Japan's traditional focus on policies of export-led growth. A close look at the history of Japanese industrial policy reveals, however, that already in the early 1960s, in order to accommodate the adopted international trade and

---

[14] For a survey of the modeling approaches used in the political economy of trade policy, see [29] or [12].

foreign exchange liberalization, the powerful ministry of international trade and industry (MITI) began to support and subsidize the supplying industry that was built up in the 1950s. Moreover in the 1960s the export industry was already strong enough to successfully compete in the world market without strong support from the MITI. The objective of generating export-led growth has thus been conducted via an industrial policy which, to a surprisingly large extent, targeted the supplying industry.[15] If industrial-policy support is at all an indicator of the political influence of the respective sector, the industrial policy conducted in Japan is thus quite compatible with our assumption of a relatively high lobbying productivity of the import-competing sector.

In the equilibrium of the lobbying contest, the election outcome w depends on the ratio of the two competing firms' respective stakes $\Delta \Pi_J = [\Pi_J(\delta_L) - \Pi_J(\delta_P)]$ and $\Delta \Phi = [\Phi(\delta_P) - \Phi(\delta_L)]$:[16]

$$w = \frac{\xi \Delta \Phi}{\xi \Delta \Phi + \Delta \Pi} = \frac{3\xi \left[\varphi - 2(1-\alpha)(\theta w_0 \sqrt{k} - \delta_L - \delta_P) \right]}{(4+3\xi)\varphi - 6\xi(1-\alpha)\theta w_0 \sqrt{k} + (4+6\xi)(1-\alpha)(\delta_L + \delta_P)}$$

where $\varphi = A + c^* - 2c - w_0 + 2\alpha\theta w_0 \sqrt{k}$. $\qquad (12)$

The two political parties act as Stackelberg leaders vis-à-vis their supporters. Anticipating the effect of the firms' lobbying (or endorsement) reaction summarized in (12), the protectionist and the liberal trade policy party choose their policy platforms δ_P and δ_P with the intention to maximize their respective probabilities of winning the election. As can be seen from (12), the slope of the iso$-w$ lines in the policy pronouncement space is $-45°$ ($d\delta_P/d\delta_L = -1$) and w increases in δ_L and δ_P. This relationship between the electoral outcome and the parties' policy pronouncements is depicted in Figure 2. Notice, first, that δ cannot be negative (i.e. the tariff cannot exceed $t = c/c^* - 1$). This is so because at $\delta = c - (1+t)c^* = 0$ the domestic price $(1+t)c^*$ of the imported input equals the cost of the domestically produced input if no relationship-specific investment has been made. The Keiretsu supplier has no interest in a tariff exceeding $c/c^* - 1$ because the J-maker can always buy from a domestic competitor at the price $p = c$; even if δ became negative, the relevant threat point would thus remain at $p = c$. Figure 2 demonstrates that the unique Nash equilibrium of the policy pronouncement game is characterized by political concordance. For interior solutions $\delta \in (0, c - c^*)$ the common policy platform δ^* results from $w(\delta_L = \delta_P = \delta^*) = 0.5$:

$$\delta^* = \frac{3\xi}{6\xi - 4}\theta w \sqrt{k} - \frac{3\xi - 4}{12\xi - 8}\frac{\varphi}{1 - \alpha}. \qquad (13)$$

---

[15] See, for example, [23] and [24].

[16] This follows immediately from the first-order conditions of (9) and (10).

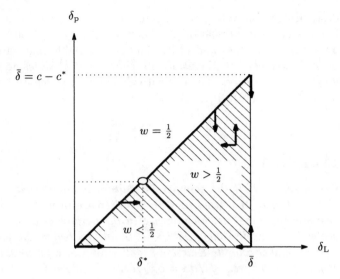

Fig. 2. Contour lines of function (12).

We thus have

Proposition 1. *If the political parties' objective is to maximize their respective probabilities of winning the election, the political process will give rise to political concordance.*

We are now in a position to analyze the first move made in the game, i.e. the investment decision made by the Keiretsu supplier. The J-maker's output follows from (6) and (13) as

$$y_J = \frac{\xi(a + 2\theta w_0 \sqrt{k})}{6\xi - 4}, \tag{14}$$

where $a = A + c^* - 2c - w_0$. The Keiretsu supplier's profit amounts to

$$\varphi = y_J(1 - \alpha) \left[\theta w_0 \sqrt{k} - \delta\right] - k = \frac{(3\xi - 4)\xi}{2} \left(\frac{a + 2\theta w_0 \sqrt{k}}{6\xi - 4}\right)^2 - k. \tag{15}$$

Notice, that ξ needs to exceed $4/3$ for the Keiretsu supplier to stay in business. Maximizing φ yields the optimal relationship-specific investment k undertaken by the Keiretsu supplier:

$$k = \left(\frac{(3\xi - 4)\theta w_0 \xi a}{(6\xi - 4)^2 - 2\theta^2 w_0^2 \xi(3\xi - 4)}\right)^2. \tag{16}$$

Let us now summarize the result derived so far. First of all, observe that in (16) the investment k does not depend on our crucial parameter α, which describes the prevailing commercial culture (i.e. α is an inverse measure of fairness in business relations). Therefore, y_J, $\pi_J = y_J^2$ and φ do not depend on a either (see (14) and (15)). The only variable that varies with α is the policy instrument δ^*. Equation (13) shows that δ^* varies negatively with α as long as δ^* is positive. The critical value of α at which $\delta^* = 0$ can be derived from (13) and (16):

$$\hat{\alpha} = 1 - \frac{3\xi - 2}{\theta^2 w_0^2 \xi}. \tag{17}$$

This gives rise to:

Proposition 2. *If the commercial culture is characterized by a sufficiently high level of mutual trust ($\alpha < \hat{\alpha}$), a decrease in mutual trust or fairness in business relations, i.e. an increase in the parameter α, gives rise to a more protectionist trade policy: $\partial \delta^* / \partial \alpha < 0$. In this regime the profits and outputs of the J-maker and the Keiretsu supplier are not influenced by changes in the commercial culture: $\partial y_J / \partial \alpha = \partial \pi_J / \partial \alpha = \partial \varphi / \partial \alpha = 0$.*

Proposition 2 indicates that the political process mitigates the redistribution brought about by changes in the commercial culture. Since k is constant for $\alpha \in (0, \hat{\alpha})$, a decrease in mutual trust as measured by an increase in α, ceteris paribus increases the J-maker's profit and decreases the profit of the Keiretsu supplier because the negotiation becomes tougher for the supplier and this results in a reduction of the price for the input. The political process, however, responds to the increase in α by increasing the tariff on imported inputs (i.e. our policy variable δ decreases). This implies that the threat point of the Nash bargaining game changes to the disadvantage of the J-maker: if bargaining with the Keiretsu supplier breaks down, the J-maker now has to buy his input from the foreign supplier at a higher price. The political process thus improves the Keiretsu supplier's bargaining position. It turns out that the exogenous *cultural effect* and the endogenous *political effect* neutralize each other. Nothing really changes as a consequence of the increase in α; only the tariff increases, but this has no real consequences since nothing is imported anyway.

4 Political Culture and Political Polarization

In order to portray changing political culture, we now generalize the objective functions of the political parties. We continue to assume that the political parties maximize their respective utility, but now we assume that the parties' utility encompasses, beside the electoral motive, an ideological component. This ideological utility component we associate with the welfare of the respective clientele interest group. Assuming that total utility is a convex combination of the two utility components, we arrive at the following utility representations for the liberal and the protectionist party, respectively:

$$z_L = (1 - \beta)(1 - w) + \beta\lambda\pi_J \qquad (18)$$

$$z_P = (1 - \beta)w + \beta\lambda\varphi. \qquad (19)$$

The parameter λ adjusts for the different dimensions of the two utility components and the parameter $\beta \in [0,1]$ measures the parties' ideological bias. If $\beta = 0$, the parties' only objective is to announce policies which maximize their respective probabilities of winning the election. If $\beta = 1$, they announce a policy which would, if implemented, maximize their respective constituency's utility, that is, in our case, the clientele firm's profit. In this case the parties are completely captured by some economic interest. Thus, β also measures to what extent the political parties are captured by economic interests, and we interpret this *interest capture* as a cultural trait.[17]

In principle, the analysis proceeds as in previous section. However, in order to focus on the influence of changing political culture, we now move the Keiretsu supplier's investment decision into the background by assuming that the supplier can either undertake an investment of given size ($k = \bar{k}$) or he can leave it ($k = 0$). Apart from reasons of analytical convenience, this assumption seems to be justified for two reasons: first, one can argue that relationship-specific investments are indeed lumpy (the supplier either moves his factory into the vicinity of the producer or he stays where he is, etc.) and, second, we have shown in part 2 that, at least in an extreme regime of political culture ($\beta = 0$), k is indeed largely independent of the prevailing commercial culture. The assumption $k \in \{0, \bar{k}\}$ does, therefore, not appear to be too restrictive. The analytical advantage is the following: if we assume that even in the most adverse of circumstances the Keiretsu supplier decides to go ahead with the investment ($k = \bar{k}$), then the cumbersome maximization calculus with respect to the investment decision disappears and the backwards induction ends with the determination of the political parties' trade policy pronouncements.

The analysis proceeds as follows. First we derive the political parties' behavior as a function of the parameter β. In a second step we then investigate the interaction of commercial culture and political culture in determining trade policy outcomes. In a final section we compare the model's implications with the stylized facts of Japanese politics.

4.1 The Impact of Political Culture

In the previous section 3 we analyzed the special case $\beta = 0$. In this section we derive the equilibrium policy pronouncements for positive values of β. If $\beta > 0$, the policy-pronouncement game is no longer a zero-sum game, and we

---

[17] Notice, that even complete interest group capture does not mean that the parties necessarily act in the best interest of their clientele group. The parties do not maximize the expected profits of the interest groups but rather announce a trade policy that maximizes the respective interest group's profit *if they are elected to public office.*

need to work out the solution with the help of the political parties' reaction functions.

We begin with the liberal trade policy party which maximizes z_L as given in (18) subject to the constraint that it announces a tax rate not exceeding the tax rate proposed by its opponent, i.e. $t_L \leq t_P$, or, alternatively, $\delta_L \geq \delta_P$. Since $1 - w$ (see (12)) and π_J are convex in δ_L, so is z_L. The liberal party's utility is thus maximized either at $\delta_L = \delta_P$, $\delta_L = \delta_P + \epsilon$ (where $\epsilon > 0$ is small), or $\delta_L = \bar{\delta}$. The values δ_P and $\delta_P + \epsilon$ need to be carefully distinguished because w is discontinuous at $\delta_L = \delta_P$. Figure 2 demonstrates that for $\delta_P > \delta^*$ ($\delta_P < \delta^*$) the choice is between $\delta_L = \delta_P$ and $\delta_L = \bar{\delta}$ ($\delta_P + \epsilon$ and $\bar{\delta}$).[18] The free trade platform $\bar{\delta}$ will be chosen if $F > 0$, where

$$F \equiv \begin{cases} (1 - \beta)[w(\delta_P, \delta_P + \epsilon) - w(\delta_P, \bar{\delta})] + \beta\lambda\langle\pi(\bar{\delta}) - \pi(\delta_P + \epsilon)\rangle, & \delta_P < \delta^* \\ (1 - \beta)\left((\frac{1}{2} - w(\delta_P, \bar{\delta}))\right) + \beta\lambda\langle\pi(\bar{\delta}) - \pi(\delta_P)\rangle, & \delta_P > \delta^*. \end{cases} \quad (20)$$

The second term in F capturing party ideology is positive, decreasing and concave in δ_P and disappears at $\bar{\delta}$. The expression in the square bracket capturing the electoral motive is negative, increasing and concave, and the corresponding expression in the large round bracket is negative, decreasing and convex. Figure 3 depicts F as a function of δ_P.

Figure 3 indicates that for sufficiently low values of β (i.e. for $\beta < \beta_1$), F is always negative, and the liberal trade policy party tries to duplicate the policy pronouncement of its opponent; to be more precise, if $\delta_P > \delta^*$, the liberal party duplicates the protectionist party's platform, and for $\delta_P < \delta^*$ it announces a trade policy that is just slightly more liberal than the policy proposal of the protectionist party. The respective reaction function is shown in panel L1 of Figure 4. For an intermediate range of values of β ($\beta_1 < \beta < \beta_3$), the liberal party deviates from the unconditional duplication policy and announces free trade if δ_P is in a neighborhood (δ'_P, δ''_P) of δ^* (see Figure 4, panels L2 and L3). For sufficiently large values of β ($\beta > \beta_3$), the liberal party announces free trade if the protectionist party announces a rather protectionist policy ($\delta_P < \delta''_P$) and duplicates the protectionist party's policy pronouncement otherwise ($\delta_P > \delta''_P$). Only at $\beta = 1$, the liberal party always announces free trade (see Figure 4, panels L4 − L6).

We now turn to the behavior of the protectionist party. The two functions entering the protectionist party's objective function z_p (see (19)) are both concave in δ_L; z_L is therefore also concave. An interior maximum is attained in the feasible policy space $\delta_P \in [0, \delta_L]$ if the first order condition

$$\frac{\partial z_P}{\partial \delta_P} = (1 - \beta)\frac{\partial w}{\partial \delta_P} + \beta\lambda\frac{\partial \varphi}{\partial \delta_P} = 0 \quad (21)$$

is satisfied, or alternatively, if $(1 - \beta)w_P = \beta\lambda|\varphi_P|$. For sufficiently low values of β, the electoral motive dominates the ideological motive and the LHS

---

[18] Notice, that $w(\delta_P) < w(\delta_P + \epsilon)$ for $\delta_P > \delta^*$. Therefore, $1 - w(\delta_P) > 1 - w(\delta_P + \epsilon)$ and $z_L(\delta_P) > z_L(\delta_P + \epsilon)$.

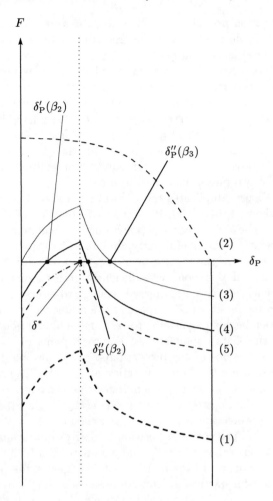

(1) $\beta = 0$
(2) $\beta = 1$
(3) $\beta = \beta_3$
(4) $\beta = \beta_2$
(5) $\beta = \beta_1$

Fig. 3. Graph of function (20).

(the marginal benefit of convergence) exceeds the RHS (the marginal cost of abandoning the ideology) even if the liberal trade policy party announces free trade: $\delta_L = \bar{\delta}$. Under these circumstances (see Figure 5, panel a), the protectionist party also announces a liberal trade policy but avoids duplicating the free trade policy of its opponent (i.e. it announces the policy $\delta_P = \bar{\delta} - \epsilon$). The protectionist party avoids policy duplication because for $\delta_L > \delta_*$ ($\delta_L < \delta^*$) the election probability $w(\delta_L - \epsilon, \delta_L)$ exceeds (falls short of) $w(\delta_L, \delta_L) = 1/2$.[19] If δ_L decreases from the free trade level $\bar{\delta}$ to δ_1, w_P increases and policy convergence continues to hold; if $\delta_L < \delta^*$, the protectionist party, of course, duplicates the liberal party's platform. This behavior is summarized in the reaction function depicted in panel P1, Figure 4.

For larger values of β (see Figure 5, panel b), the marginal benefit and marginal cost curves intersect in the feasible policy space of the protectionist party if the liberal party announces free trade, $(\delta_L = \bar{\delta})$. If the liberal party moves towards the left $(\delta_L < \bar{\delta})$, the $(1 - \beta)w_P$-curve shifts upwards and the protectionist party announces a more liberal policy.[20] This convergence of the two platforms comes to a halt at $\tilde{\delta}_L$; for $\delta_L \leq \tilde{\delta}_L$ the protectionist party (almost) duplicates the platform of its opponent. The reaction functions in Figure 4, panels P2-P4, depict this reaction of the protectionist party.

For high values of β (see Figure 5, panel c), marginal cost exceeds marginal benefit if the liberal party announces free trade. The protectionist party thus announces the highest tariff (i.e. $\delta_P = 0$). Only if the liberal party, at smaller value of β announces sufficiently protectionist trade policies, the marginal benefit curve shifts upwards enough to intersect with the marginal cost curve in the feasible policy space of the protectionist party. The protectionist party then begins to converge towards more liberal policies until it reaches the platform of its opponent (see Figure 4, panel c). Notice, that for $\delta_L < \delta^*$ the convergence of the protectionist party may be discontinuous because of the discontinuity of the w-function at $\delta_L = \delta_P$. The reaction function depicted in Figure 4, panel P5, summarizes this behavior. For very high values of β the marginal cost of convergence is always higher than the marginal benefit and the protectionist party always announces $\delta_P = 0$ (see Figure 4, panel P6).

We are now in a position to derive equilibrium platform combinations for various values of our crucial parameter β, which portrays the prevailing political culture. In the panels I1-I6 in Figure 4 the reaction functions of the two political parties are superimposed. For low values of β the electoral motive dominates the ideological motive and the result of section 3 of this paper carries over: in equilibrium the two parties announce the same trade policy δ^*, i.e. the two reaction functions "intersect" at $\delta_L = \delta_P = \delta^*$ (see panel I1). For very high values of β (see the panels I5 and I6) the ideological motive dominates the electoral motive and the two parties announce extreme policies: the liberal trade policy party announces free trade and the protectionist party announces a tariff which neutralizes the price advantage of the foreign suppliers, i.e. the two reaction functions intersect at the point $(\delta_P, \delta_L) = (0, \bar{\delta})$.

Starting out from this regime of complete political polarization, we now decrease the value of β. If the election motive becomes more prominent in the calculus of the political parties they begin to ponder political conver-

---

[19] See Figure 2.

[20] The fact $\partial \delta_P / \partial \delta_L < 0$, can also be inferred from equation (21) via the implicit function rule.

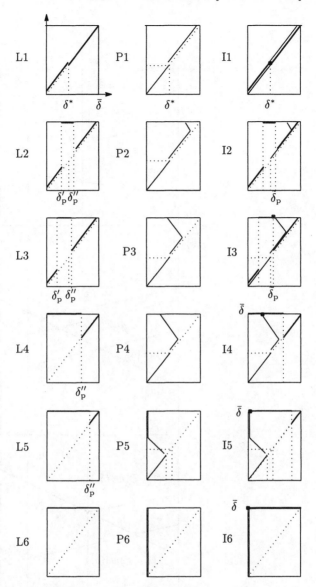

Fig. 4. Reaction functions of the political parties.

gence since convergence increases the probability of winning the election. The protectionist party's objective function z_P is concave. This party therefore ponders *marginal* adjustment of its trade policy stance. The liberal party's objective function z_L is convex; the liberal party therefore ponders *dramatic policy shifts* (i.e. duplication of the policy stance of the opponent). We envisage here a development in which the protectionist party has first reason

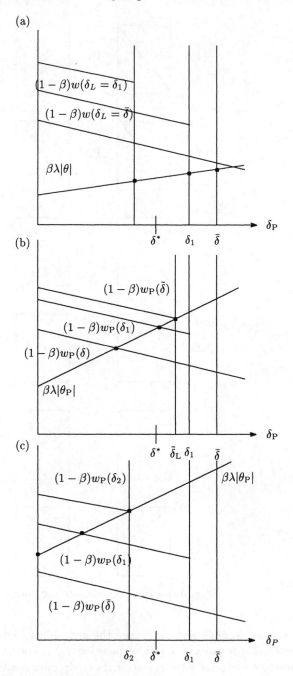

Fig. 5. Graph of equation (21).

to adjust its trade policy stance. In the panels I4 and I3 of Figure 4 the intersection of the two reaction functions is located at $\delta_L = \bar{\delta}$, whereas δ_P increases from 0 to $\delta_P'' > 0$. For the respective range of β-values we have a regime of (partial) political convergence. This regime, however, breaks down when δ_P'' exceeds $\tilde{\delta}_P$ ($\delta_L = \bar{\delta}$). Panel I2 in Figure 4 demonstrates that for a range of β-values no equilibrium exists.[21] This situation arises because the liberal party, at the platform combination $(\bar{\delta}, \delta_P'' - \epsilon)$, would like to duplicate the trade policy announcement of its opponent for electoral reasons; the protectionist party, however, would react to this policy shift by moving away from its original policy stance and announcing a somewhat more protectionist policy in order to distinguish its policy from the liberal party. This more protectionist policy is, for ideological reasons, not acceptable anymore for the liberal party, which, under these circumstances, prefers its original stance $\bar{\delta}$. To this reversal, however, the protectionist party responds by moving back to where it was in the first place, etc.

Figure 6 shows how political polarization depends on our crucial parameter β. We summarize this insight in

Proposition 3. *Depending on the prevailing political culture as measured by parameter β, four qualitatively different regimes of political interaction between the two competing parties can emerge: (1) (complete) political polarization, (2) (incomplete) political convergence, (3) a regime of political turmoil in which the two parties often readjust their respective trade policy stances without converging to an equilibrium, and (4) political concordance in the sense of Hoteling and Downs.*

4.2 The Interaction of Commercial Culture and Political Culture

We now return to the analysis of the influence of commercial culture (as measured by the parameter α) on trade policy formation. As compared to part 2, we now, however, investigate the general case in which $\beta \in [0, 1]$.

In the previous section we implicitly assumed a value of α which is compatible with a $\delta^* \in (0, \bar{\delta})$ (i.e. with an interior solution of δ^*). Equation (13), however, reveals that for α sufficiently close to 1, the common trade policy platform which materializes for sufficiently low values of β will be $\delta_P = \delta_L = 0$, since $\delta^* < 0$. Analogously, it can be seen that for low values of a the common platform of the two contestants may well be $\delta_P = \delta_L = \bar{\delta}$ since δ^* can exceed $\bar{\delta}$. If $\delta^* \notin [0, \bar{\delta}]$, the sequence of equilibria depicted in Figure 6 does no longer apply: for low and high values of α the regimes 2 and 3 (i.e. the regimes of political convergence and turmoil) need not be encountered if the development of political culture is characterized by a steady decline of the parameter β from 1 to 0. If the prevailing commercial culture is not based on mutual trust

---

[21] We only consider equilibriums in pure strategies to represent solutions of our game.

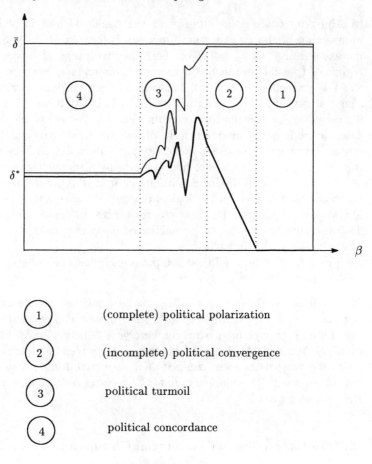

1	(complete) political polarization
2	(incomplete) political convergence
3	political turmoil
4	political concordance

Fig. 6. Political polarization and political culture.

(α high), increasingly election motivated politicians will eventually cause the political equilibrium of complete polarization to break down and to transform into an equilibrium of political concordance. The same clean transformation occurs in a system characterized by a very high degree of mutual trust in the commercial sphere (α low, i.e. α close to 1/2).

Figure 7 provides an impression of the interaction of business and political culture in determining the trade policy stances of the political parties. The figure is based on a numerical example. The sequence of equilibria depicted in Figure 4 and 6 corresponds to the development of the parameter constellation (α, β) characterized by arrow B. The arrows A and C correspond to a development of the prevailing culture giving rise to a sudden transformation of political polarization into political concordance. Keeping political culture constant, we can also look at the influence of changes of the prevailing commercial culture. If, for a given political culture β, a commercial culture strongly based on mutual trust is eroded over time and gives way to a commercial culture characterized by interactions "at arms length," we are faced with a development of the parameter constellation (α, β) as portrayed by the arrows A through D. Inspection of Figure 7 yields our final

Proposition 4. *The interaction of commercial and political culture in trade policy determination is rather complex. Depending on the cultural development as represented in our model by the time paths of the parameter constellation (α, β), almost any sequence of the four possible policy regimes identified in Proposition 3 may emerge.*

Proposition 4 implies that an empirical test of the interaction between commercial and political culture as proposed in our model - which, at least in principle, is general enough to portray a large variety of cultural settings - needs to be based on a historical development in which cultural traits went through substantial changes. We believe that the Japanese experience since WWII represents a historical incident which is very well suited to contrast the predictions of our model with the observed changes in political relations.

5 The Japanese Experience

In this section we compare the development of trade policy making in Japan with the predictions of the model developed above. We begin with a brief description of the development of the party landscape in Japan. Our presentation relies heavily on the recent monograph by [28]. From this account we derive some stylized facts, which we then compare with the behavior of our model.

Even though elections in pre-WWII Japan were not completely insignificant, the Japanese history of electoral democracy begins with the first postwar election held in April 1946 (still under the Meiji Constitution) in which some 363 political parties officially campaigned. The outcome confirmed the demise of the once powerful prewar party elite and the empowerment of the political left. The Japan Socialist Party (JSP) won the largest number of seats in the 1947 election under the new constitution and formed Japan's first socialist-led cabinet. The postwar chaos and uncertainty in Japanese politics came to an end when, in 1955, the socialist movement overcame its division and, as a reaction, the conservatives formed the Liberal Democratic Party (LDP). After this consolidation, the LDP and the JSP dominated the party landscape for a long time; as late as the 1967 election the two largest parties still won 86% of the seats. Whereas in most democracies the extreme differences between capital and labor disappeared soon after WWII, the class cleavage continued to be the major issue in Japan. The JSP, for example, did not abolish the idea of a "dictatorship of the proletariat " until the end of the 1980s. This political polarization resulted in an extended period of conservative hegemony.

The party duopoly began to crumble when the Democratic Socialist Party (1960) and the Clean Government (Komeito) Party (1974) formed as "parties of the center." The extreme political polarization of the early period of the conservative regime was further softened up when, in 1976, the New Liberal Club split from the LDP and the Japan Communist Party transformed into a "lovable" party. During this intermediate period the sharp ideological left-right division between government and opposition thus slowly disappeared and the electoral contests became more competitive, since voters identified themselves more and more as independents (1960 fewer than 10%, 1995 about 50%). The ruling LDP lost as early as 1967 the majority of votes cast; the biased electoral system, however, still furnished it with a majority of seats. Nevertheless, the secular decline in the vote share of the ruling LDP began to threaten the conservative hegemony. To counter this trend, specific economic policies became more narrowly targeted and explicitly politicized in order to gain the political support of major interest associations, large socioeconomic blocs, and big donors.

The overt politicization of important aspects of economic policy proved to be beneficial to the LDP, but ultimately these adjustments came back to haunt the conservatives and to contribute to their toppling in the 1990s, largely as a result of corruption scandals ([28], p. 185). The end of the LDP dominance was the consequence of its unexpected break-up in June 1993 when the Hata faction supported the no-confidence motion against the cabinet and formed the Japan Renewal Party. In the following July 1993 election three new conservative parties, the Japan Renewal Party, the Japan New Party and the New Party Sakigake competed with the LDP for conservative votes. The result was that the LDP lost its majority and a coalition government formed that comprised all of the LDP's opponents with the exception of the Communist Party. This government broke down in 1994 when the JSP and Sakigake walked out of the coalition. A minority government formed but was very short-lived and was replaced by a hitherto imponderable coalition between the LDP and the JSP with Sakigake as a broker. This coalition, which documents more than anything the increasing abandoning of ideological principles and the move towards a more election oriented political environment, held together until the 1996 elections.

The period up to the 1996 election was marked by great political instability; Japan had eight prime ministers in five years and the party landscape continued to undergo significant changes. A number of non-LDP parties merged into the New Frontier Party, the JPS, in order to signal its ideological transformation, changed its name to the Social Democratic Party of Japan (SDPJ), and a new liberal party, the Democratic Party, was formed. Four conservative parties thus competed in the 1996 election, where the big loser was the SDPJ. Even though the LDP was back in power by the end of 1996, its hold was far from secure. The party system had been undeniably transformed and more fragmentation, realignment, and false starts are likely before any new equilibrated regime can be identified. Indeed, there is no guarantee that clarity will emerge for some time ([28], p. 205). Pempel even goes so far to compare Japan in the 1990s with the countries transforming from socialism: "that the old regime had been displaced was clear; that transition was under way was beyond question; but precisely how that transition would play out, and what new equilibrium would replace the old, was less evident. What was clear, however, was that like Humpty Dumpty, the old regimes in Japan just as in the former communist countries could not be put back together again" (p. 167).

Apart from the continual recombination of political parties, the most recent period of Japanese politics has been characterized by a struggle for power in which the contesting parties hardly articulated any clear-cut and distinctive policy positions. The traditional pattern of political support underwent a process of dramatic realignment. The conservatives lost the unequivocal political support of farmers and small business, whereas labor stood far closer to the conservatives on numerous issues than it had three decades earlier. The business-labor divisions have given way to sectoral differences that pitted business and labor in single industries or firms against business and labor in others ([28], p. 164). Trade policy issues, in particular, have generated sharp cleavages within the business sector; internationally highly competitive manufacturers in areas such as electronics, machine tools, and automobiles increasingly favor an open market policy, whereas less competitive industries look to the government for protection from foreign competition and guaranteed profitability within the domestic marketplace (see [28], pp. 165-166).

We are now in a position to summarize the stylized facts of the development of the political interaction in post-WWII Japan. Broadly speaking, one can distinguish three different regimes after the chaotic initial period that lasted until 1955. The *first regime* (mid 1950s – mid 1970s) was characterized by a strict political polarization based on the traditional ideological left-right cleavage. The conservative LDP enjoyed in Parliament a safe majority of seats vis-à-vis the socialist opposition and implemented an economic policy, which has been described by [28] as a policy of "embedded mercantilism". Nevertheless, this policy was, of course, much more liberal than the economic policy advocated by the anti-capitalist opposition. In the course of the *second regime* (mid 1970s – 1980s) the sharp ideological left-right division between government and opposition dissolved: new centrist parties formed in the middle of the political spectrum and the anti-capitalist opposition (the JSP and the Communist Party) began to endorse policies which appealed to a larger segment of the electorate. The observed *political convergence* was clearly instigated by a political class, which became more and more election oriented.[22] *The third regime* covers the 1990s and the contemporary political interaction

---

[22] Unfortunately, no *quantitative* studies exist that analyze the *development* of party platforms in Japan. The only relevant study undertaken so far refers to the election year 1996 (see [20]).

in Japan. It is characterized by an incessant recombination of political parties, a frequent repositioning of vague political platforms, and a continual realignment of political support. Whether this process, which we describe as *political turmoil*, has come to an end with the election of the present Prime Minister Junichiro Koizumei in April 2001 remains to be seen.

We believe that our model is suitable to portray these stylized facts and to provide some insights into the underlying mechanisms. Needless to say that we do not want to claim that this simple model represents a sufficiently complete representation of the complex political-economic interactions that have taken place in modern Japan. From the outset, our objective has been much less haughty, namely to demonstrate that the observed (trade) policy positions held by Japanese politicians over the last fifty years can be portrayed with the help of a simple model employing as a driving force two key aspects of the Japanese commercial and political culture.

Our case is summarized in Figure 7 by the fat arrow depicting the development of the commercial and political culture as we see it. We interpret the evidence relating to the prevailing fairness standards in the Japanese business community to entail an initial increase in fairness (inverse of α) during the early period of Keiretsu -building, followed by a steady decline over the last decade in which the globalization of the Japanese economy significantly deepened. As far as the political culture is concerned, we concur with the received wisdom of the political scientists and presuppose over the whole period of investigation a continuous weakening of ideological considerations in the politicians' motivation (i.e. an increasingly election oriented political class). We thus are faced with a steadily decreasing value of the parameter β. The parameter constellation depicted by the fat arrow in Figure 7 moves through the regimes 1, 2 and 3. This course of events is perfectly consistent with the historical development: after an initial regime of political polarization, Japanese politics entered a regime of political convergence in the mid 1970s, and in the beginning of the 1990s a regime of political turmoil.

We leave it to those who are more inclined than we to speculate whether, and if so, when, the underlying cultural forces will bring about a stable regime of political concordance. Some signs appear to indicate that the election of Prime Minister Junichiro Koizumi has heralded a new era of purely election based politics which will render Japanese politics in the near future more akin to the political interaction observed in "mature" democracies such as Great Britain and Germany with their "New Left" or the United States with George W. Bush's "Compassionate Conservatism". A similarly speculative exercise would be to ask the counterfactual question as to whether the political instability in the 1990s would have been avoided if the commercial culture had sustained even more or, alternatively, less fairness and trust than it actually did (see the dotted arrows in figure 7).

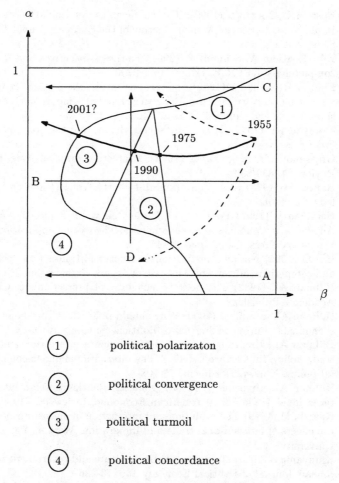

①	political polarizaton
②	political convergence
③	political turmoil
④	political concordance

Fig. 7. Interaction of political and commercial culture.

References

1. Aoki M (1988) Information, incentive, and bargaining power in the Japanese economy, Cambridge, Cambridge University Press
2. Clark K, Fujimoto T (1991) Product development performance: Strategy, organization, and management in the world auto industry, Harvard Business School Press, Boston, Massachusetts
3. Dyer J (1995) From arms-length relationships to supplier partnerships: The Chrysler case, Working Paper
4. Dyer J (1996) Specialized supplier networks as a source of co mpetitive advantage: Evidence from the auto industry, Strategic Management Journal 17: 271-291
5. Dyer J, Chu W (1997) The determinants and economic outcomes of trust in supplier-buyer relations, Working Paper

6. Epstein G, Nitzan S (1999): The endogenous determination of public policy, Paper presented at the Annual Meeting of the European Public Choice Society, Siena 26-29
7. Fehr E, Klein A, Schmidt K (2001) Fairness, Incentives and Contractual Incompleteness. CEPR Working Paper 2790
8. Findley R, Wellisz S (1982) Endogenous tariffs, the political economy of trade restriction, and welfare, In: Bhagwati J (eds.), Import competition and response, Chicago University Press, Chicago: 238-243
9. Fukuyama F (1995) Trust: The social virtues and the creation of prosperity, FreePress, New-York
10. Grossman GM, Helpman E (1994): Protection for sale, American Economic Review 84: 833-850
11. Hayek FA (1973) Law, legislation and liberty, Vol 1 (Rules and order), Routledge, London
12. Helpman E (1997) Politics and Trade Policy, In: Kreps D, Wallis K (eds.), Advances in economics and econometrics: Theory and applications. Cambridge University Press, Cambridge: 19-45
13. Hill C (1995) National institutional structures, transaction cost economizing and competitive advantage: The case of Japan, Organization Science 6: 119-131
14. Hillman AL (1982) The political economy of protectionism, Chur, Harwood Academic Publishers
15. Hillman AL, Swank O (2000) Why should political culture be in the lexicon of economists? European Journal of Political Economy 16, 1-4
16. Hillman AL, Ursprung H (1994) Environmental protection and international trade policy, In: Carraro C (eds.), The international dimension of environmental policy. Kluwer, Dordrecht: 75-108
17. Hillman AL, Ursprung H (1988) Domestic Politics, Foreign Interests, and International Trade Policy, American Economic Review 78: 719-45
18. Kaneda M (1999) The evolution and interaction of norms: Firm objectives and the effects of international trade and integration, Working Paper, Georgetown University
19. Katayama S (2000): Japanese political culture and government regulation, European Journal of Political Economy 16: 273-286
20. Kato J, Laver M (1998): Theories of government formation and the 1996 general election in Japan, Party Politics 4: 229-252
21. Knack S, Keefer P (1997): Does social capital have an economic payoff? A cross-country investigation, Quarterly Journal of Economics 112: 1251-1288
22. Mayer W (1984) Endogenous tariff formation, American Economic Review 74: 970-985
23. MITI (1985) History of commercial and industrial policy, No. 19, Machinery industry (2): 235-246 (in Japanese)
24. MITI (1990) History of trade and industrial policy, No. 6, chapter 5, Fostering Machinery and electronics industry: 549-617 (in Japanese)
25. Miyashita K, Russell D (1994) Keiretsu - inside the hidden Japanese conglomerates, McGraw-Hill, New York
26. Nelson D (1999) The political economy of trade policy reform: Social complexity and methodological pluralism, Journal of International Trade and Economic Development 8: 3-26
27. Paldam M, Svendsen G (2000) An essay on social capital: Looking for the fire behind the smoke, European Journal of Political Economy 16: 339-366

28. Pempel T (1998) Regime shift: Comparative dynamics of the Japanese political economy, Ithaca and London, Cornell University Press

29. Rodrik D (1995) Political Economy of Trade Policy, In: Grossman G, Rogoff K (eds.), Handbook of international economics, 3, North-Holland, Amsterdam: 1457-94

30. Sako M, Helper S (1998) Determinants of trust in supplier relations: Evidence from the automotive industry in Japan and the United States, Journal of Economic Behavior and Organization 34: 387-417

31. Schlicht E (1998) On custom in the economy, Clarendon Press, Oxford

32. Spencer B, Qiu L (2000) Keiretsu and relationship-specific investment: A barrier to trade? the International Economic Review 42: 871-901

33. Ursprung H (1990) Public Goods, Rent Dissipation, and Candidate Competition, Economics and Politics 2: 115-32

34. Young L, Magee S (1986) Endogenous protection, factor returns, and resource allocation, Review of Economic Studies 53: 407-419

Protection and Jobs: Explaining the Structure of Trade Barriers Across Industries*

Scott Bradford

Economics Department, Brigham Young University, Provo, UT 84602, USA
bradford@byu.edu

1 Introduction

Protection persists despite its weighty costs, and many studies have investigated its causes. Still unresolved is the question of why some industries receive significantly more protection than others. Shedding light on what explains the variation of trade barriers across industries may suggest more effective strategies for reducing protection (see [19]; and [30]). Also, incorporating the politics of trade is likely to improve trade theory (for example, see [8]).

Within the theoretical literature, [20] pioneered the political support approach to trade barriers, in which policy makers choose protection levels to maximize support from special interest groups and society at large. [17] extended this work by developing a framework that explicitly models lobbying. Many have built insightfully on their foundation ([23], among others). So far, however, the theoretical literature has tended to neglect the impacts of employment levels and of industry characteristics, such as number of firms, on protection levels. Also, almost all such models imply that protection increases with output. There are numerous econometric analyses of the structure of protection across industries.[1] Formal modeling does not guide most such studies, making the results hard to interpret. Recent work, however, has advanced

---

* I thank Donald Davis, Seiichi Katayama, Jeffry Frieden, Gene Grossman, Elhanan Helpman, Dale Jorgenson, Hiro Lee, Aaron Tornell, Heinrich Ursprung and David Weinstein for their help. Special thanks go to Arye Hillman, Val Lambson, Robert Lawrence, and three anonymous referees. I thank Daniel Trefler for sharing his data and Kishore Gawande for data help. Various members of the USC and BYU economics faculty have made helpful comments on this work. I have also been helped by comments from participants in the International Economics seminar and International Economics and Political Economy workshops at Harvard University and the RIEB trade policy conference held at Kobe University in March 2000. Any errors are mine alone.

[1] [3] and [32] survey this large literature. [34] is especially noteworthy. Our model below combines two of the informal models that [3] summarizes: the pressure

this literature by basing regressions strictly on theory. For instance, [15] and [16] examine the Grossman-Helpman (GH) model empirically and confirm the main GH prediction that protection is increasing in the ratio of output to imports. They also find that jobs and industry characteristics do not significantly affect protection levels. They do not, however, explicitly model these factors, only adding them to the regressions in an ad hoc way.

This paper provides additional evidence on the pattern of protection across industries by estimating a structural equation derived from a new model. We also use alternative measures of protection that we believe are more trustworthy than previous ones. In the model (presented and discussed in Sections 2 and 3), policy makers choose protection levels to maximize votes, producers and import rent seekers lobby for rents, and workers and consumers vote according to protection's effect on their economic well-being. The model implies that protection increases with workforce size and decreases with lobbying costs (as proxied, for instance, by the number of firms). The predicted effects of output and imports are ambiguous. This paper's primary results are in Section 4, which takes the model to the data and confirms its main predictions. The results also imply that the government weights a dollar of campaign contributions about 15% more heavily than a dollar of consumer surplus and that each $1000 reduction in consumer surplus results in the loss of one vote.

2 The Model

2.1 The Economic Structure

Consider a small economy whose consumers maximize $u = x_0 + \sum_{i=1}^{n} u_i(x_i)$. x_0 is the numeraire and is traded freely at a price of 1. Each u_i is differentiable and strictly concave. The population is normalized to 1. Consumer surplus for each non-numeraire good is $s(p_i) = u_i[d_i(p_i)] - p_i d_i(p_i)$, where p_i is the price and $d_i(p_i)$ is demand.[2]

For production, consider a modified version of the specific factors model. There are constant returns to scale and perfect competition. Capital is specific, and labor is mobile. Unlike the standard model, though, we follow [10] and [7] and assume that each sector's wage is fixed above market-clearing and each worker's reservation wage, causing involuntary unemployment.[3] Thus, $L^i = L_i^d(\bar{w}_i/p_i)$ where L_i is the amount of labor in industry i, and w_i is the

---

group model and the adding machine (voting) model. (These are the two models that [14] finds to be most important.)

[2] This consumption structure follows GH.

[3] The working paper, available upon request, shows one way to endogenize rigid wages. As long as the wage is rigid and leads to unemployment, all of the results below hold. Allowing wages to move might be interesting further work, though [29] shows that employment is much more flexible than wages in the short run.

fixed wage. Since $L_i^{d\prime} < 0$, $dL_i/dp_i > 0$.[4] The total reward to specific capital depends only on the price: $\pi_i = \pi_i(p_i)$, with $\pi' > 0$.

The government chooses trade barriers of any type for each industry.[5] No matter the barrier, it raises the domestic price p_i above the fixed world price, denoted by p_i^w. We assume no lump-sum rebating of trade tax revenues or import rents. Instead, lobbies compete for these.

2.2 The Political Structure

Import-competing producers form lobbies. We also allow for a second type of lobby. Since non-tax protection generates rents for importers,[6] we assume that importer lobbies form, one per sector. (Lobbies may also vie for trade taxes. See [5].) We assume that the effect of lobbying on any lobby's consumer surplus is negligibly small. Thus, welfare for each producer lobby is simply profits, $w_i^P(p_i) = \pi_i(p_i)$, while welfare for each importer lobby is the value of import rents, $w_i^{IM}(p_i) = (p_i - p_i^w)m_i(p_i)$ where m_i is the quantity of imports.

Lobbying consists of making contributions. We assume that each lobby engages in a bilateral Nash cooperative game with the government, so that total surplus is maximized, with the division of the surplus indeterminate.[7] Each lobby takes prices in all other sectors as given. Most models assume that contributions are frictionless transfers, but we allow for transactions costs. Contributions received by the government from the producer and importer lobbies, respectively, are $C_i^P(p_i) = b_i^P[\pi_i(p_i) - B_i^P]$ and $C_i^{IM}(p_i) = b_i^{IM}[(p_i - p_i^w)m_i(p_i) - B_i^{IM}]$, where b_i^P and b_i^{IM} (both ≤ 1) are lobbying friction coefficients,[8] and B_i^P and B_i^{IM} are the rents that the lobbies retain in the bargain. In this Nash set-up, the price chosen does not affect these B terms. The government has the following objective function:

$$V(\mathbf{p}) = \sum_{i=1}^{n} \left[(L_i^d(p_i) - L_i^w) + c \left[C_i^P(p_i) + C_i^{IM}(p_i) \right] + a \left(s_i(p_i) - s_i^w \right) \right] \quad (1)$$

---

[4] Labor is not specific in this model. Laid off workers can move to any sector. Employed workers do feel attached to their sectors, since the alternative is a period of unemployment. [9] discusses how unemployment blurs the distinction between Heckscher−Ohlin and specific factors models.

[5] We do not analyze why protection is chosen over more efficient tools, taking as given that protection is ubiquitous. [31] and [25] model the choice of protection over subsidies.

[6] See [21] and [23] for models with such lobbying.

[7] See [19] for a discussion of why a series of bilateral bargains might be a more reasonable approach than that of a single multilateral menu auction game.

[8] The lobbying frictions are exogenous and thus compatible with efficient bargaining: the parties still end up on the Pareto frontier, even though frictions may affect the position of the frontier.

where $V(\mathbf{p})$ is total votes; L_i^{w} and s_i^{w} are free trade levels of employment and consumer surplus, respectively; c is the fraction of a vote that a dollar of contributions buys; and a is the votes lost per dollar of lost consumer surplus.

The first term, $L_i^{\mathrm{d}}(p_i) - L_i^{\mathrm{w}}$, gives the number of votes won from workers in protected industries. Specifically, each worker hired due to protection switches from voting against the government (because he or she was unemployed) to voting for it.[9] Thus, employment is assumed to override price changes in determining how workers vote. The second pair of terms captures contributions induced by protection; the government uses these funds to 'buy' votes at a rate of c votes per dollar.[10] The last pair of terms captures lost support from consumers who face higher prices, with the number of votes lost directly proportional to the loss of consumer surplus.

The government chooses the price in each sector so as to maximize votes.[11] Taking the derivative of V with respect to a representative price, p_i, yields:

$$\tilde{P}_i = \frac{p_i^* - p_i^{\mathrm{w}}}{p_i^*} = \frac{e_{(L,p),i}L_i + c\left(b_i^{\mathrm{P}}\bar{y}_i + b_i^{\mathrm{IM}}\bar{m}_i\right) - a\left(\bar{y}_i + \bar{m}_i\right)}{e_{(L,p),i}L_i + cb_i^{\mathrm{IM}}e_{(m,p),i}\bar{m}_i} \qquad (2)$$

where, in each sector i, $e_{(L,p),i}$ is the elasticity of labor demand, $e_{(L,p),i}$ is the elasticity of import demand (> 0), $\bar{y}_i = y_i p_i^{\mathrm{w}}$ is the value of output at free trade prices, and $\bar{m}_i = m_i p_i^{\mathrm{w}}$ is the value of imports at free trade prices.[12]

3 Discussion and Implications of the Model

Three main features distinguish our model from most of the literature: treating workers as a separate source of support, instead of lumping them in with

---

[9] The results do not depend on having each worker switch her or his vote. As long as some fraction switch, the results go through. Thus, we could express the model in terms of probabilistic voting. An extension of this framework would be to model more explicitly who will switch. Note that party affiliation and the ideology of the government (e.g. whether it is 'free trading' or not) do not play roles in this model.

[10] See [27] for a model of how campaign spending buys votes.

[11] In doing so, we follow [26] and [2]. We could easily reformulate the model to have policy makers maximize 'power' or 'wealth'. See Becker's comments on Peltzman. Also, although democratic governments only need a simple majority of votes to stay in office, super-majorities have value because they make it easier for governments to implement their overall agenda.

[12] $\tilde{P}_i$ maps protection onto the $[0, 1)$ interval. This formulation follows GH and Goldberg and Maggi. Also, we assume no negative protection, which would imply import subsidies. This appears to be innocuous since all the industries in our sample get positive protection. For notational convenience, we have suppressed the dependence of labor demand, output, imports, and the two elasticities on the price.

consumers as a whole; not assuming lump-sum rebating of trade barrier revenue or rents; and allowing for lobbying frictions. In order to capture these forces while preserving tractability, we have assumed that all potential lobbies organize and that the impact of lobbying on that lobby's consumer surplus is negligible.

To help in interpreting (2), consider how each of the three main features affects it. The L_i terms in (2) capture the independent influence of workers on protection. Without rigid wages and unemployment, these terms would disappear, and the equilibrium equation would be

$$\bar{P}_i = \frac{c\left(b_i^{\mathrm{P}}\bar{y}_i + b_i^{\mathrm{IM}}\bar{m}_i\right) - a\left(\bar{y}_i + \bar{m}_i\right)}{cb_i^{\mathrm{IM}}e_{(m,p),i}\bar{m}_i}.$$

This resembles more closely GH-type models, in which protection depends on the ratio of output to imports, the weight that contributions get relative to consumer surplus (c vs. a), and the elasticity of import demand.

Nevertheless, this expression is still more complicated because it does not assume lump-sum rebating of trade barrier revenue or rents and because there are lobbying frictions that vary by industry. To assume rebating would set $cb_i^{\mathrm{IM}} = a$, which means that the revenues or rents get the same weight as consumer surplus. This would reduce (2) to

$$\tilde{P}_i = \frac{e_{(L,p),i}L_i + \left(cb_i^{\mathrm{P}} - a\right)\bar{y}_i}{e_{(L,p),i}L_i + ae_{(m,p),i}\bar{m}_i}$$

with unemployment and

$$\tilde{P}_i = \frac{\left(cb_i^{\mathrm{P}} - a\right)\bar{y}_i}{ae_{(m,p),i}\bar{m}_i} = \frac{\left(cb_i^{\mathrm{P}} - a\right)y_i}{ae_{(m,p),i}m_i}$$

without.

If contributions are assumed to be frictionless transfers, then the b_i^{P} and b_i^{IM} terms in any of the above equilibrium expressions would equal 1. Applying this change to the previous equation, so that all three of the main features are dropped, gives

$$\tilde{P}_i = \frac{(c-a)y_i}{ae_{(m,p),i}m_i}.$$

Adopting the GH convention of letting $c = 1 + a$, further reduces this to

$$\tilde{P}_i = \frac{y_i}{ae_{(m,p),i}m_i}.$$

This is the expression for protection that comes out of their framework (with separate bilateral bargains) when all industries lobby and each lobby's consumer surplus is ignored.[13] Our model, therefore, is an alternative to the GH

---

[13] Referring to [19], all industries being organized means that the equation on p. 22 of that article applies to all industries, and abstracting from changes in lobbies' consumer surplus means that $\alpha_j = 0$.

model but not a generalization of it: we have abstracted from certain features of their model while adding new elements. The model implies several ceteris paribus results for import-competing industries.

Result 1 *Sectors with more workers receive more protection.*[14]

The intuition for this is straightforward. More workers in an industry means more potential votes for the government when it imposes protection. The empirical literature finds a robust connection between workforce size and trade barriers. By incorporating involuntary unemployment, this model differs from others in providing a theoretical backing for the claim, accepted by most observers, that jobs do matter.

Result 2 *Sectors with higher elasticities of labor demand receive more protection.*

Holding all other variables fixed, industries that hire many workers in response to a price increase also provide many votes if granted protection and thus will receive more of it. As with result 1, this is unique, as far as we know, to the theoretical literature.

Result 3 *Sectors with lower lobbying transactions costs (higher b_i^P) receive more protection.*

Lower transactions costs imply that the producer lobby will have more clout with the government, since the government will actually receive more of the resources that the lobby dedicates to lobbying. Such transactions costs are probably closely connected to the extent of free riding, which, in turn, is probably related to such variables as industry concentration and the number of firms. Thus, we expect protection to be correlated with such variables. This result springs from Becker's idea [4] that the pressure applied by interest groups may not actually equal the amount of resources that they devote to such lobbying. We have chosen exogenous friction coefficients as a reduced form operationalization of this idea, but more explicit modeling of such transactions costs would be interesting future work.

Result 4 *Sectors with higher levels of output receive more protection only if $cb_i^P > a$.*

Large industries have more resources to contribute to politicians in order to acquire more rents. If, however, c or b_i^P is quite low (or both are), meaning that contributions are not valued enough or that lobbying costs are high (or both), then larger industries may get less protection. In this case, large industries cannot muster enough contributions to counteract the large amount

---

[14] $\tilde{P}_i$ is monotonically increasing in L_i. Increasing L_i may also decrease $e_{(L,p),i}$ but, as long as $L^d(\bar{w}/p)$ is decreasing, this secondary effect will not outweigh the direct effect of increasing L.

of consumer surplus that protection in those industries would wipe out. This result goes against the conventional theoretical wisdom that protection increases with output. Much empirical work, however, finds the opposite. [23] is another formal model which allows for the possibility that protection can be decreasing with output. Their result arises not from lobbying frictions but from distortionary taxation.

Result 5 *Import rent seekers want neither free trade nor autarky but some intermediate level of protection that maximizes their rents.*

To see this, note what would happen to the price if all other special interests were removed from the game, i.e., if a, b_i^P, and $e_{(L,p),i}$ were all set equal to 0. Then,

$$\tilde{P}_i = \frac{1}{e_{(m,p),i}},$$

which is the expression for the maximum revenue tariff, or, more generally, the maximum rent trade barrier. Import rent seekers want the price that maximizes rents. Unlike with producers, higher prices do not necessarily benefit them.[15]

Result 6 *Sectors with lower levels of imports receive more protection if $cb_i^{IM} \leq a$; otherwise, the connection between protection and imports is ambiguous.*[16]

Intuitively, if $cb_i^{IM} \leq a$, then the clout of import rent seekers is smaller than that of consumers. In this case, industries with more imports get less protection, because more imports means that protection for such an industry will result in a larger loss of consumer surplus. If, on the other hand, import rent seekers have more clout than consumers so that $cb_i^{IM} > a$, then the fact that import rent seekers want an intermediate level of imports creates an ambiguous connection between imports and protection. The model in [23], like ours, has import rent seekers, so that results like ♯5 and ♯6 could be derived from their framework.

Result 7 *Sectors with lower elasticities of import demand receive more protection.*

Since more elastic demand leads to greater deadweight loss when prices are propped up, more elastic import demand leads to less protection. This accords with all GH-type models and is implicit in other frameworks, as [19] shows.

---

[15] This requires that $e_{(m,p),i} > 1$. Even if $e_{(m,p),i}$ is less than or equal to 1 at world prices, as the price rises, $e_{(m,p),i}$ will exceed 1 at some point, as long as there is an upper limit on the price that consumers are willing to pay for imports.

[16] The derivation is available upon request.

4 Empirics

We now turn to the task of empirically testing the model's predictions. Section 4.1 develops an empirical model based on the theoretical model. Section 4.2 briefly describes the data. Section 4.3 presents and analyzes the regression results.

4.1 An Econometric Model

In (2), production, imports, and labor demand are all endogenous with respect to the level of protection.[17] [16] and [34] instrument for the ratio of imports to output using industry-level factor shares. We follow them and instrument for these variables in the same way. The presumption is that factor shares are correlated with imports and output but not with the price. Since labor is endogenous (because it is mobile), we do not include labor shares in the instruments. We also instrument for labor using non-labor factor shares. For a given technology, the amount of labor demanded will depend on the amount of other factors present.[18]

As mentioned above, we expect b_i^P to be a function of variables that reflect the extent of transactions costs in lobbying. The Trefler data set has four such variables: 4-firm concentration ratio, geographical concentration, number of firms, and the unionization rate. We do not fully develop a model of the relation between these variables and lobbying transactions costs. Instead, we specify a simple linear relation between b_i^P and each of the variables: $b_i^P = b_0^P + b_1^P x_{ij}$, where x_{ij} is the value of the jth lobbying cost variable in industry i. The data will then tell us whether, within the theoretical framework developed, these proxies for lobbying costs influence protection. Note that we are only trying to proxy for lobbying effectiveness. We are not trying to measure directly the amount of lobbying since this is not determined in our Nash set-up.

We do not proxy for importer lobbying frictions since we do not have the needed data. Instead, we assume that b_i^{IM} is constant across sectors. Thus, our econometric model can be written as:

$$\tilde{P}_i = \frac{\epsilon \text{LAB}_i + \chi \left(\left[\beta_0^P + \beta_1^P \text{LOB}_{ij} \right] \text{OUT}_i + \beta^{IM} \text{IMP}_i \right) - \alpha \left(\text{OUT}_i + \text{IMP}_i \right)}{\epsilon \text{LAB}_i + \chi \beta^{IM} (\text{ELAS}_i)(\text{IMP}_i)} + u_i$$

(3)

where LAB_i is the number of workers (L_i); OUT_i is the value of output ($\tilde{y}$); IMP_i is the value of imports ($\bar{m}_i$); LOB_{ij} is one of the lobbying costs variables (x_{ij}); and α, β_0^P, β_1^P, β^{IM}, χ and ϵ are parameters to be estimated or fixed, corresponding to a, b_0^P, b_1^P, b^{IM}, c, and $e_{L,p}$, respectively.

---

[17] We assume that both elasticities are constant around equilibrium.

[18] The factor instruments are physical capital, inventories, cropland, pasture land, forest land, coal, petroleum, and minerals. The data is from [34]. The main results are robust to the choice of instruments, although a shorter list of instruments reduces the standard errors, as one would expect.

Notice that the elasticity of labor demand has become a parameter (ϵ). This is because we do not have data on the industry-level elasticities of labor demand for our sample. We estimate the model using non-linear two-stage least squares (NL2S; see [1]).[19]

4.2 The Data

We use mid-1980s US data for 191 SIC 4-digit industries. This choice of country and time period stems from the fact that the endowments data needed for the instruments are only readily available for the US in 1983 ([34]).

We use new, industry-level measures of protection from 1985.[20] Specifically, detailed price data from a sample of six OECD countries were used to construct tariff equivalent price gaps that capture all kinds of barriers to trade. See Appendix A for an overview. [6] provides further details and discusses why they are probably more trustworthy than other commonly used measures, such as NTB indices and unit value comparisons. The employment data also come from Trefler and are 1983 US data. These data were adjusted to account for intra-industry trade. Since some output from almost all industries gets exported, we multiplied the number of workers by the ratio of non-exported production to total production, to arrive at an estimate of the number of import-competing workers for that sector.

The imports and exports data are from the Feenstra data set, and the output data are from the Bartelsman, Becker, and Gray data set. Both data sets are from 1983 and are on the NBER web site. As with employment, we adjusted output downward to reflect import-competing production. We did so by subtracting exports from output. These data sets give the value of imports and output at current (protected) prices. We converted these to values at world prices by dividing the current value by the ad valorem protection rate.

The lobbying cost variables-4-firm concentration, geographical concentration, number of firms, and unionization rates-are all from Trefler and are from 1983, as well.

---

[19] The dependent variable falls within the $[0, 1]$ interval but is neither truncated nor censored. There are no zeros in our data, indicating no truncation. Also, we have dropped no industries because their protection level was below zero, indicating no censoring.

[20] These protection measures are nominal, even though specific capital owners care about effective protection, which could, theoretically, differ substantially from nominal protection. Unfortunately, it is most difficult to calculate effective protection. The standard measures assume no substitutability among inputs and thus overstate true effective protection. Some researchers have tried to overcome this problem, but there are no reliable estimates of effective protection for the 191 sectors. In the end, it appears to make little difference. According to data from [11], the correlation between nominal and effective protection for 18 2-digit sectors in the US was 0.99. (It was 0.93 for the EU and 0.87 for Japan.)

Like [16] and [15], we take the import demand elasticity data from [33]. These estimates are considered to be the best available at the level of disaggregation used in this empirical analysis. For a few industries, the elasticity estimates were positive, and we dropped these from the sample. Since the elasticity data are estimated, we used the errors-in-variables correction presented in [13] to 'purge' the elasticities data. Summary statistics for all variables are shown in Table 1.

4.3 Results

Estimating the Model

The equation for protection is homogeneous of degree 0 in α, χ, and ϵ, meaning that we must peg one of these parameters in order to estimate the model.[21] Doubling the units in which we convert dollars to votes (α and χ) and doubling the elasticity of labor demand will have no impact on $\tilde{P}$.

We peg α and let the regressions generate results for ϵ and χ. These latter two parameters indicate whether jobs and contributions, respectively, play important roles in the protection game. What value should be chosen for α? Given that ϵ, the elasticity of labor demand, is a parameter that others have estimated, we choose α such that the estimate for ϵ comes out in a reasonable range. Estimates of labor demand elasticities at the industry level in [18] range from 0.20 to 1.03. It turns out that, in the regressions below, setting α at 0.001 generates point estimates for ϵ that range from 0.30 to 0.77.[22] This value of α implies that each \$1000 drop in consumer surplus results in the loss of one vote.[23]

It also turns out that we also need to peg one of β_0^P, β_1^P, β^{IM} and χ: Multiplying all of the β's by a positive constant and dividing χ by the same constant also would not affect $\tilde{P}$. We peg β^{IM} and generate results for β_0^P and β_1^P. Unlike with α, however, there is no empirical work that sheds light on reasonable values for β^{IM}. Thus, the equations were estimated 10 times, with set β^{IM} equal to all multiples of 0.1 ranging up to 1. (Recall that β^{IM} is bounded by 0 and 1.) The sign and significance of all three estimated parameters are robust to all choices of β^{IM}. We will focus on the results for $\beta^{IM} = 0.9$, because it seems likely that, despite some transactions costs associated with importer lobbying, the majority of contributions from importers are not dissipated. Picking lower values for β^{IM}, meaning higher transactions costs, would unequivocally strengthen all the conclusions below. We discuss the implications of assuming no transactions costs ($\beta^{IM} = 1$) in footnote 23.

---

[21] This stems from not normalizing the weight on either consumer surplus or contributions to be 1, as GH and others have done.

[22] Increasing α by a factor of 10 increases ϵ by a factor of 10. Thus, setting α equal to 0.01 would lead to estimates for ϵ between 3.0 and 7.7. Similarly, a 10-fold reduction in α would decrease the ϵ estimates by a factor of 10.

[23] Changing α changes only the point estimate for ϵ, not affecting the substantive results below.

Table 1. Summary statistics (191 US Industries, 1983).

	MEAN	MEDIAN	MIN	MAX	S.D.
Regression variables					
Protection: $\tilde{P} = \frac{p^* - p^W}{p^*}$	0.188	0.138	0.000999	0.627	0.150
Employment (thousands): LAB	53.2	24.6	1.59	994	101
Production (\$ million, valued at world prices):					
OUT	4360	1920	42.1	165,000	12,800
Imports (\$ million, valued at world prices): IMP	443	144	0.0129	16,224	1410
Elasticity of import demand (corrected):					
$e_{m,p}$ or ELAS	1.62	1.33	0.221	3.78	0.876
Lobbying cost variables:					
4-firm concentration ratio: LOB_1	0.373	0.350	0.0300	0.940	0.188
Geographical concentration: LOB_2	0.691	0.692	0.300	0.996	0.155
Number of firms (scaled by output): LOB_3	0.277	0.150	0.00155	2.10	0.351
Uniozation rate: LOB_4	0.333	0.308	0.0630	0.754	0.126
Underlying data					
Tariff equivalent: $\frac{p^*}{p^W}$	1.28	1.16	1.001	2.68	0.295
Raw employment (thousands)	57.4	26.0	2.20	999	106
Raw production					
(\$ million, valued at domestic prices)	5640	2690	73.1	183,000	14,600
Raw imports (\$ million, valued at domestic prices)	509	187	0.0167	17,500	1150
Exports (\$ million)	424	124	0	10,400	1150
Alternative data for robustness checks					
NTB/Tariff index: as is	1.15	1.05	1.00	2.00	0.249
NTB/Tariff index: doubled	1.30	1.10	1.00	3.00	0.498
NTB/Tariff index: tripled	1.45	1.15	1.00	4.00	0.747
Uncorected elasticities	2.00	1.07	0.0420	23.9	2.65

Results for the Unrestricted Model

The first four columns of Table 2 show the results of estimating the equation with each of the four lobbying cost variables. In each case, the point estimate for ϵ is significantly positive at the 5% level or better, indicating that, ceteris paribus, industries with a greater number of workers do receive more protection. Thus, regressions stemming from a structural model that accounts for job concerns confirm the widely held belief that workforce size has a positive independent influence on protection.

The results for χ provide unambiguous evidence that lobbying contributions influence protection, just as votes do. The point estimate is significantly positive in all cases. Also, the estimate for χ is significantly greater than the pegged value of α in each case. This implies that contribution dollars are more valuable to policy makers than consumer surplus dollars.[24] The point estimate of χ indicates that politicians find contributions to be about 15%

---

[24] This is the only conclusion that does not hold for all calibrations of β^{IM}. In particular, if $\beta^{IM} = 1$, then χ is not significantly greater than α when using geographical concentration, number of firms, or unionization. The reason that the result weakens when we set β^{IM} at a higher level is that imputing more influence to importers for a given amount of protection means that producers' contributions need to receive less weight in order to best estimate the model with the given data. When using 4-firm concentration, χ is significantly greater than α

Table 2. Non-linear 2-stage least squares estimation of the general model.

Parameter	Lobbying cost	variable	used		
	4-Firm concentration Estimate (t-stat.)	Geographical concentration Estimate (t-stat.)	Number of firms Estimate (t-stat.)	Unionization rate Estimate (t-stat.)	None Estimate (t-stat.)
ϵ	0.351** (1.90)	0.433** (2.05)	0.562*** (2.47)	0.588** (1.80)	0.299*** (2.45)
$\chi^{\sharp}$	0.00117*** (4.49)	0.00116*** (4.04)	0.00115*** (3.78)	0.00115*** (3.13)	0.00117*** (5.12)
$\beta_0^{P\,\sharp\sharp}$	0.857*** (6.41)	0.860*** (4.95)	0.868*** (4.36)	0.868*** (7.56)	0.854*** (5.99)
β_1^P	0.00120 (0.496)	0.00227 (1.08)	-0.00581** (-1.89)	0.00936 (1.02)	
Pseudo-SSR	1.4307	1.4767	1.2333	1.3302	1.3442
Variance of the residuals	0.04641	0.04757	0.04272	0.05090	0.046

Dependent variable: $\tilde{P} = \frac{p^* - p^w}{p^*}$. Number of observations:191. α is set equal to 0.001. β^{IM} is set equal to 0.9. Standard errors are robust White.

*, **, * * * Significant at the 10%, 5%, or 1% level, respectively. All are 1-tailed tests.

$\sharp$ Asterisks and t-stats refer to whether $\chi > \alpha$. If this is so, then contributions get more weight than consumer surplus.

$\sharp\sharp$ Asterisks and t-stats refer to whether $\beta_0^P < 1$. Given the results for β_1^P, this implies that there are transactions costs in lobbying.

more valuable in terms of how many votes they can buy than is consumer surplus. This estimate seems more reasonable than that of [16], which implied a value of about 2%.

The results for the lobbying parameters indicate significant transactions costs associated with lobbying: β_0^P is significantly less than 1, and the estimate for β_1^P never significant and large in absolute value. Thus, $\beta_0^P + \beta_1^P \text{LOB}_j$ is always significantly less than 1 for all values of the four LOB_j variables. This casts doubt on the standard assumption in lobbying models that contributions are frictionless. Of the four lobbying cost variables, only the number of firms is significant (at the 5% level). The point estimate is so low, though, that the estimated impact of this variable on lobbying transactions costs is quite small. For instance, halving the number of firms from its mean would only reduce transactions costs by about 0.6%.[25] Thus, the one political variable that is statistically significant has little economic significance.

---

at the 10% level, and, with no lobbying costs variables, χ is significantly greater than α at the 5% level.

[25] Number of firms is measured in firms per one million dollars, and the mean for this variable is 0.28. Since the estimate for the producer lobbying coefficient is given by $\hat{b}_i^P = \beta_0^P + \beta_1^P \text{NUM}_i$ (where NUM_i is the number of firms), the estimate for b_i^P evaluated at the mean value of 0.28 is $0.868 + (-0.00581)(0.28) = 0.8664$. Cutting the mean in half increases the estimate for b_i^P to $0.868 + (-0.00581)(0.14) = 0.8672$. Thus, the estimate for transactions costs, which equals $1 - b_i^P$, is reduced from 0.1336 to 0.1328, a 0.6% reduction.

Given these weak results for the lobbying variables, we re-estimated the equation without one. Thus, we assumed that b_i^{P} simply equals a constant, β_0^{P}. The result of this model is in the fifth column of Table 2. As with all the other regressions, ϵ, χ, and β_0^{P} are significantly positive. Notice also that β_0^{P} is significantly less than β^{IM}, which has been set at 0.9. This implies that transactions costs for producer lobbies exceed those for importers. The estimate of 0.854 implies that producer transactions costs are 14.4% (1- 0.854), given the assumption that import transactions costs are 10% $(1 - 0.1)$.

Is protection increasing in output? The GH model says unequivocally that it is, while [15] and [16] have found empirical evidence for this proposition.[26] Recall from Result 5 above that, in our framework, protection increases in output if $cb_i^{\mathrm{P}} > a$. Thus, if $\chi(\beta_i^{\mathrm{P}} + \beta_1^{\mathrm{P}} \mathrm{LOB}_{ij})$ is significantly greater than α, that constitutes empirical evidence that protection increases in output. Imposing the restriction $\chi(\beta_i^{\mathrm{P}} + \beta_1^{\mathrm{P}} \mathrm{LOB}_{ij}) = \alpha$ does not significantly worsen the fit, for all five specifications. Thus, we have no evidence that protection is increasing in output. While policy makers do value contributions more than consumer surplus, the presence of transactions costs apparently diminishes producer influence to the point where contributions from large producers cannot outweigh the large consumer costs inflicted by protecting those large producers.

A Restricted Model Without Import Rent Seekers

Our modeling has sought to account for possible lobbying by import rent seekers, since casual observation suggests that this occurs. It turns out, though, that we can ignore import rent seeking and assume lump-sum rebating because doing so does not significantly worsen the fit.

As discussed above, imposing lump-sum rebating changes the prediction to:

$$\tilde{P}_i = \frac{e_{L,p}L_i + \left(cb_i^{\mathrm{P}} - a\right) \bar{y}_i}{e_{L,p}L_i + ae_{(m,p),i}\bar{m}_i}$$

The econometric equation becomes:

$$\tilde{P}_i = \frac{\epsilon \mathrm{LAB}_i + \left[\chi \left(\beta_0^{\mathrm{P}} + \beta_1^{\mathrm{P}} \mathrm{LOB}_{ij}\right) - \alpha\right] \mathrm{OUT}_i}{\epsilon \mathrm{LAB}_i + \alpha(\mathrm{ELAS}_i)(\mathrm{IMP}_i)} + u_i \tag{5}$$

Once again, we need to peg either χ or one of the β's, as well as α. Thus, we set β_0^{P} equal to the point estimates from the previous results in Table 2.[27]

We report the results for this restricted model in Table 3. Quasi-likelihood ratio tests ([12]) for each of the five pairs of models never reject the restricted model, even at the 10% level. In this simpler model, the estimates for ϵ are

---

[26] These papers also imply that protection decreases with imports, but, since we do not estimate b^{IM}, we cannot test this proposition. [20] shows that output and protection can move in opposite directions when world prices change.

[27] The results are robust to the choice of β_0^{P}.

strongly significant in all cases (at the 1% level), confirming that jobs matter. As before, the estimate for χ is significantly positive and is significantly greater than the calibrated value of α, confirming that politicians do indeed value contributions more than wealth spread across the populace. We also get stronger results for the lobbying cost variables: geographical concentration and unionization rate join number of firms in being significant at the 5% level, with the predicted signs. As before, though, the point estimates are so small that these variables have limited economic significance.

Table 3. Non-linear 2-stage least squares estimation of the model without import rent seekers.

Parameter	Lobbying cost	variable	used		
	4-Firm concentration	Geographical concentration	Number of firms	Unionization rate	None
	Estimate (t-stat.)	Estimate (t-stat.)	Estimate (t-stat.)	Estimate (t-stat.)	Estimate (t-stat.)
ϵ	0.616*** (4.25)	0.712*** (4.33)	0.754*** (4.56)	0.769*** (3.94)	0.477*** (4.38)
$\chi^\sharp$	0.00116*** (72.2)	0.00116*** (49.4)	0.00115*** (238)	0.00114*** (28.9)	0.00117*** (635)
β_1^P	0.00364 (1.25)	0.00482** (1.88)	−0.00768*** (−2.51)	0.00143** (1.69)	
Pseudo-SSR	1.4980	1.5185	1.2685	1.3553	1.4705
Reject this model for the unrestricted one? (5% significance)	NO	NO	NO	NO	NO

Dependent variable: $\tilde{P} = \frac{p^* - p^w}{p^*}$. Number of observations: 191. α is set equal to 0.001. β^{IM} is set equal to point estimates in Table 2. Standard errors are robust White.

*, **, * * * Significant at the 10%, 5%, or 1% level, respectively. All are 1-tailed tests.

$\sharp$ Asterisks and t-stats refer to whether $\chi > \alpha$. If this is so, then contributions get more weight than consumer surplus.

Since it has been standard procedure to use NTB indices to measure protection, let us compare our results with such empirical studies. [14], [15], and [22], all find a positive significant relation between workforce size and NTB protection, while [16] and [34] find a positive but insignificant relation. So, using a new model and data, we confirm the NTB literature's presumption that protection increases with the number of jobs at stake. As for the lobbying variables, though, our results diverge more sharply from the literature. In particular, our significant, positive results on geographical concentration and unionization are unique. Most papers find no significant relation, while [28] and [15] get significant, negative coefficients on geographical concentration and unionization, respectively. We find robust evidence that protection decreases with number of firms; only [34] examines this, and he finds no significant correlation. Finally, while we find no connection between four-firm concentration and protection, [24] and [28] find a negative relation, while [34] and [14] find a positive relation.

Robustness Checks

We checked the robustness of these results in five ways. (1) We used an alternative protection measure based on the NTB indices used in many other papers. (2) We tried a quadratic, instead of linear, functional form for lobbying costs. (3) We experimented with different sets of instruments. (4) We estimated the system using limited information maximum likelihood (LIML), instead of NL2S. (5) We used uncorrected elasticities, instead of those corrected for errors-in-variables.

NTB coverage ratios are fraught with problems, but, as a check on whether our new measures drive the results (which still would not invalidate our results, if our measures are superior), we estimated the equation using the NTB measures. These data are censored at zero (53% of the observations[28]), however, and trying to incorporate some kind of Tobit correction into our non-linear framework lies beyond this paper. So, zeros in the NTB data were replaced with tariff rates. Nearly all of these rates are small, so the effect of this modification was to replace zeros with small numbers. Another problem with the coverage ratios is that they are bounded above at 1, which, in effect, limits the maximum protection rate to 100%. We thus followed Goldberg and Maggi and considered three different cases: using the NTB data as is; doubling the data, so that the maximum tariff equivalent becomes 200%; and tripling the data, so that the maximum becomes 300%. Using the NTB/ tariff data as is, with no upward scaling, workforce size is only significant in the unrestricted model when the number of firms is the lobbying cost proxy. In the restricted model, workforce size is significant in all cases except when using unionization rate. We reject this streamlined model, however, when using 4-firm concentration, geographical concentration, or no lobbying cost variable. So, in the end, workforce size is only significant when using number of firms. Thus, using the NTB/ tariff data as is gives mixed results, but this is precisely the data that is most dubious.

Doubling the NTB/ tariff data yields more robust results. Tripling the data improves the results even more. When the data is doubled, all the results are robust, with the following exceptions. We reject the streamlined model (no import rent seekers) when using geographical concentration or no lobbying cost proxy. Workforce size is not significant under the geographical concentration specification. Also, among the political variables, neither geographical concentration nor unionization rate is significant (at the 5% level). When the data are tripled, we reject the streamlined model when no lobbying cost proxy is used, but, otherwise, all the results carry through.

Using a quadratic specification for the lobbying cost variables does not affect our conclusions that workforce size matters and that assuming lump-sum rebating is justified. In only one case out of eight (four regressions each

---

[28] The fact that such a high fraction of industries show zero protection, when each one of them has positive tariffs, casts further doubt on the usefulness of this NTB data.

for the full model and the restricted model), did the quadratic term come out significant at the 5% level (restricted model, 4-firm concentration). The conclusions regarding these political variables were largely unchanged.

We also experimented with different instruments and found no change in the main results. Using no instruments, however, did undermine the results. We need to correct for endogeneity. We also estimated the system using LIML and got very similar results. Using LIML was problematic, however, because we rejected normality of the residuals. Dropping outliers so that normality was not rejected also produced very similar results. Finally, we ran the regressions using uncorrected elasticities, and this did not affect any of the main results.[29]

5 Conclusion

We have developed a protection model that incorporates the incentives of politicians to win support through creating or preserving jobs, as well as through campaign spending. In fact, we may think of job preservation as a direct way, and campaign spending as an indirect way, of winning votes.[30] The theory predicts that protection for an industry will be increasing in the number of workers in that industry and that there is no necessary connection between protection and either output or imports. In particular, if industries cannot organize well enough, protection may be decreasing in output. Also, the impacts of both imports and output on protection are conditioned by workers' ability to influence policy makers through voting. The result also implies that protection is decreasing in lobbying costs.

The empirical results provide strong evidence that protection increases with the number of workers in that industry.[31] We also do not find that protection increases with output. We have provided some evidence that variables that affect lobbying (geographical concentration, unionization rates, and, especially, the number of firms) affect protection levels. We find that there are significant transactions costs in lobbying: contributions are not frictionless transfers. The empirics also imply that one does not need to replace the

---

[29] The adjusted R^2 for the regressions range from 0.02 to 0.05. Using adjusted R^2 to measure goodness-of-fit, however, is problematic because 2-stage least squares does not minimize the sum of the squared errors. It minimizes the errors after projecting them onto the instruments matrix. The minimized value of this objective function is the pseudo-SSR that we have reported.

[30] [16] also find that "there is some evidence that factors linked to unemployment may affect protection through channels different than the ones suggested by the GH theory." They go on to say: "This suggests that it might be fruitful to $\cdots$ allow for $\cdots$ unemployment and examine the impact that this has $\cdots$." We have done precisely this.

[31] This contrasts with the claim made in [17] that "our formula suggests that only two variables (the elasticity of import demand and the ratio of domestic output to imports) should explain the cross-industry variation in protection levels."

lump-sum rebating assumption with a formal specification of the role that import rent seekers play in the protection game. Finally, this work implies that politicians place about 15% more weight on a dollar of campaign contributions than on a dollar of consumer surplus.

Our framework can be modified to test other hypotheses. For instance, to test whether there is a sympathy motive for protection, we could let c depend on skill levels or industry growth, just as we have let b_i^P depend on lobbying cost variables. It would also be useful to see whether this paper's conclusions hold with more recent data or data from other countries or both. On the theoretical side, modeling the labor market and unemployment more explicitly within a political economy model such as this may prove quite fruitful. For instance, such modeling would make it possible to explicitly incorporate the influence of wages on protection into the analysis. While much work remains to be done, we hope that this paper has shed light, and will stimulate further research, on the complex connections among protection, jobs, voting, and lobbying.

Appendix A. New Protection Measures

Nations protect their industries in many ways. Aside from standard instruments, health and safety standards, labeling laws, certification requirements, biased government procurement, burdensome customs procedures, and threats can all restrict trade. Thus, measuring protection is not straightforward. Here, we briefly describe our method. See [6] for more details and a discussion of other methods.

We infer protection levels from price gaps. The philosophy is that international barriers to arbitrage should be considered barriers to trade. This implies that, after accounting for shipping costs between countries, a price gap for equivalent goods in different countries indicates protection (even if policies not explicitly designed to impede trade are responsible).

The underlying data come from the OECD, which collects carefully matched retail prices in order to calculate Purchasing Power Parity estimates. The data cover 124 traded final goods categories (103 household goods and 21 capital goods) and are from 1985. All prices were converted to US dollars using 1985 market exchange rates.

We need to convert these consumer prices to producer prices to measure protection. We did so using data on distribution margins.[32] We have such data, for six countries – Australia, Canada, Japan, the Netherlands, the UK, and the US – which comprise our sample. Thus,

$$p_{ij} = \frac{p_{ij}^c}{1 + m_{ij}}$$

[32] These cover retail trade, wholesale trade, transportation costs and taxes collected by retailers.

where p_{ij}^{P} is the producer price of good i in country j, p_{ij}^{c} is the consumer price (from the OECD data), and m_{ij} is the margin.[33]

We infer protection by comparing the domestic producer price to the landed (world) price of the foreign good. We infer the world price by using data on export margins and international transport costs, as follows. By adding the export margins to the producer prices, we calculated the export price for each product in each country. This price is given by $p_{ij}^{e} = p_{ij}^{P}(1 + em_{ij})$, where p_{ij}^{e} is the export price of good i for country j , and em_{ij} is the export margin of good i for country j. The common world price was then found by adding the international transport cost to the lowest export price in the sample $p_{i}^{w} = p_{iM}(1 + tm_{i})$, where, for each good i, p_{i}^{w} is the world price, $p_{iM} = \min(p_{i1}^{e}, \cdots, p_{i6}^{e})$ is the minimum of the 6 export prices, and tm_{i} is the international transport margin.

We then used the ratio of each country's producer price to the world price as a preliminary protection measure:

$$ppr_{ij} = \frac{p_{ij}^{P}}{p_{i}^{w}}$$

These measures will be biased downward if each country has substantial barriers to imports. For such goods, the calculated world price exceeds the true world price. At the same time, if just one of the countries has no barriers in that good, then these measures will not be biased downward, since, in this case, prices in the free trading country will approximate world prices. With fairly free traders such as Australia, Canada, and the US in the sample, we believe that the low price approximates the world price the great majority of the time. Nevertheless, we use data on trade taxes to correct, at least partially, for the possible downward bias. The final measure of protection is $pr_{ij} = \max(ppr_{ij}, 1 + tar_{ij})$, where tar is the tariff rate for good i in country j. We simply use the fact that trade taxes provide a lower bound on protection. After this correction, these measures will only be biased downward if all countries in the sample have non-tariff barriers against the rest of the world.

References

1. Amemiya T (1983) Non-linear regression models, In: Griliches Z, Intriligator M (eds.) Handbook of Econometrics 1, North-Holland, Amsterdam
2. Baldwin RE (1987) Politically realistic objective functions and trade policy. Economics Letters 24: 287-290
3. Baldwin RE (1984) Trade policies in developed countries. In: Jones RW, Kenen PB (eds.) Handbook of International Economics, 1 North-Holland, Amsterdam
4. Becker GS (1983) A theory of competition among pressure groups for political influence. Quarterly Journal of Economics 98: 371-400

---

[33] m_{ij} is the fraction by which the consumer price exceeds the producer price. Thus, if the consumer price is 25% higher, then m_{ij} is 0.25.

5. Bhagwati JN, Srinivasan TN (1980) Revenue seeking: a generalization of the theory of tariffs. Journal of Political Economy 88: 1069-1087
6. Bradford SC (2003) Paying the price: final goods protection in OECD countries, Review of Economics and Statistics 85: 24-37
7. Brecher RA (1974) Minimum wage rates and the pure theory of international trade. Quarterly Journal of Economics 88: 98-116
8. Cassing JH, Hillman AL (1986) Shifting comparative advantage and senescent industry collapse, American Economic Review 76: 516-523
9. Davidson C, Martin L, Matusz S (1999) Trade and search generated unemployment, Journal of International Economics 48: 271-299
10. Davis DR (1998) Does European unemployment prop up American wages: national labor markets and global trade, American Economic Review 88: 478-494
11. Deardorff AV, Stern RM (1984) The effects of the Tokyo round and the structure of protection. In: Baldwin RE, Krueger AO. (eds.) The Structure and Evolution of Recent US Trade Policy. University of Chicago Press, Chicago
12. Gallant AR, Jorgenson DW (1979) Statistical inference for a system of simultaneous, non-linear, implicit equations in the context of instrumental variables estimation, Journal of Econometrics 11: 275-302
13. Gawande K (1997) Generated regressors in linear and non-linear models. Economics Letters 54: 119-126
14. Gawande K (1998) Comparing theories of endogenous protection: Bayesian comparison of Tobit models using Gibbs sampling output, Review of Economics and Statistics 80: 128-140
15. Gawande K, Bandyopadhyay U (2000) Is protection for sale? Evidence on the Grossman-Helpman theory of endogenous protection, Review of Economics and Statistics 82: 139-152
16. Goldberg PK and Maggi G (1999) Protection for sale: an empirical investigation, American Economic Review 89: 1135-1155
17. Grossman GM, Helpman E (1994) Protection for sale, American Economic Review 84: 833-850
18. Hammermash DS (1986) The demand for labor in the long run. In: Ashenfelter O, Layard R (eds.), Handbook of Labor Economics. North-Holland, Amsterdam
19. Helpman E (1995) Politics and trade policy, NBER Working Paper No. 5309
20. Hillman AL (1982) Declining industries and political-support protectionist motives, American Economic Review 72: 1180-1187
21. Krueger AO (1974) The political economy of the rent-seeking society, American Economic Review 64: 291-303
22. Lee JW, Swagel P (1997) Trade barriers and trade flows across countries and industries, Review of Economics and Statistics 79: 372-382
23. Maggi G, Rodriguez-Clare A (2000) Import penetration and the politics of trade protection, Journal of International Economics 51, 287-304
24. Marvel HP and Ray EJ (1983) The Kennedy round: evidence on the regulation of international trade in the United States. American Economic Review 73: 190-197
25. Mitra D (2000) On the endogenous choice between protection and promotion, Economics and Politics 12: 33-51
26. Peltzman S (1976) Toward a more general theory of regulation, Journal of Law and Economics 19: 211-248

27. Potters J, Sloof R, van Winden FW (1997) Campaign expenditures, contributions, and direct endorsements: the strategic use of information and money to influence voter behavior, European Journal of Political Economy 13: 1-31

28. Ray EJ (1981) The determinants of tariff and nontariff trade restrictions in the United States, Journal of Political Economy 89: 105-121

29. Revenga AL (1992) Exporting jobs? The impact of import competition on employment and wages in US manufacturing, Quarterly Journal of Economics 107: 255-284

30. Richardson M (1993) Endogenous protection and trade diversion, Journal of International Economics 34: 309-324

31. Rodrik D (1986) Tariffs, subsidies, and welfare with endogenous policy, Journal of International Economics 21: 285-296

32. Rodrik D (1995) What does the political economy literature on trade policy (not) tell us that we ought to know? In: Grossman, GM amd Rogoff K (eds.). Handbook of International Economics 3. North-Holland, Amsterdam

33. Shiells CR, Stern RM, Deardorff AV (1986) Estimates of the elasticities of substitution between imports and home goods for the United States, Welfwirtschlaftiches Archiv: 497-519

34. Trefler D (1993) Trade liberalization and the theory of endogenous protection, Journal of Political Economy 101: 138-160

Part II

The Political Economy of International Relations

Unemployed Immigrants and Voter Sentiment in the Welfare State[*]

Gil S. Epstein[1,2,3] and Arye L. Hillman[1,2]

[1] Department of Economics, Bar-Ilan University, Israel
esteig@mail.biu.ac.il   hillman@mail.biu.ac.il
[2] CEPR, Houghton Street, London W2A 2AE, UK
[3] IZA, Bonn, Germany

1 Introduction

Studies of the political economy of immigration policy investigate voters' attitudes to immigrants (see for example [2], [10], [17]). Such studies require an underlying basis that explains why a voter might personally support or object to immigration. One basis that identifies personal gains and losses from immigration is the standard full-employment model of international trade and factor movements (see [22]), where voter sentiment to immigration is derived from changes in real incomes, with some persons (generally described as factor owners) gaining from immigration and others losing.

There are, on the other hand, circumstances where there are no domestic losers from immigration. [8] propose, for example, that immigration can result in skill upgrading that is beneficial for all domestic workers. Alternatively, everyone in a local population can benefit when immigration reduces the domestic per capita tax burden for financing collective goods ([1]). Or there can more generally be mutual benefit for a local population when immigration expands the domestic tax base, and for example allows public financing of intergenerational transfers that might otherwise be unsustainable because of demographic imbalance in the local population (see [3], [12], [14], [20]).

Such benefits from an expanded tax base require that immigrants add to the tax-paying population. If unemployed immigrants are beneficiaries of tax-financed income transfers, immigrants increase government expenditures rather than adding to the domestic tax base. Voters perceiving the tax-financed income transfers to immigrants might then raise questions about the benefits from immigration.[1]

---

[*] We thank Joseph Deutsch, Abraham Lioui, Dennis Snower, Avi Weiss, Kar-yiu Wong and Thomas Piketty for helpful comments.
[1] For empirical evidence on tax-financed income transfers to unemployed immigrants in a welfare state (the Swedish case), see [9]. [21] correspondingly point

There are however circumstances where tax-financed transfers to unemployed immigrants can be socially beneficial, with no personal losses whether voters earn income from labor or from ownership of capital. The circumstances arise when unemployment is explained by efficiency wages (see [19]).

In this paper we investigate the efficiency-wage case for benefit from immigration in a welfare state. There are of course explanations of unemployment other than efficiency wages. A minimum-wage explanation of unemployment views unemployed immigrants as unable to find jobs because immigrants' productivity does not justify payment of the minimum wage. An insider–outsider theory of unemployment (see [15]) views insiders as paying themselves above market-clearing wages and using contrived means to protect their rents from outsiders who wish to work but remain unemployed. Immigrants according to insider–outsider theory are unemployed because they are natural outsiders.

If the reason for unemployment of immigrants is minimum wages or insider rent protection, there are no benefits to national voters from the presence of unemployed immigrants receiving tax-financed income transfers, other than the altruistic feeling of giving to the less unfortunate or participating in humanitarian assistance. There is of course also the possibility in principle that unemployed immigrants are content not to work, given the income transfers of the welfare state in which they have chosen to reside (see [4]).

An efficiency-wage view of unemployment suggests, however, a source of benefit for voters from welfare-assisted unemployed immigrants. Given the inevitably of unemployment in the efficient worker-disciplining equilibrium[2], domestic labor might prefer that someone else be unemployed. Immigrants accept this role, against the alternative of the quality of life offered in the countries that they have chosen to leave.

In our model, employed workers pay the taxes that finance income transfers to the unemployed, and immigrants at first displace national workers from the unemployment pool. The real wage declines because of immigration, but the probability of a local worker being employed increases. Although employed workers finance the income transfers to the unemployed, immigration within designated bounds increases the expected utility of local workers. Since employers benefit from immigration, immigration policies exist that are mutually beneficial for all voters whether voters are local employees or employers, although employers will want more immigrants than workers.

Efficiency wages can therefore rescue the welfare state from adverse voter sentiment when immigrants are unemployed and benefit from tax-financed income transfers. The credibility of unemployed immigrants as a labor-market discipline requires, however, that immigrants receive job offers and are willing

---

out how the welfare state can affect the choice between free trade in goods and free immigration.

[2] The efficiency-wage explanation for unemployment has, of course, similarities with Karl Marx's ([16]) idea of the 'reserve army of the unemployed' as a device by employers to maintain worker discipline.

to accept the offers. If the job offers are made and accepted, immigrants over time displace local workers from employment. Employment displacement compromises the efficiency wage as a counter to adverse voter sentiment to immigration. Adverse voter sentiment is then however not based on the income transfers of the welfare state, but on the loss of jobs to immigrants.

We proceed in Section 2 to set out the model. Section 3 is concerned with policies. The final section summarizes the conclusions.

2 The Model

We consider a population that consists of owners of capital and workers. Workers consist of N_L nationals and N_F immigrants. All workers are risk neutral and averse to effort. The utility of workers is separable and linear in private consumption that is provided through expenditure of a wage w and in the level of effort e,

$$U(w, e) = w - e. \tag{1}$$

Effort is dichotomous, at zero or positive. An unemployed worker receives benefits of w_0 from the state and exerts no effort so that $e = 0$. Welfare payments are the same for nationals and immigrants (immigrants are legal). An immigrant has greater expected income than in the country he or she has left.

A worker of type j ($j = F, L$) has a probability p_j of becoming unemployed for exogenous reasons that do not depend on the employer. All workers maximize present discounted utility, with a rate of time preference $r > 0$. The model is set in continuous time. The only choice that a worker makes is selection of effort e. A worker who does not shirk performs at a customary level of effort for the job, receives the wage w, and retains his or her job until he or she exogenously becomes unemployed. Employers imperfectly monitor effort. Workers who shirk are detected and fired with probability per unit of time q

$V_e(s, j)$ and $V_e(n, j)$ are expected lifetime utilities of an employed worker of type j when shirking (s) and when not (n). V_u is the expected lifetime utility of an unemployed person. For a shirker,

$$rV_e(s, j) = w - (p_j + q)(V_e(s, j) - V_u) \tag{2}$$

and for a non-shirker,

$$rV_e(n, j) = w - e - p_j(V_e(n, j) - V_u). \tag{3}$$

From (2) and (3), we have:

$$V_e(s, j) = \frac{w + (p_j + q)V_u(j)}{r + p_j + q} \quad \text{and} \quad V_e(n, j) = \frac{(w - e) + p_j V_u(j)}{r + p_j} \tag{4}$$

No shirking takes place if and only if $V_e(s, j) \leq V_e(n, j)$ i.e.,

$$w \geq rV_u(j) + \frac{(r + p_j + q)}{q}e. \tag{5}$$

Production functions for firms are $\tilde{f}(\bar{K}, L)$ where $\bar{K}$ is available capital and L is the number of employed workers. The incomes of owners of capital (or employers) increase when the number of workers who are employed increases[3]. Demand for workers is given by their value of marginal product, and is a decreasing function of the wage w. An equilibrium is defined as an outcome where owners of capital, taking as given wages and employment levels at the other firms, find it optimal to offer the going wage rather than a different wage, that is, there is a Nash equilibrium in wages paid by employers. The sole variable determining employers' decisions is the disciplining of employed workers through V_u, the expected utility of an unemployed worker.

Since all unemployed workers receive the same welfare benefits w_0, V_u is common to all employees. An unemployed person's utility is thus independent of the identity of his or her previous employer. Hence

$$rV_u(j) = w_0 + k_j(V_e(j) - V_u(j)) \tag{6}$$

where k_j is the rate at which workers who are unemployed find jobs and $V_e(j)$ is the expected utility of an employed worker of type j, which in equilibrium equals $V_e(n, j)$. Substituting (6) into (4), we obtain

$$rV_e(j) = \frac{(w - e)(k_j + r) + w_0 p_j}{k_j + p_j + r} \quad \text{and} \quad rV_u(j) = \frac{(w - e)k_j + w_0(r + p_j)}{k_j + p_j + r}. \tag{7}$$

Then, substituting (7) into (5), we determine that worker j will not shirk if

$$w \geq w_0 + e + \frac{e}{q}(k_j + p_j + r). \tag{8}$$

The *efficiency wage* is defined as the lowest wage that satisfies (8).

We wish to express the efficiency wage as depending on the level of unemployment. We therefore denote by L_j total employment of individuals of group j and by N_j the total potential labor supply of group j, with $N_{\mathrm{L}} > N_{\mathrm{F}}$. In a steady state,

$$k_j - p_j \frac{L_j}{N_j - L_j}. \tag{9}$$

The probability of job loss independent of the employer's decision quit rate, p_j, is an increasing function of the rate of employment L/N where $N = N_{\mathrm{L}} + N_{\mathrm{F}}$ and $L = L_{\mathrm{N}} + L_{\mathrm{F}}$ (since the lower is unemployment, the more willing is a worker to leave a job for extraneous personal reasons). Hence

$$p_j = f_j\left(\frac{L}{N}\right) \quad \text{such that} \quad \frac{\partial\left(f_i\left(\frac{L}{N}\right)\right)}{\partial\left(\frac{L}{N}\right)} > 0. \tag{10}$$

---

[3] Because of diminishing marginal product of labor.

From (10), (9), and (8), the condition that a worker of type j will not shirk is

$$w \geq w_0 + e + \frac{e}{q} \left(f_i \left(\frac{L}{N} \right) \frac{N_j}{(N_j - L_j)} + r \right) \tag{11}$$

and the equilibrium efficiency wage is where (11) holds with equality. We see that immigration affects the efficiency wage through

$$\frac{\partial w}{\partial N_F} \geq \frac{e}{q} \frac{\partial f_L \left(\frac{L}{N} \right)}{\partial N_F} \frac{(\eta - 1)L}{N^2} \frac{N_L}{(N_L - L_L)}. \tag{12}$$

η is the elasticity of the aggregate employment with respect to the potential work force

$$\left(\eta = \frac{\partial L}{\partial N} \frac{N}{L} \right).$$

In the efficiency-wage model, $\eta < 1$: that is, the number of employed workers cannot increase proportionately more than an increase in the total potential workforce. An increase in the number of immigrants therefore increases unemployment, so enhancing labor-market disciplining, and the efficiency wage in (12) falls.

2.1 Income Transfers to the Unemployed

We now establish how income transfers to the unemployed affect the equilibrium. Substituting the steady-state relationship $k_j = f_j L_j / (N_j - L_j)$ (see (9) and (10)) into (8), we see that a worker of type j will not shirk if

$$w \geq w_0 + e + \frac{e}{q} \left(f_j \frac{N_j}{N_j - L_j} + r \right) \quad \forall j \neq i \text{ and } j, i = L, F. \tag{13}$$

From (13), the willingness-to-exert effort function is

$$L_j = N_j \left(1 - \frac{f_i e}{qw - qw_0 - er - eq} \right) \quad \forall j = L, F. \tag{14}$$

The aggregate function is therefore

$$L = L_L + L_F = N - \frac{(N_L f_L + N_F f_F) e}{qw - qw_0 - er - eq}. \tag{15}$$

From (8), $qw - qw_0 - er - eq > 0$. (15) therefore expresses the positive relation between the efficiency wage w and willingness-to-exert-effort that underlies the efficiency wage explanation for unemployment. We also observe that *the higher are income transfers, the lower is willingness to exert effort*.

2.2 Labor-Market Equilibria

From (14), since

$$\frac{\partial f_{\mathrm{L}}}{\partial \left(\frac{L}{N}\right)} > 0, \quad \frac{\partial \left(\left(\frac{L}{N}\right)\right)}{\partial N} < 0,$$

and

$$\frac{\partial N}{\partial N_{\mathrm{F}}} = \frac{\partial N}{\partial N_{\mathrm{L}}} = 1,$$

we have

$$\frac{\partial L_{\mathrm{L}}}{\partial N_{\mathrm{F}}} = -\frac{N_{\mathrm{L}}e}{qw - qw_0 - er - eq} \frac{\partial f_{\mathrm{L}}}{\partial \left(\frac{L}{N}\right)} \frac{\partial \left(\frac{L}{N}\right)}{\partial N} \frac{\partial N}{\partial N_{\mathrm{F}}} > 0 \qquad (16)$$

and

$$\frac{\partial L_{\mathrm{L}}}{\partial N_{\mathrm{L}}} = \left(1 - \frac{f_{\mathrm{L}}e}{qw - qw_0 - er - eq}\right) - \frac{N_{\mathrm{L}}e}{qw - qw_0 - we - wq} \frac{\partial f_{\mathrm{L}}}{\partial \left(\frac{L}{N}\right)} \frac{\partial \left(\frac{L}{N}\right)}{\partial N} \frac{\partial N}{\partial N_{\mathrm{L}}}$$
$$> 0 \qquad (17)$$

That is, immigrants increase local workers' willingness-to-exert effort, and a downward shift takes place in the willingness-to-exert effort function. Wages in the new equilibrium are determined by equality of demand and the aggregate willingness-to-exert effort that takes account of both the domestic and immigrant workers. In equilibrium, wages decrease. When effort does not decline precipitously in response to the lower wage, and when demand for labor is sufficiently elastic, employment of domestic workers increases[4].

An important question is who obtains the new jobs. If national workers have priority, immigrants 'push' national workers into employment? ––at a lower wage than before immigration (otherwise the additional jobs would not be available).

2.3 The Financing of Income Transfers

We shall place the entire tax burden of financing income transfers received by the unemployed on employed labor. For benefits w paid to both local and immigrant unemployed workers, the tax per employed worker that finances the income transfers is:

$$\mathrm{Tax} = \frac{(N - L)}{L} w_0 = \frac{(N_{\mathrm{L}} + N_{\mathrm{F}} - L_{\mathrm{L}} - L_{\mathrm{F}})}{L_{\mathrm{L}} + L_{\mathrm{F}}} w_0 \qquad (18)$$

Employed workers do not shirk if

---

[4] Completely inelastic demand would of course allow for no increase in employment, nor would an extreme effort response. See Appendix A for more detail.

$$w \geq w_0 \left(1 + \frac{N-L}{L}\right) + e + \frac{e}{q}\left(f_L\left(\frac{L}{N}\right)\frac{N_L}{(N_L - L_L)} + r\right). \qquad (19)$$

An increase in the number of immigrants affects the efficiency wage through:

$$\frac{\partial w}{\partial N_F} = w_0 \left(\frac{(1-\eta)L}{L^2}\right) + \frac{e}{q}\left(\frac{\partial f_L\left(\frac{L}{N}\right)}{\partial N}\frac{L(\eta-1)}{N^2}\frac{N_L}{(N_L - L_L)}\right). \qquad (20)$$

There are two countervailing effects on the willingness of workers to exert effort. More immigrants increase the tax levied on employed workers, which reduces willingness-to-exert effort. However, as the number of immigrants increases, the threat of dismissal to local workers increases, which increases employed workers' willingness to exert effort. A necessary and sufficient condition for immigration to increase the willingness of the local individuals to exert effort is

$$\frac{\partial w}{\partial N_F} = w_0 \left(\frac{(1-\eta)L}{L^2}\right) + \frac{e}{q}\left(\frac{\partial f_L\left(\frac{L}{N}\right)}{\partial N}\frac{L(\eta-1)}{N^2}\frac{N_L}{(N_L - L_L)}\right) < 0. \qquad (21)$$

We therefore establish an upper bound on income transfers for immigrants to increase discipline on employed workers. Income transfers cannot exceed

$$w_0 < \frac{e}{q}\left(\frac{\partial f_L\left(\frac{L}{N}\right)}{\partial N}\left(\frac{L}{N}\right)^2\frac{N_L}{(N_L - L_L)}\right). \qquad (22)$$

Clearly, income transfers to the unemployed that are too high blunt the disciplining effect of an increase in the unemployment pool (or, to Karl Marx's term, the size of the reserve army), since being unemployed is less attractive. The taxes levied on employed workers to finance welfare payments at the same time make effort exertion less attractive, because of the lower loss of net income if found shirking.

There is also a lower bound to income transfers $\underline{w}$. The lower bound is the minimum income required to attract immigrants, or to have them stay and not go elsewhere.

The lower and upper bounds on income transfers establish the condition ensuring that additional immigrants increase willingness to exert effort:

$$\underline{w} < w_0 < \bar{w} = \frac{e}{q}\left(\frac{\partial f_L\left(\frac{L}{N}\right)}{\partial N}\left(\frac{L}{N}\right)^2\frac{N_L}{(N_L - L_L)}\right). \qquad (23)$$

We can therefore summarize that willingness to exert effort depends on taxes paid to finance income benefits for the unemployed. If benefits are in the range determined by (23), immigration increases discipline on employed workers.

At the same time, if income benefits to the unemployed are sufficiently high, or the number of immigrants is sufficiently large, immigrants displace national workers from employment. Also, the upper bound on benefits decreases with the number of immigrants.

2.4 Low Benefits for Immigrants

If immigrants receive differentially lower benefits, or no benefits at all, then immigrants may be placed in a position of offering to join the labor force *at any wage offered*. National workers, if they receive higher unemployment or welfare benefits, at the same time do not mind being unemployed as much as immigrants. From (11), national workers' willingness-to-exert-effort is a function of the efficiency wage: $L_L = v_L(w)$. The total willingness-to-exert-effort function is

$$L_L^S = L_L + L_F = v_L(w) + N_F \tag{24}$$

where N_F is the number of immigrants. An increase in labor supply due to immigration decreases the equilibrium efficiency wage and now *also decreases employment of local workers*. Yet an increased probability of employment or exit from the unemployment pool is the sole source of gain for national workers from increased immigration.

If benefits for unemployed immigrants are discriminately low and immigrants displace local workers in employment, national workers therefore cannot gain from immigration.[5] National workers therefore can gain from immigration only if the immigrants receive tax-financed income transfers.

3 Policy Decisions

We now apply the above analysis to consider policy decisions. The upper part of Fig. 1 shows the level of tax-financed income transfers to the unemployed w_0 and the number of immigrants N_F. The preferred policies of employers and national workers are at the points A and B respectively, and AB is the contract curve for the choice of policies.

Employers wish income transfers w_0 to the unemployed to be low, to increase the attractiveness of being employed. Employers would therefore choose income transfers at the lower bound $\underline{w} = w_0 \leq \bar{w}$, as shown at the point A. National workers want higher income transfers, between the lower and upper bounds such as at the point B.

Immigrants benefit employers by increasing employment decreasing the wage.

Employers want more immigrants than national workers (there are more immigrants at A than at B).

Expected utility of workers is given by

$$E^L U(w, e) = \left[\Pr_j \left(w^* - w_0 \frac{N - L}{L} - e \right) + (1 - \Pr_j) w_0 \right] \frac{1}{r}. \tag{25}$$

$\Pr_j$ is the probability that the national worker is employed and has utility

---

[5] For proof see Appendix B.

$$\left(w^* - w_0 \frac{N-L}{L} - e \right).$$

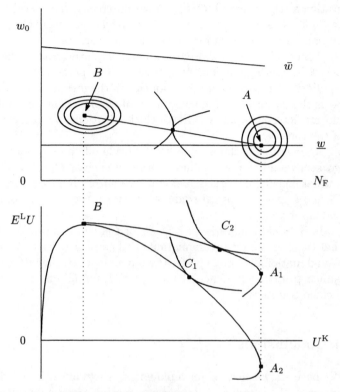

Fig. 1. Policy choice.

The probability of unemployment is $(1 - \mathrm{Pr}_j)$, in which case the worker receives benefits w_0 and exerts no effort $(e = 0)$. The probability that a local worker is employed is, in the steady state, equal to the proportion of employed persons, $\mathrm{Pr}_j = L_{\mathrm{L}}^* / N_{\mathrm{L}}$. At the workers' preferred point B,

$$\frac{\mathrm{E}^{\mathrm{L}} U(w, e)}{\partial w_0} = 0, \quad \frac{\mathrm{E}^{\mathrm{L}} U(w, e)}{\partial N_{\mathrm{F}}} = 0.$$

The lower part of Fig. 1 shows the expected utility of workers $\mathrm{E}^{\mathrm{L}} U$ and the utility of employers U^K. The number of immigrants increases from the origin along OB and workers' expected utility is again maximized at the point B. Along the segment OB, both national workers and owners of capital benefit from increases in the number of immigrants. Employers want more immigrants than at B, but beyond B the expected utility of workers declines.

Two alternative forms for the utility possibility frontier beyond B show preferred immigration for employers at A_1 and A_2. If the utility-possibility frontier is OBA_1, immigration at levels between B and A_1 (such at C_1) is beneficial for both workers and employers compared to a policy of no immigration at the origin O. OBA_2 shows outcomes where workers and employers can both lose from immigration, but policies are available (such at C_2) that are mutually beneficial for employers and workers.

Along OB there is consensus among employers and workers that the number of immigrants should be increased. The point B is the majority voting equilibrium if workers are the majority (if the median voter is a worker). A_1 or A_2 is the majority voting equilibrium if employers are the majority (or if employers determine policy through the institutions of representative democracy of the society).

A government choosing policy to trade-off the interests of employers and workers would choose a policy at a point such as C_1, or at C_2, where there is mutual benefit to workers and employers from immigration. The contours at C_1 and C_2 show political trade-offs between the interests of national workers and employers.

In political equilibria such at C_1 or C_2, workers would express discontent that there are too many immigrants and employers that there are too few. Although national workers prefer the outcome at B, they have nonetheless have gained from the presence of unemployed immigrants receiving tax-financed income transfers.

4 Conclusions

We have shown how, if unemployment is explained by efficiency wages, the presence of unemployed immigrants receiving tax-financed income transfers can be beneficial for both national workers, as well as employers -- although workers and employers[6] will be in disagreement about whether immigration should be decreased or increased.

Our model has supposed that local workers have advantages that provide priority in receiving job offers, and that immigrants remain disproportionately unemployed. The benefit from unemployed immigrants requires that unemployed immigrants receive and accept job offers. Should immigrants refuse to accept job offers that are made, taxpayers can come to see themselves as caught in the type of social dilemma described by [4], where some people prefer to receive income transfer payments rather than work for a living.

If immigrants however accept job offers, as they are required to do for their unemployed status to be a credible efficiency-enhancing discipline, then immigrants displace local workers from employment. We have observed that such

---

[6] We do not suggest by the distinction between workers and employers that we have used in this paper that employers do not work.

displacement will in particular tend to occur if unemployed national workers receive higher income transfers than unemployed immigrants. A source of anti-immigrant sentiment is then the feeling by national workers that they have lost their jobs to immigrants.

Unemployment need not, of course, be due to efficiency wages. The efficiency wage explanation for unemployment is an assumption of our model. Unemployment might be due to minimum wages or insider rents, or can be a response to social transfers at levels that, for some people, do not make the exertion of effort in employment worthwhile. In these cases, unemployed immigrants receiving tax-financed income transfers offer no sources of economic gain for the local population.

We have also presumed that only economic motives underlie voter attitudes to immigration. Voter discontent can also arise independently of economic motives, if parts of the domestic population are averse to the ethic and cultural diversity that in general accompanies immigration. [13] found for example that the propensity to commit acts of violence against immigrants in unified Germany was independent of income. Non-economic objections of voters to the presence of immigrants can also reflect disutility from fear of change in social norms and customs and loss of identity (see [12]), or a more fundamental dislike that [18] has described as a form of faith[7].

A further question is why do immigrants undertake the personal upheaval of relocation to choose unemployment and the stigma of living off the state in preference to opportunities in their own countries-and to choose to encounter at times the lack of acceptance by parts of the local population? This question is not the topic of the present paper. For purposes of this paper, we have simply assumed that immigrants are available when welfare payments are sufficiently high. An answer to why immigrants are available points to foreign living standards, and also to standards of governance and political culture in countries from which immigrants come[8].

Our model has considered only legal immigration[9]. Legal presence allows immigrants to receive tax-financed income transfers when not earning income through reported employment. Illegal immigrants have unreported jobs, and in general neither pay taxes nor benefit from the income transfers provided by the state in the event of unemployment. The illegal immigrants may be quite visibly present. In [10], visible presence of illegal immigrants is explained as a means of containing immigrants to particular employment. Tax-base con-

---

[7] For example, commenting on election results that favored politicians who had taken anti-immigration positions, the President of Switzerland (Ruth Dreifuss) observed that: 'Nationalism and xenophobia of the kind that underpinned big election gains last year for the Swiss and Austrian far right have always existed in Europe. What is new is the return of what was repressed' (*Herald Tribune*, January 24, 2000).

[8] See [8], [11].

[9] On illegal immigration, see for example [6]. For a perspective on efficiency wages with illegal immigration in a dual labor market model, see [5].

siderations suggest that, as well, permissible illegal immigration is a means of preempting welfare payments to immigrants.

Appendix A

In this appendix we derive the conditions under which an increased number of immigrants results in efficiency-wage equilibrium with lower wages and more employment. The local and immigrants willingness-to-exert-effort function are given respectively by: $L_L(w, L_F)$ and $L_F(w, a)$ (a is the number of immigrants entering the country). We have:

$$L_w = \frac{\partial L_L(w, L_F)}{\partial w} > 0, \quad \tilde{L}_F = \frac{\partial L_L(w, L_F)}{\partial L_F} > 0$$

$$F_w = \frac{\partial L_F(w, a)}{\partial w} > 0 \quad \text{and} \quad F_a = \frac{\partial L_F(w, a)}{\partial a} > 0.$$

In equilibrium the demand for labor, $D(w)$, equals the aggregate willingness-to-exert effort:

$$L_w(w, L_F) + L_F(w, a) = D(w) \tag{A.1}$$

Denoting $F = L_F(w, a)$ and $D_w = \partial D(w)/\partial w < 0$ and using the total differential of (A.1) with respect to a we confirm that increasing the number of immigrants decreases the equilibrium wage:

$$\frac{dw}{da} = \frac{\tilde{L}_F F_a + F_a}{D_w - L_w - F_w} < 0 \tag{A.2}$$

From (A.2), the effect of a change in number of immigrants on the equilibrium size of the local employed workforce is:

$$\frac{dL}{da} = \frac{L_w F_a + D_w L_a \tilde{L}_F}{D_w - L_w - F_w} \tag{A.3}$$

The denominator is negative. Thus $dL/da > 0$ if $\eta_L^S F_a/(L_a, \tilde{L}_F) < -\eta^D$ where η_L^S is the elasticity of the willingness-to-exert effort and η^D is the elasticity of demand (which is negative). The outcome therefore depends on the elasticities of demand and willingness-to-exert-effort function.

Appendix B

If unemployed immigrants receive no income transfers, immigrants may offer to join the labor force at any wage offered. In this case $\tilde{L}_F = \partial L_L(w, L_F)/\partial L_F < 0$ and $F_a = \partial L_F(w, a)/\partial a = 1$. (A.2) holds. However, dL/da becomes negative. Immigrants therefore displace local workers in employment.

References

1. Arad RW, Hillman A (1979) The collective good motive for immigration policy. Australian Economic Papers 18: 243-257
2. Benhabib J (1996) On the political economy of immigration. European Economic Review 40: 1737-1743
3. Bonin H, Raffelhuschen B, Walliser J (2000) Can immigrants alleviate the demographic burden? An assessment with generational accounting. Finanzarchiv 57: 1-21
4. Buchanan JM (1975) The samaritan's dilemma. In: Phelps E (eds.), Altruism, Morality and Economic Theory. Russell Sage, New York: 71-85
5. Carter TJ (1999) Illegal immigration in an efficiency wage model. Journal of International Economics 49: 385-401
6. Djajic S (1997) Illegal immigrants and resource allocation. International Economic Review 38: 97-117
7. Epstein GS, Hillman AL, Ursprung HW (1999) The king never emigrates. Review of Development Economics 3: 107-121
8. Fuest C, Thum M (2001) Immigration and skill formation in unionised labour markets. European Journal of Political Economy 18: 557-573
9. Hansen J, Lofstrom M (1999) Immigration assimilation and welfare participation: Do immigrants assimilate into or out of welfare? Paper presented at CEPR/ TSER workshop on Labor Demand, Education, and the Dynamics of Social Exclusion, Bar-Ilan University
10. Hillman A, Weiss A (1999) A theory of permissible illegal immigration. European Journal of Political Economy 15: 585-604
11. Hillman A, Ursprung HW (2000) Political culture and economic decline. European Journal of Political Economy 16: 189-213
12. Hillman A (2002) Immigration and intergenerational transfers. In: Siebert H (eds.), Economic Policy For Aging Societies. Kluwer Academic Publishers, Dordrecht: 204-217
13. Krueger AB, Pischke JS (1996) A statistical analysis of crime against foreigners in unified Germany. NBER working paper 5485, Cambridge, MA
14. Lee RD, Miller TW (1998) The current fiscal impact of immigration and their descendants: beyond the immigrant household. In: Smith JP, Edmonston B (eds.), The Immigration Debate. National Academy Press, Washington, DC.: 183-205
15. Lindbeck A, Snower D (1988) The Insider and Outsider Theory of Employment and Unemployment. MIT Press, Cambridge, MA
16. Marx K (1887) Translated from the third German, In: Moore S, Aveling E, Engels F (eds.) A Critical Analysis of Capitalist Production. Capital, Progress Publishing, Moscow
17. Mazza I, van Winden FW (1996) A political economy analysis of labor migration and income distribution Public Choice 88: 333-363
18. Sartre JP (1965) Anti-Semite and Jew 1965, Schocken Books, New York
19. Shapiro C, Stiglitz J (1984) Equilibrium unemployment as a worker discipline device. American Economic Review 74: 433-444
20. Storesletten K (2000) Sustaining fiscal policy though immigration. Journal of Political Economy 108: 300-323
21. Wellisch D, Walz U (1997) Why do rich countries prefer free trade over migration?: The role of the welfare state. European Economic Review: 42 1595-1612

22. Wong KY (1995) International Trade in Goods and Factor Mobility. MIT Press, Cambridge, MA

Strategic Emission Tax-Quota Non-Equivalence under International Carbon Leakage[*]

Kazuharu Kiyono[1] and Jota Ishikawa[2]

[1] School of Political Science & Economics, Waseda University, 1-6-1 Nishiwaseda Shinjuku-ku, Tokyo 169-8050, Japan kazr@mn.waseda.ac.jp
[2] Faculty of Economics, Hitotsubashi University, Naka 2-1, Kunitachi, Tokyo 186-8601, Japan jota@econ.hit-u.ac.jp

1 Introduction

A growing anticipation of global warming has spurred a lot of discussion among economists not only in environmental economics but also in international trade.[1] One of the theoretically new issues in economics is which system of environmental regulation is desirable for the world, a decentralized regulation based on each country's individual policy decision or a centralized one using the regional or international cooperation of environmental policies such as coordination in the emission tax policies and creation of the international tradeable emission permit market as proposed in the Kyoto protocol.[2]

In the decentralized regulation system, each country has several alternative policy instruments. Among them, the emission tax and quota (including creation of a domestic emission permit market) are major ones. The previous literature on environmental regulation finds that these two instruments are equivalent in a closed economy as far as neither uncertainty nor incomplete information exists. Its simple application to the international environmental cooperation implies that a single issue is how to coordinate policies. When each country sticks to the emission tax, there are no methods of coordinating each country's emission tax rate that enhances every country's welfare unless there are some means of international income transfers to compensate

[*] This paper is written by incorporating relevant extracts from our discussion paper [18]. We wish to thank the participants of RIEB International Conference 2000 held at Kobe University for their valuable comments. All remaining errors are our own. We also acknowledge the financial support from the Ministry of Education, Culture, Sports, and Technology of Japan under both the Grant-in-Aid for Scientific Research and the 21st Century Center of Excellence Project.
[1] See the papers in [11].
[2] Gains from international coordination of environmental policies are discussed in [2], [3], [8], for example.

those which are worse off.[3] The situation is essentially the same even when the countries set up a tradeable emission permit market among them. The problem of income transfer is now replaced by the problem of deciding on the total issue of permits and their allocation among the countries.[4]

However, we believe that the analyses in the previous studies have failed to fully capture a critical factor for discussing regional and international cooperation against global warming, i.e., the effect of *carbon leakages* through the trade on fossil fuel, the greatest source of green-house gases (GHGs) worsening the global environment quality. It has double-fold implication.[5]

First, the traditional equivalence between the emission tax and quota critically hinges on the absence of carbon leakages.[6] For example, when several countries employ the emission taxes, a country's tax-raise lowers the fuel price through a decrease in her fuel demand, boosting the fuel demand and thus the GHG emissions by other tax-employing countries, which is the so-called "carbon leakage". If this carbon leakage effect is so strong that the world total GHG emissions increase, each country tends to lax her environmental

---

[3] See also [17]. He attempts to characterize the optimal tariff-cum-transfer policies which improve coordinating their environmental policies among countries. His world is the second-best one in the sense that no countries use the emission taxes. As will be made clear, our world is also the second-best in the sense that no countries use the import tariffs on the fuel.

[4] An optimal way to allocate the permit endowments can be discussed in the contest of cooperative game theory. See [30] regarding this literature.

[5] Carbon leakage works through several routes. The first is through the change in the country's industrial structure (see [10], for example). That is, when a country takes some environemntal policy, the comparative advangate of the pollution-intensive industry shifts towards abroad. The second is through relocation of the plants by firms, pariculary those in the pollution-intensive industries (see [27], [28], and [41]). The last is through a change in the fuel price as is discussed in [18]. But the listed studies consider imperfect competition among firms. See also [17].

[6] In this paper, the emission quota actually means the creation of a domestic tradeable permit market where the total permits issued by the government are given. In this regard, the tax-quota equivalence means that when maximizing national welfare, the government can achieve the same resource allocation either by the emission tax or by the emission quota. However, the term has been used also in a different way. That is, the emission tax and quota are equivalent when replacement of the emission tax with the quota set equal to the tax-ridden equilibrium emissions gives rise to the same resource allocation across the economies. Within a partial equilibrium framework in the absence of uncertainty and incomplete information, such equivalence holds in a perfectly competitive market (see [38]) as well as in an imperfectly competitive market without firms' strategic abatement investment before the government policy decision (see [37]). However, the equivalence breaks down in a general equilibrium model as is shown by [18] or [19]. This is mainly because the emission quota puts a cap over country's total GHG emissions whereas its volume is endogenously determined under the emission tax policy.

regulation. However, its effect vanishes once the other countries employ the emission quotas, for their GHG emissions are directly controlled by those governments. The other countries' choices over the policy instruments thus alter each country's toughness against the global warming.

In other words, the emission tax and quota are unilaterally equivalent for each country when the policy decisions by the other countries are given (*unilateral equivalence*), but they are not once the countries understand that the others' policy choices, particularly their choices of the policy instruments, may be affected by the own choice under strategic interdependence among the countries subject to the carbon-leakage effect (*strategic non-equivalence*).[7] [8]

Second, the above strategic non-equivalence between the emission tax and quota gives rise to differences in each country's environmental toughness and thus the global environmental quality, which depends on the choice of environment regulation instruments among the countries.

In this paper, we demonstrate the above results more rigorously.[9] In section 2, we construct our model of two fuel-consuming countries emitting GHG and one fuel-supplying country. In section 3, we discuss the properties of the equilibrium in which neither of the two fuel-consuming countries restrict the GHG emissions as a benchmark for the succeeding analysis. In section 4, we explore the effects of the individual efforts to protect the global environment by imposing the emission quota over the own national economy.[10] More specifically, in the subsection 4, we characterize the emission quota equilibrium where both countries employ and simultaneously decide the emission quota policies, and in the subsection 4 we inquire into the effect of an individual country's effort of environmental protection over the world. The results in these subsections imply that the unilateral effort of an individual country's environment protection might rather deteriorate the global environmental quality through a decrease in the world fuel price (the carbon-leakage effect through the fossil fuel market). In section 5, we examine the tax-quota equivalence in the strategic international interdependence and discuss the importance of distinction between the unilateral equivalence and the strategic equivalence. The last section 6 summarizes some further implications of the present paper.

---

[7] The issue of unilateral equivalence and strategic non-equivalence was discussed rigorously in [22] within essentially the same framework as in the present paper.

[8] Even in the absence of carbon leakage, the tax-quota equivalence may break down in a general equilibrium framework when the pollution intensities differ across the industries. See [18] and [19].

[9] These issues have already been discussed in the first part of [17] in a much simpler and cruder framework. We demonstrate that the results there are robust.

[10] Throughout the present paper, the emission quota policy means the creation of a free competitive domestic tradeable emission permit market where the government sets a specific volume of the total permits within the country.

2 Structure of the Model

Consider a world consisting of three countries, 1, 2 and 3. Countries 1 and 2 use fossil fuels for production and emit green-house gases (GHG). Neither of them can produce fossil fuels for themselves, and both import them from country 3. Country 3 produces fossil fuels but does not emit any GHG.[11]

The welfare of country 3 consists only of the profits from selling its fossil fuels to the rest of the world. Let X denote the total amount of fossil fuels produced, $C(X)$ the associated total cost function and p the world price of the fossil fuel. Then the welfare of country 3 is assumed to be expressed by

$$u_3 = pX - C(X). \tag{1}$$

For simplicity of exposition, we assume that country 3 is a price taker in the world fossil fuel market.[12] Thus it determines its fossil fuel supply so as to equate the world price p with the marginal cost $C'(X)$, which is assumed to be increasing in the output. Thus its supply price of fossil fuel is given by its marginal cost, which is expressed by

$$p = P_s(X) \left(= C'(X) \right). \tag{2}$$

Since the marginal cost of producing fossil fuel is increasing, country 3's supply curve is upward sloping with respect to the fuel price.

We now depict the structures of the two fuel consuming countries, countries 1 and 2. When we assume away the effects of abatement activities, there must be a one-to-one technological relationship between country i's amount of fuel consumption x_i and its amount of GHG emission z_i. We call this relationship the emission technology and express it by[13]

$$z_i = G_i(x_i) \text{ for } i = 1, 2. \tag{3}$$

By consuming the fossil fuel, each fuel-consuming country can produce various goods and services, the value of which we express by the GDP function $f_i(x_i)$. Since the fuel must be imported from abroad with a unit price p, its net benefit is assumed to be given by $f_i(x_i) - px_i$.

---

[11] In this paper, we essentially employ a partial equilibrium approach and assume that the welfare of each country is measured by her real income. However, even a model to take a full account of each country's welfare does not alter the rest of the analysis. See [18].

[12] An alternative formulation is that the oil-producing country is a monopolist in the world market. But even under this alternative formulation, insofar as an increase in the oil-import tariff by either oil-importing country lowers the world oil price, our analysis applies. The assumption of the price-taking behavior by country 3 is merely for simplicity of exposition.

[13] We consider more general emission technology which allows substitution between fuel and other factors against a change in the emission tax rate or the tradeable emission permit price in [18].

However, this is not an end of the story. Since each fuel-consuming country emits GHG as much as z_i, the world total GHG emission becomes $Z = z_1 + z_2$. This GHG emission damages the global environment as much as measured by the global warming damage function $D(Z)$. We assume that the marginal global warming damage $D'(Z)$ is increasing in the total GHG emission and that country i perceives its $(100 \times \theta_i)\%$ as its own damage where $\theta_i > 0$.[14]

To sum up, country i's welfare is given by

$$u_i = f_i(x_i) - px_i - \theta_i D\left(\sum_j G_j(x_j)\right). \tag{4}$$

By substituting (2) into (4), one can express each fuel-consuming country's national welfare as a function of the fuel consumption profile (x_1, x_2) as below:

$$u^i(x_i, x_j) = f_i(x_i) - P_s(x_i + x_j)x_i - \theta_i D\left(\sum_k G_k(x_k)\right). \tag{5}$$

3 Free Emission Equilibrium

At first, we consider the equilibrium when countries 1 and 2 impose no GHG emission controls and allow their private sectors to seek for their own profit maximization. The resulting fuel consumption level should equate the marginal value product of fossil fuel $f'(x_i)$ with its world price p:

$$f_i'(x_i) = p. \tag{6}$$

Assume that the marginal value product of fossil fuels is decreasing. Then an increase in the world price of the fossil fuel decreases each country's fuel consumption, leading to a reduction in GHG emission.

An important point is that each country's GHG emission is not independent of the other's. It follows from (2) that facing the other country's increase in its GHG emission, each country has an incentive to reduce its GHG emission due to an increase in the world price of fossil fuel. This interdependent optimizing behavior of each fuel-consuming country is captured by the following equation, which is obtained by putting (2) into (6):

$$f_i'(x_i) = P_s(x_i + x_j). \tag{7}$$

Application of the implicit function theorem assures that the optimal private consumption of the fossil fuel by country i is a decreasing function of the other

---

[14] Note that we do not impose a condition $\sum_i \theta_i = 1$. This is because there may be damages from global warming on the areas with no human beings or there may be externalities in damage perception, i.e., there may be some countries which value the well-being of other countries.

country j's fuel consumption, the relation of which we express by $x_i = R_i^p(x_j)$. We call it country i's private reaction function.

The private reaction function of country i is depicted by curve R_i^p in Figure 1. The intersection of the two reaction curves, denoted by E_{pp}, is the free-emission equilibrium where the private sectors can freely and competitively choose their fuel consumption levels when there are no GHG controls by countries 1 and 2.

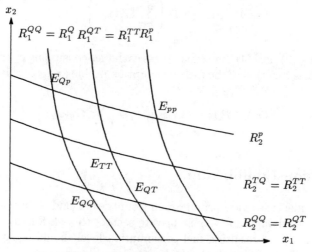

Fig. 1. Strategic choices of emission controls.

4 GHG Emission Control by Direct Regulations

We next introduce the regulation on the GHG emission level. We first consider the case when the government employs emission quotas over the country's total GHG emission volume.[15]

---

[15] In general, the emission quota to control the total emissions has a problem of how the quota should be assigned among firms. Improper quota assignment yields additional distortion over the economy. To avoid such additional distortion and clarify the role of direct quantitative restriction compared with indirect tax policies, we in fact assume that the total emission volume is set as a cap over the national economy by creating the domestic tradeable emission permit market. Free and competitive trade on permits equalizes each and every domestic firm's opportunity costs of emissions, thus leading to no additional distortion.

Emission Quota Equilibrium

A large country importing fuels may have a strategic incentive to restrain her import to lower the world fuel price and thus improve her terms of trade. When global warming matters, she may find further gains from the strategic fuel import control, for the resulting change in the fuel price affects other countries' fuel consumption and thus their GHG emission volumes. She can indirectly alter the damages from global warming. To clarify these strategic effects, we assume hereafter that the two fuel-consuming countries are large in the world fuel market.

Assume that each fuel-consuming country's government regulates her total GHG emission and thus indirectly intervenes in fuel trade. Since each country's fuel consumption has a one-to-one relationship with the amount of GHG emissions as expressed by (3), the quota on GHG emissions is equivalent to that on the fuel consumption. In the succeeding analysis, we can thus assume that the government i controls the fuel consumption $x_i(i = 1, 2)$ when imposing emission quotas.[16]

To describe the resulting equilibrium, we draw each government's reaction curve. We call country i's government "government i", and let $R_i^{QQ}(x_j)$ present government i's reaction function. When country i's fuel consumption x_i is equal to $R_i^{QQ}(x_j)$, it should maximize country i's welfare (5), given country j's fuel consumption x_j. Thus, it should satisfy the following first-order condition for welfare maximization:

$$0 = f_i'(x_i) - P_s(x_i + x_j) - P_s'(x_i + x_j)x_i - \theta_i D'(Z)G_i'(x_i) \qquad (8)$$

The first term on the RHS represents the marginal value product of fossil fuel, the second term the world fuel price (the marginal fuel consumption costs for a small country), the third term the marginal loss from terms-of-trade (TOT) deterioration due to an increase in the own fuel consumption, and the last term the marginal global warming effect, i.e., the marginal damage from aggravation in global warming. Assuming that the payoff function is strictly concave in her own fuel consumption, country i's best response fuel consumption depends on country j's through the TOT effect and the marginal global warming effect. The reaction curve associated with $x_i = R_i^{QQ}(x_j)$ is shown by curve R_i^{QQ} in Figure 1. The intersection of the two reaction curves, E_{QQ} represents an equilibrium where both fuel-consuming country's governments directly control their total GHG emission volumes.

The reaction curves in Figure 1 are described as downward sloping curves. This is the case in which each country's fuel consumption is a strategic substitute to the other's. In general, it may not be the case. The reaction curve of a country's government may be upward sloping, i.e., a country's fuel consumption may become a strategic complement to the other's. A factor giving the

---

[16] [18] consider a case with more general technology, in which we explicitly consider a quota on the GHG emissions. But the analysis differs little from the present paper.

dividing line between strategic substitutes and complements is a size of the change in the TOT effect due to an increase in the other country's fuel consumption. In fact, an increase in the other country's fuel consumption raises the world fuel price and the marginal global warming effect, both of which increase the country's marginal fuel consumption costs. However, the direction and the size of the changes in the TOT effects are generally ambiguous, which makes it difficult for us to predict whether the reaction curves are downward or upward sloping.

However, fortunately, the succeeding analysis does not depend on the assumptions on strategic substitutes and complements. What is necessary for inquiry is the so-called equilibrium stability condition, i.e., the absolute value of the slope of each reaction curve is strictly smaller than unity: [17]

$$\left| R_i^{QQ\prime}(x_j) \right| < 1 \text{ for } i, j = 1, 2 \ \ (j \neq i). \tag{9}$$

We impose this stability condition for each possible reaction curve of both countries including the private reaction ones.

Free Emission vs. Direct Total Emission Control

Before comparing the two equilibria, E_{pp} and E_{QQ}, we first discuss the effects of the direct total emission control by a single country, say country 1, when the other country 2 maintains laissez-faire in GHG emission. As is shown in Figure 1, the reaction function of country 1's government R_1^{QQ} is located left to the private counterpart R_1^p. There are two factors causing this inward shift.

First, the government takes into account the TOT deterioration effect which is neglected in the private decision over fuel consumption. Second, the government also cares an increase in the marginal global warming effect, which is also neglected by the private sector. These two factors make the government restrain its national fuel consumption compared with the private decision.

When country 1's reaction curve shifts inward from R_1^p to R_1^{QQ} by the government intervention, the equilibrium shifts from the initial free emission equilibrium E_{pp} to E_{QP}. Insofar as the absolute value of the slope of each reaction curve is less than unity (recall the equilibrium stability condition), there must be a decrease in the world total fuel consumption, leading to a drop in the world fuel price. This result has the following implications.

First, the decrease in the world fuel price lets country 2, which has no emission controls, have an incentive to expand its fuel consumption, leading to an increase in its GHG emission. This is what is called the "carbon leakage" effect.

---

[17] More specifically, we assume the following adjustment process at disequilibrium.

$$\dot{x}_i = \alpha_i \left\{ R_i^{QQ}(x_j) - x_i \right\} \ (i = 1, 2),$$

where $\alpha_i (> 0)$ denotes a parameter to express the adjustment speed.

Second, and more importantly, a country's emission control does not necessarily lead to a decrease in the world total GHG emission. Since the emission volume of country 1 decreases by the total emission volume control but that of country 2 increases by virtue of the carbon leakage effect, it is generally ambiguous whether the world total GHG emission decreases or not. More specifically, when country 2's energy efficiency is sufficiently lower than country 1's in the sense of more GHG emission per input of fuel, the result is an increase in the world total GHG emission.[18]

Proposition 1 *When only country 1 controls her own GHG emission volume, it has the following three effects.*

1. *The world fuel price decreases.*
2. *Country 2 without GHG emission quotas expands its fuel consumption as well as its GHG emission.*
3. *The world total GHG emission volume increases if country 2's energy efficiency is sufficiently lower than country 1's.*

As has been made clear, GHG emission quotas by the countries with higher energy efficiently cannot effectively restrain the world total GHG emission without the cooperation from those with lower energy efficiency.

When both countries 1 and 2 (i.e., all the fuel-consuming countries) undertake emission quotas, there would be a decrease in the world total GHG emission. This state is depicted by point E_{QQ} in Figure 1.

5 Tax-Quota Equivalence

As a policy instrument to control GHG emission, a country can also employ emission taxes. In the case of emission quotas, the country's total GHG emission volume is kept at the target level regardless of the world fuel price, while in the case of emission taxes, the emission volume changes along with the

---

[18] In the present paper, we assume away the income effect on the demand for higher environmental quality. If this effect exists and the higher income strengthens demand for the more improved global environment, then a sufficient decrease in the world fuel price may give country 2 an incentive to regulate its GHG emission volume. This is because the drop in the world fuel price increases country 2's real income. This is what [9] discussed. However, their argument seems to lack reality. First, the size of real income increase to trigger emission control may be too large to realize, particularly for developing countries. Second, there may be many countries, like oil-producing ones, which suffer from a decrease in the real income due to the drop in the world fuel price. If these countries initially employ any GHG emission quotas but become less environment-minded after the real income loss, then the world total GHG emission may increase even if there are some countries starting to control their emissions.

world fuel price level through a change in the fuel consumption. In this section, we examine the case where one of the two countries employs emission taxes as a means to control the national GHG emission.

Assume that initially country 2 as well as country 1 employs direct emission control, and consider country 1's choice between emission taxes and emission quotas. First of all, we should note that given country 2's fuel consumption, the choice does not matter for country 1 insofar as the two policies achieve the best-response fuel consumption against country 2's.

When country 1 employs emission taxes and country 2 employs emission quotas, their reaction curves should be depicted over the plane of country 1's emission tax rate and country 2's fuel consumption volume. However, when we transform them into the plane of fuel consumption volumes, country 1's reaction curve should be the same as if it employs direct controls. That is, country 1's transformed reaction curve with emission taxes, expressed by R_1^{TQ}, is identical with R_1^{QQ}.[19]

Similarly, when country 2 initially employs emission taxes, insofar as country 2's policy level is given, it is indifferent for country 1 between emission taxes and emission quotas. That is, $R_1^{QT} = R_1^{TT}$. It should be noted that each country's transformed reaction curve in Regime (T, T), expressed by R_i^{TT}, should be located left to the private reaction curve R_i^p, for the government has an incentive to restrain fuel consumption for the reasons stated earlier.[20]

Proposition 2 *Given the other country's policy tool, the choice between emission taxes and emission quotas does not matter for a country's government.*

We may call this result the *unilateral tax-quota equivalence* theorem, for it shows equivalent effects of the two policies given the policy choice by the other country. However, the equivalence does not hold once the other country switches from one policy instrument to the other. Such *strategic non-equivalence* between taxes and quotas is captured by the relation between R_1^{QQ} and R_1^{QT}, when inquiring into what effects arise to country 1's incentive for GHG emission when country 2 switches from emission quotas to emission taxes. In fact, this has a significant effect.

As discussed earlier, country 1's optimal fuel consumption should equate the marginal value product of fuel, $f_i'(x_i)$, with the sum of the the following three marginal cost of fuel consumption:

1. the direct purchase cost of fuel, p
2. the TOT deterioration effect
3. the marginal global warming effect

---

[19] The superscripts, for example TQ, represent the state in which country 1 employs emission taxes (T) and country 2 direct controls (Q).

[20] The result below is an extension of the tariff-quota equivalence theorem in trade to the choices over the environmental policies in the international setting.

When country 2 commits to a certain specified emission level, the second and third marginal costs arise only from country 1's own increase in fuel consumption. However, when country 2 employs emission taxes, the increase in the world fuel price due to country 1's consumption expansion gives country 2 an incentive to reduce its fuel consumption.[21] This decrease in country 2's fuel consumption eases the second and third marginal cost effects, which lets country 1 expand further its fuel consumption than before. We thus obtain the following strategic tax-quota non-equivalence theorem.

Proposition 3 *Given the rival country's fuel consumption volume, a country's best response fuel-consumption volume is greater when the rival employs emission taxes than when it employs emission quotas.*

The results obtained so far are summarized in Figure 1. We can obtain the following implications from the figure. First, when either country controls the own GHG emission, the world total fuel consumption decreases as well as the fuel price as is shown by a shift of an equilibrium from E_{pp} to E_{Qp}. We have already discussed the resulting effect regarding the carbon leakage effect.

Second, the world total fuel consumption volume tends to be the smallest when both countries regulate the own GHG emission by emission quotas. Thus, the world total GHG emission volume would be the smallest at equilibrium E_{QQ}.

Third, for a country committing to emission quotas, it is often more beneficial if the other country employs emission taxes rather than emission quotas. This is because the country with emission quotas can strategically expand the own fuel consumption at the expense of the other country through a price hike in the world fuel market.

---

[21] More specifically, country 1's best response fuel consumption given country 2's emission tax rate is obtained as follows. First, let t_2 denote country 2's specific emission tax. Then given the world fuel price p, its fuel consumption should satisfy

$$f_2'(x_2) = P_s(x_1 + x_2) + t_2 G_2'(x_2),$$

where one should note that $G_2'(x_2)$ represents the marginal GHG emission of fuel in country 2. As is expressed in the above equation, country 2's fuel consumption depends on its own emission tax rate t_2 and country 1's x_1, the relation of which we express by $x_2 = x_2^{QT}(x_1, t_2)$. And this fuel demand function of country 2 satisfies

$$-\frac{\partial x_2^{QT}}{\partial x_1} = \frac{P_s'}{P_s' - f_2''} \in (0, 1)$$

$$-\frac{\partial x_2^{QT}}{\partial t_2} = \frac{1}{P_s' - f_2''} > 0.$$

As the first equation shows, given the initial fuel-consumption pair, if country 2 commits to a specified rate of emission tax, then an increase in country 1's fuel consumption decreases country 2's fuel consumption as discussed in the text.

We inquire into this strategic gains of country 1 more in detail with the aid of Figures 2 and 3. For this inquiry, one may resort to the use of iso-welfare contours. They take the same shapes as the iso-profit curves in homogeneous Cournot duopoly, for an increase in the other country's fuel consumption aggravate the TOT as well as global warming.

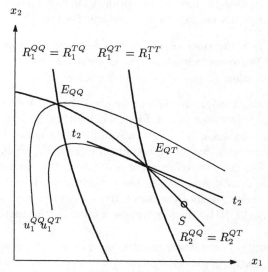

Fig. 2. Country 1's gains from commitment to emission quota.

The curves u_1^{QQ} and u_1^{QT} show two iso-welfare curves of country 1, where the former is associated with equilibrium E_{QQ} and the latter with E_{QT}. Since in Figure 2 country 2's fuel consumption is a strategic substitute to country 1's and an increase in country 2's fuel consumption hurts country 1, the best fuel consumption profile for country 1 along country 2's reaction curve is the one such as point S requiring an increase in country 1's consumption and a decrease in country 2's compared with a non-cooperative equilibrium for emission quotas E_{QQ}. It is a point achieved when country 1 acts as Stackelberg leader against country 2.

Since E_{QT} is an equilibrium when country 1 chooses quotas and country 2 taxes, country 1's iso-welfare contour u_1^{QT} should touch its feasibility locus t_2t_2 showing a locus of feasible fuel consumption profiles given country 2's equilibrium emission tax rate, which we call the iso-emission tax rate curve. Then if the situation is the one in Figure 2, that is, if the equilibrium is located to the left of country 1's Stackelberg equilibrium S, country 1's welfare is higher when country 2 chooses emission taxes.

However, this is not the only possibility. As is shown in Figure 3, country 1's welfare may be lower at E_{QT} than at E_{QQ}. The critical difference between the two figures is whether the iso-emission tax rate curve of country 2 is flatter in the absolute value than its reaction curve. If the iso-emission tax rate curve of country 2 is steeper in the absolute value than its reaction curve, then country 1 tends to overconsume fuel compared with its Stackelberg leader equilibrium S. If this overconsumption effect is sufficiently strong, country 1 may ultimately lose from country 2's policy switch from export quotas to taxes.

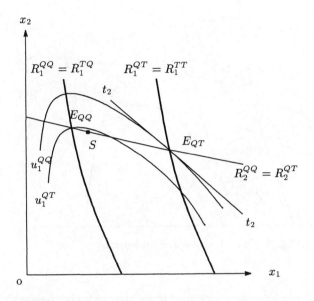

Fig. 3. Country 1's losses from commitment to emission quota.

These results can be extended to the case where each country's fuel consumption is a strategic complement to the other's as is shown in Figure 4. Since each country's reaction curve is now upward sloping, country 2's iso-emission tax rate curve, which is always downward sloping, has the smaller slope than country 2's reaction curve. Therefore, it is straightforward to verify that country 1 is hurt by country 2's switch from quotas to taxes.[22][23]

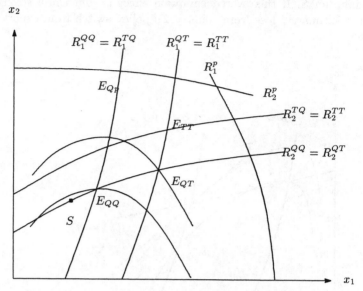

Fig. 4. Case of strategic complements.

---

[22] By using the results in footnote 21, we may prove the resultmore rigorously. To prove the result, it suffices to prove that country 1's welfare is still increasing along country 2's reaction curve $R_2^{QQ} = R_2^{QT}$ at equilibrium E_{QT}. This can be computed as below

$$\left.\frac{du_1^{QQ}(x_1, R_2^{QQ}(x_1))}{dx_1}\right|_{x_1=x_1^{QT}} = f_1' - P_s - x_i P_s' \left(1 + R_2^{QQ\prime}\right) - \theta_1 D' \left(G_1' + G_2' R_2^{QQ\prime}\right)$$

$$= \left(x_1 P_s' + \theta_1 D' G_2'\right) \left(\frac{\partial x_2^{QT}}{\partial x_1} - R_2^{QQ\prime}\right),$$

where use was made of country 1's equilibrium condition at E_{QT}, i.e.,

$$0 = \frac{\partial u_1^{QT}}{\partial x_1} = f_1' - P_s - x_1 P_s' \left(1 + \frac{\partial x_2^{QT}}{\partial x_1}\right) - \theta_1 D' \left(G_1' + G_2' \frac{\partial x_2^{QT}}{\partial x_1}\right).$$

Thus, we obtain

$$\left.\frac{du_1^{QQ}(x_1, R_2^{QQ}(x_1))}{dx_1}\right|_{x_1=x_1^{QT}} > 0 \iff \frac{\partial x_2^{QT}}{\partial x_1} > R_2^{QQ\prime}$$

[23] Similar results hold even when we allow international emissions trading designated in the Kyoto mechanism as discussed in Kiyono (2000).

Proposition 4 *Country 2's policy switch from emission quota to emission tax benefits country 1 employing emission quota only if country 2's fuel consumption is a strategic substitute to country 1's and country 2's iso-emission tax rate curve has the larger slope than its own reaction curve at the equilibrium when country 1 chooses quotas and country 2 taxes. Otherwise, it tends to hurt country 1.*

Note that the conditions using the slopes of the iso-emission tax rate curves and the reaction curves can be used to rank the welfare levels of each country among other possible equilibria. But the essence of the argument is the same, so we leave such welfare comparison to readers.

6 Concluding Remarks

What we have attempted to clarify is potential effects of choices over the domestic GHG emission controls. We conclude the paper by pointing out three major implications of our results.

First, a fight against global warming requires each and every country's commitment to global environment management. Although the world is now going towards international cooperation against the global warming by proposing the Kyoto mechanism, the mechanism lacks (i) really global cooperation, covering only advanced countries, and (ii) international enforceability of the cooperative measures. The proposed solutions calls for self-discipline of each member participating the Kyoto mechanism, particularly with respect to what domestic environmental policies are allowed to achieve the aim of the group as a whole. In this respect, we believe that our results shed some light for discussing the need to further promote international cooperation against the global warming.

Second, international carbon leakage critically affects efficacy of the countries' environment management efforts. Emission tax policy by other countries dampens a country's incentive to keep the environmental quality compared with emission quota, because the effort by the latter lowers the world fuel price, boosting other countries' demand for fuel and their GHG emissions. We have inquired into the further effect of this carbon leakage in [19], and showed that one of the new policy proposal in the Kyoto mechanism, i.e., the creation of an international tradeable emission permit market may not lead to Pareo-improvement even for the fuel-consuming countries.

Third, the ways of international cooperation critically hinge on the policies employed by each country before agreeing on cooperation. One of the standard approaches to cooperation is to formulate the problem as a bargaining game. The bargaining outcome depends on each country's payoff at the disagreement, which depends on the policy choices, either emission tax or quota. Strategic non-equivalence between emission taxes and quotas implies that each country may further strategically decides on which policy to employ before sitting at the bargaining table. Setting aside such a strategic pre-bargaining behavior, we still have a problem of the policy choice by the countries. We have already tackled this problem in [19] and obtained the conditions for each policy combination equilibrium to emerge.

References

1. Antweiler A, Copeland B, Taylor MS (2001) Is free trade good for the environment, American Economic Review 91: 877-908
2. Barrett S (1990) The problem of global environmental protection," Oxford Review of Economic Policy 6: 68-79
3. Barrett S (1994) Strategic environmental policy and international trade, Journal of Public Economics 54: 325-338
4. Cheng L (1985) Comparing Bertrand and Cournot equilibria: a geometric approach, Rand Journal of Economics 16(1): 146-152
5. Conrad K (1993) Taxes and subsidies for pollution-intensive industries as trade policy, Journal of Environmental Economics and Management 25: 121-135
6. Copeland BR, Taylor MS (1994) North-south trade and the global environment, Quarterly Journal of Economics 109: 755-87
7. Copeland BR, Taylor MS (1995) Trade and transboundary pollution, American Economic Review, 85: 716-737
8. Copeland BR, Taylor MS (1999) Trade, spatial speration, and the environment, Journal of International Economics: 137-168
9. Copeland BR (1996): Pollution content tariffs, environmental rent shifting, and the control of cross-border pollution, Journal of International Economics 40: 459-476
10. Copeland BR, Taylor MS (2000) Free trade and global warming: a trade theory view of the Kyoto Protocol, Discussion Paper 7657, NBER Working Paper
11. Dean, JM (eds.) (2001): International Trade and the Environment, International Library of Enivronmental Economics and Policy. Ashgate, Aldershot
12. Goulder LH, Parry IWH, Burtraw D (1998) The cost-effectiveness of alternative instruments for environmental protection in a second-best setting, Discussion Paper 6464, NBER Working Paper
13. Grossman G, Helpman E (2001) Special Interest Politics. The MIT Press
14. Hoel M (1991a) Efficient international agreements for reducing CO_2, The Energy Journal 12: 93-107
15. Hoel M (1991b) Global environmental problems: the effects of unilateral actions taken by one country, Journal of Environmental Economics and Management 20: 55-70
16. Hoel M (1997) Environmental policy with endogenous plant location," Scandinavian Journal of Economics, 99(2): 241-259
17. Hoel M (2001) International trade and the environment: how handle carbon leakage, In: Frontiers of Environmental Economics, Folmer, Gabel, Gerkin and Rose(eds.) Edward Elgar:176-191
18. Ishikawa J, Kiyono K (2000) International trade and global warming, Discussion Paper CIRJE-F-78, CIRJE Discussion Paper Series, Faculty of Economics

19. Ishikawa J, Kiyono K (2003) Greenhouse-Gas Emision Controls in an Open Economy, COE-RES Discussion Paper Series, No. 8, Graduate School of Economics and Institute of Economic Research, Hitotsubashi University

20. Janeba E (1998) Tax competition in imperfectly competitive markets, Journal of International Economics 44: 135-153

21. Kato K, Kiyono K (2003) Environmental policies and market structure: Equivalence of environmental regulations, Presented at the Annual Meeting of the Japanese Economic Association held at Meiji University in 2003

22. Katsoulacos Y, Xepapadeas A (1996) Emission Taxes and Market Structure, In: Environmental Policy and Market Structure, Carraro YKC, and Xepapadeas A (eds) Kluwers Academic Publishers

23. Kennedy PW (1994) Equilibrium pollution taxes in open economies with imperfect competition, Journal of Environmental Economics and Management 27: 49-63

24. Kiyono K (1985) Trade-policy game - an inquiry into tariff quota equivalence (Boueki-seisaku gemu - Kanzei to suryo wariate no douchi meidai ni kansuru ichi kousatsu-), Studies on Trade and Industrial Policies (Tsusho-Seisaku Kenkyu) (10): 1-16, in Japanese

25. Kiyono K, Ishikawa J (2002) Environment Management Policy under International Carbon Leakages, a paper presented at the fourth European Trade Study Group Meeting held in Kiel, Germany, 2002

26. Kiyono K, Okuno-Fujiwara M (2003) Domestic and international strategic interactions in environment policy formation, Economic Theory 21: 613-633

27. Long NV, Soubeyran A (1999) Pollution, Pigouvian taxes and asymetric international oligopoly, In: S. Petrakis E, Xepapadeas A (eds.) Environmental Regulation and Market Power: 175-194. Edward Elgar

28. Markusen J, Morey E, Olweiler N (1995) Noncooperative equilibria in regional environmental policies when plant Locations are endogenous, Journal of Public Economics 56: 55-77

29. Markusen J, Morey E, Olweiler N (1993) Environmental policy when market structure and plant location are endogenous, Journal of Environmental Economics and Management, 24: 69-86

30. Meade JE (1952) External economies and diseconomies in a competitive situation, Economic Journal 62(245): 54-67

31. Missfeldt F (1999) Game-theoretic modelling of transboundary pollution, Journal of Economic Surveys 13(3): 287-321

32. Motta M, Thisse J (1999) Minimum quality standard as an environmental policy: domestic and international effects, In: Petrakis SES, Xepapadeas A (eds) Environmental regulation and market power: 27-46. Edward Elgar

33. Perroni C, Rutherford TF (1993) International trade in carbon emission rights and basic materials: a general equilibrium calculations for 2000, Scandinavian Journal of Economics 95: 257-278

34. Perroni C, Wigle RM (1994) International trade and environmental quality: how important are the linkages, Canadian Journal of Economics, pp. 551-567

35. Petrakis E, Xepapadeas A (1999) Does government precommitment promote environmental innovation?, In: Petrakis, SE, Xepapadeas A (eds.) Environmental regulation and market over, pp. 145-161 Edward Elgar

36. Ulph A (1996a) Environmental policy instruments and imperfectly competitive international trade, Environmental and Resource Economics, 7: 333-355

37. Ulph A (1996b) Strategic environmental policy and international trade — the role, of market conduct In: Carraro YC, and Xepapadeas A (eds) Environmental policy and market structure: 99-127 Kluwer Academic Publishers
38. Ulph A (1997) Environmental policy and international trade — a survey of recent economic analysis, In: Holmer H, Tietenberg T (eds.) International Yearbook of Environmental and Resource Economics, Edward Elgar, Aldershot
39. Ulph A (1998): Environmental policy and international trade, In: Carraro C, Siniscalco D (eds.) New Directions in the Economic Theory of the Environment : 147-192. Cambrigde University Press
40. Ulph A, Valenti L (1997) Plant location and strategic environmental policy with inter-sectoral linkages, Resource and Energy Economics: 363-383
41. Ulph A, Valenti L (2001) Is environment dumping g reater when plants are footloose?, Scandianvian Journal of Economics 103(4): 673-688
42. Xepapadeas A (1997) Advanced Principles in Environmental Policy. Edward Elgar Publishing, Inc.

Allocation of Aid Between and Within Recipients: A Political Economic Approach

Sajal Lahiri

Southern Illinois University, Carbondale, IL. 62901-4515, U.S.A. lahiri@siu.edu

F35

1 Introduction

One reason for giving foreign aid to a recipient country is the benefit of the poor in that country.[1] However, it is well established that it is very difficult for donor countries to enforce that aid reaches intented targets, and foreign aid is highly fungible (see [3], [7], [13], [24]). This is rather surprising given that the total amount of aid that a donor country gives out is limited and there is strong competition from developing countries for access to this limited fund.[2] One would expect that recipient countries would set their house in order to receive a greater amount of aid.

This paper attempts to examine the relationship between fungibility and allocation of aid. In particular, it develops a stylised model of foreign aid allocation in which a donor country allocates a fixed amount of aid between two recipient countries in order to reduce poverty in the recipient countries. The donor's motive to give aid is thus altruistic. However, an organized interest group in each recipient country bribes its government's officials and diverts part of the aid away from the poor. For expositional simplicity, we shall call this group 'the rich'. We examine how the equilibrium allocation aid between the recipient countries is related to the degree of corruption in those countries. Does the less corrupt country, *ceteris paribas*, receive a bigger share of aid? This is one of the questions that we shall examine.

The present paper is part of a (small) literature on the political economy of foreign aid, surveyed by [6].[3] However, as far as aid fungibility is concerned, the relevant papers are [28], [10] and [18]. They also provide a political economic

---

[1] See footnote 3 on motives for giving foreign aid.

[2] Although developed countries agreed, after the publication of the United Nations sponsored Pearson Commission Report in 1969, to allocate 0.7% of GNP as overseas development assistance, the actual figure for the major donor countries is about 0.25%. For an analysis of competition for aid see [16].

[3] In this literature also the motive for giving foreign aid is altruistic, but clearly other motives may exist and these may vary from donor to donor. Strategic and

explanation of why aid fungibility takes place. However, the framework and the principal focus of analysis in the first two papers differ significantly from the present one. Whereas the political economic model in [28] is a rent-seeking one where a number of lobby groups compete each other for access to foreign aid budget, [10] considers a recipient government that finances the production of public goods with the help of a distortionary income tax, and where foreign aid can reduce this tax. In contrast, in the present paper the interactions between the behaviour of the recipient governments, the donor government and the lobby groups are at the heart of the analysis. The present paper is an extension of [18] to the case of multiple recipients. Whereas [18] focuses on the time of actions between one donor and a single recipient country, this paper focuses on the allocation of aid between the two recipient countries.

As far as the allocation aid within each recipient country is concerned, we try to explain the allocation of aid within the recipient country by a domestic political process *a la* the political contribution approach of [9]. This political contribution approach, derived from the common agency problem analysed by [2], was first introduced by [9] in modelling the political economy of trade protection. However, one of the shortcomings of that framework is that preferences of everyone in the country are assumed to be of the quasi-linear type which gives rise to constant marginal utilities of income. This assumption is particularly inappropriate for any problem where redistribution matters, as it is the case in the present analysis. [5] have generalised the Bernheim-Whinston framework to allow for general preferences and therefore variability in marginal utilities of income, and it is their approach that we follow in this paper. Needless to say, there are many alternative approaches in modelling the political process – see [27] for a survey – including the unproductive rent-seeking activities approach ([14]), the tariff-formation function approach ([8]), the political support function approach ([11]; [12]), median voter approach ([22]), the campaign contribution approach ([21]).

After the presentation of the basic framework in section 2, section 3 provides the comparative static exercises. Concluding remarks are to be found in section 4.

2 The Basic Framework

In our model there are two countries: a donor country (labeled α) and two recipient countries (labeled β and γ). The population in the donor country is homogeneous. However, there are two types of individuals in the recipient countries: labeled 1 and 2. For expositional simplicity we shall call 1 'poor' and 2 'rich'. The size of population of these groups are L_α, L_{β_1}, L_{β_2}, L_{γ_1} and

---

economic self-interest have been found to be important for bilateral official aid for many donor countries (for empirical work see, for example, [20], [29], [4], [1], and for theoretical work see, for example, [19]).

L_{γ_2}. Without any loss of generality, we shall assume $L_\alpha = 1$. Both countries are small in the international goods market so that the commodity prices are exogenous. This together with the additional assumption that all factors are internationally immobile and inelastically supplied also mean that the factor prices do not vary in our analysis.[4] Therefore per-capita factor incomes, before any lump-sum transfers are made, can be taken as given, and these are denoted by $\bar{Y}_i$, $i = \alpha$, β_1, β_2, γ_1, γ_2.

We assume that people in the donor country are altruistic only towards the poor in the recipient countries. The per-capita utility level, u_α, of the donor is given by:[5]

$$u_\alpha = V_\alpha + \lambda_\beta L_{\beta_1} u_{\beta_1} + \lambda_\gamma L_{\gamma_1} u_{\gamma_1} \tag{1}$$

where V_α is the direct utility derived from consumption, u_{j_1} is the per-capita utility levels of the poor in the jth recipient country ($j = \beta$, γ), and λ's are the altruism parameters. $\lambda_\beta > \lambda_\gamma$ means that the donor country cares more about the poor people in country β than those in country γ.[6]

The total amount of aid given by the donor is denoted by T, and it is assumed to be fixed. The donor government allocated a fraction, θ, to country β and the remainder, $1 - \theta$ to country γ. These amounts are given to the recipient governments for the purpose of benefiting the poor in those countries.[7] However, rich people in the recipient countries lobby their respective governments and obtain a part of it. The allocation of this aid between the two groups in each recipient country is endogenous, and we denote by μ_i the proportion of aid that is allocated to the poor in country i ($i = \beta$, γ). In other words, the government in each recipient country decides how much of the aid should reach its intended destination. However, in deciding the allocation, each recipient government may need to take into consideration possible 'sanctions' that the donor country may impose by lowering the amount of aid allocated to it. The recipients governments thus compete for a given amount of aid and each tries to influence the amount it receives by 'optimally' deciding the allocation of aid between the rich and the poor. There are thus three types of allocations: (i) the allocation by the donor country of the total amount of aid between the two recipients, (ii) the allocation by the government in country β of the amount of aid it receives between the rich and the poor, and (iii) the allocation by the government in country γ of the amount of aid it receives between the rich and the poor. The three allocation variables are determined in a political equilibrium to be discussed later on.

---

[4] For a model that incorporates factor price changes in a political economy explanation of foreign aid, see [23]. Politics in the above paper is in the donor country.

[5] We follow [17] in modeling altruism.

[6] Historical (colonial) ties between donor and recipient countries, *inter alia*, can explain differences in the altruism parameters.

[7] Official bilateral and multilateral aid are usually given to the recipient government. As many NGOs have found, it is often impossible not to channel even private aid via governments in recipient countries.

Assuming that aid is distributed among the poor in a lump-sum fashion by the recipient governments, and that aid is financed in the donor country by lump-sum taxation, the per-capita utility in the donor country and that of the poor in the recipient countries are given respectively by

$$u_\alpha = V_\alpha(\bar{Y}_\alpha - T) + \lambda_\beta L_{\beta_1} u_{\beta_1} + \lambda_\gamma L_{\gamma_1} u_{\gamma_1}, \tag{2}$$

$$u_{\beta_1} = V_{\beta_1}\left(\bar{Y}_{\beta_1} + \frac{\mu_\beta \theta T}{L_{\beta_1}}\right), \tag{3}$$

$$u_{\gamma_1} = V_{\gamma_1}\left(\bar{Y}_{\gamma_1} + \frac{\mu_\gamma(1-\theta)T}{L_{\gamma_1}}\right), \tag{4}$$

where V_i's are the indirect utility functions. Throughout the paper we shall assume positive and diminishing marginal utility of income for the consumers, i.e.

$$V_i' > 0 \quad \text{and} \quad V_i'' < 0, \quad (i = \alpha,\ \beta_1,\ \beta_2,\ \gamma_1,\ \gamma_2). \tag{5}$$

Equation (2) implies that the net income in the donor country is equal to its factor income minus the amount of foreign aid it gives. Similarly, (3) and (4) imply that the total income of the poor in each recipient country is equal to their total labour income plus the part of the aid that they receive.

The aid allocation parameters μ_β and μ_γ are policy instruments for the governments in the recipient countries and they are determined endogenously in the political equilibrium. We shall follow [5] (henceforth to be referred to as DGH) in specifying the equilibrium. The poor in the recipient countries do not lobby the government, but the rich do by making contributions to the political party in power. Contribution in the context of our framework is best interpreted as bribes paid to ministers and/or bureaucrats, and these are spent on purchases of goods and services. The contribution schedules for the rich are denoted by $c_\beta(\mu_\beta)$ and $c_\gamma(\mu_\gamma)$. The objective function of the two recipient governments are given respectively by

$$G_\beta = \rho_\beta c_\beta + (L_{\beta_1} u_{\beta_1} + L_{\beta_2} u_{\beta_2}), \tag{6}$$

$$G_\gamma = \rho_\gamma c_\gamma + (L_{\gamma_1} u_{\gamma_1} + L_{\gamma_2} u_{\gamma_2}), \tag{7}$$

where ρ_β and ρ_γ are positive constant parameters. They are the weights given by the recipient governments to political funds in their objective functions and as such they indicate the degree of corruption in the respective recipient governments. A bigger value of ρ means a higher degree of corruption. It is implicit in the above specification of the governments' objective functions that they care about the total welfare of their nationals, and also about the amount of contributions that they receive.[8]

---

[8] Rather than considering the sum total of individual welfare levels (which we do for analytical convenience), we could have considered a more general social welfare function as the second term in the above objective function, without changing the qualitative nature of our results.

The political equilibrium in each recipient country is an outcome of a two-stage game, and each recipient government takes allocation by the donor government (represented by θ) as given. In describing the game, we shall only consider the recipient country β. However since the two countries are symmetric in structure, after describing the political equilibrium in country β, we shall simply write down the equilibrium conditions for country γ. In stage one of the game, the rich choose their contribution schedule. Government sets policy in stage two. A political equilibrium is given by (i) a contribution schedule $c_\beta^*(\mu_\beta)$, such that it maximizes the welfare of the rich given the anticipated political optimization by the government, and (ii) a policy variable, μ_β^*, that maximizes the government's objective given by (6), taking the contribution schedule as given.

As discussed in DGH, the model can have multiple sub-game perfect equilibria. Following DGH, we consider a refinement called the *truthful* equilibrium. We shall first state formally the equilibrium conditions and then we shall explain them.

Let $\left(c_\beta^0(\mu_\beta^0, u_{\beta_2}^0), \mu_\beta^0\right)$ be a truthful equilibrium in which $u_{\beta_2}^0$ is the equilibrium per-capita utility level of the rich. Then $(c_\beta^0(\mu_\beta^0, u_{\beta_2}^0), \mu_\beta^0, u_{\beta_2}^0)$ is characterized by: (i) the truthful contribution schedules chosen by the lobby group

$$c_\beta(\mu_\beta, u_{\beta_2}^0) = \max(0, A_\beta),$$ (8)

where A_β is defined in

$$u_{\beta_2}^0 = V_{\beta_2}\left(\bar{Y}_{\beta_2} + \frac{(1-\mu_\beta)\theta T - A_\beta}{L_{\beta_2}}\right),$$ (9)

(ii) the optimal allocation of aid, μ_β^0, chosen by the recipient government

$$\mu_\beta^0 = \text{Argmax}_{\mu_\beta}\left\{\rho_\beta c_\beta(\mu_\beta, u_{\beta_2}^0) + \left(L_{\beta_1} u_{\beta_1}(\mu_\beta) + L_{\beta_2} u_{\beta_2}^0\right)\right\},$$ (10)

and (iii) the following equation that ties down the utility level of the lobby group

$$L_{\beta_1} u_{\beta_1}(\mu_\beta^1) + L_{\beta_2} u_{\beta_2}(\mu_\beta^1) = \rho_\beta c_\beta(\mu_\beta^0, u_{\beta_2}^0) + L_{\beta_1} u_{\beta_1}(\mu_\beta^0) + L_{\beta_2} u_{\beta_2}^0,$$ (11)

where μ_β^1 is defined in

$$\mu_\beta^1 = \text{Argmax}_{\mu_\beta}\left\{L_{\beta_1} u_{\beta_1}(\mu_\beta) + L_{\beta_2} u_{\beta_2}(\mu_\beta)\right\},$$ (12)

and $u_{\beta_1}(\mu_\beta)$ is defined in (3).

Intuitively equations (8) and (9) state that the truthful contribution schedule is never negative and is set to the level of compensating variation relative to the equilibrium utility level of the rich, i.e. the rich offer exactly the amount of money that would keep them at the same equilibrium utility level for all actions μ of the government (see [5], p.759). Equation (10) is self explanatory:

given that the government acts at stage two of the game, it takes the utility level of the lobby group as given and chooses its aid allocation parameter so as to maximize its objective function. Equation (11) completes the characterization of the truthful equilibrium and is derived from the premise that the rich would pay the lowest possible contribution to induce the government pursuing the equilibrium policy given in (10). For this to be the case (11) must hold, i.e. the government must be indifferent between implementing the equilibrium policy and receiving contributions from the rich (right hand side term) and implementing a policy by accepting no contribution (left hand side term).[9] Finally, (12) describes the equilibrium allocation of aid when no group lobbies, i.e. when the government is a pure social welfare maximizer.

The parallel equilibrium equations for the recipient country γ can be written similarly as follows:

$$c_\gamma(\mu_\gamma,\ u^0_{\gamma 2}) = \max(0,\ A_\gamma), \tag{13}$$

$$u^0_{\gamma 2} = V_{\gamma 2}\left(\bar{Y}_{\gamma 2} + \frac{(1-\mu_\gamma)(1-\theta)T - A_\gamma}{L_{\gamma 2}}\right), \tag{14}$$

$$\mu^0_\gamma = \mathrm{Argmax}_{\mu_\gamma}\{\rho_\gamma c_\gamma(\mu_\gamma, u^0_{\gamma 2})$$
$$+ \left(L_{\gamma 1}u_{\gamma 1}(\mu_\gamma) + L_{\gamma 2}u^0_{\gamma 2}\right)\}, \tag{15}$$

$$L_{\gamma 1}u_{\gamma 1}(\mu^1_\gamma) + L_{\gamma 2}u_{\gamma 2}(\mu^1_\gamma) = \rho_\gamma c_\gamma(\mu^0_\gamma, u^0_{\gamma 2}) + L_{\gamma 1}u_{\gamma 1}(\mu^0_\gamma) + L_{\gamma 2}u^0_{\gamma 2}, \tag{16}$$

$$\mu^1_\gamma = \mathrm{Argmax}_{\mu_\gamma}\{L_{\gamma 1}u_{\gamma 1}(\mu_\gamma) + L_{\gamma 2}u_{\gamma 2}(\mu_\gamma)\}, \tag{17}$$

and $u_{\gamma 1}(\mu_\gamma)$ is defined in (4).

When the rich in a recipient country does not lobby, its government maximizes only the aggregate utility of its nationals given by the right hand sides of (6) (or, (7)), and if the solution is in the interior the marginal utilities of the two groups in that country will be equalised, i.e. $V'_{j_2} = V'_{j_1}$, $(j = \beta, \gamma)$. However, under the realistic assumption that the amount of aid is not large enough, or the income differential between the rich and poor in each is too big, to equalize marginal utilities, the optimization problems will result in

$$\mu^1_\beta = 1 = \mu^1_\gamma.$$

Thus, if a recipient government maximizes social welfare, all aid will go to the poor. This is exactly what the donor country wants.

However, when the rich lobby, the two recipient governments maximize (6) and (7) respectively, and they allocates aid according to:

$$\rho_\beta = V'_{\beta_1}, \tag{18}$$

$$\rho_\gamma = V'_{\gamma_1}. \tag{19}$$

---

[9] As is well known, it follows from this condition that a single lobby group is able to acquire the entire rent from its agency relation with the government. See also [26] for a model where political contributions are provided only by a single lobby group.

That is, the benefit of allocating an extra unit of aid to the poor in a country (the right hand side) should be equal to the cost of allocating an extra unit of aid to the poor (the left hand side). This extra allocation to the poor means less transfer to the rich which, in turn, implies less political contribution from the rich. This is clearly a cost to the government. Thus, if a recipient government cares about contributions from the lobby group, it will choose to distribute aid differently from what a donor would want it to.[10]

It only remains to specify the determination of the allocation of aid by the donor country, i.e. the variable θ. For this we assume that the donor government acts simultaneously with the recipient country governments. In particular, we assume that the donor government chooses θ to maximize the welfare of its nationals, given by u_α in (2), taking the allocation variables of the recipient countries μ_β and μ_γ as given. This gives the optimality condition as:

$$\lambda_\beta \mu_\beta^0 V_{\beta_1}' = \lambda_\gamma \mu_\gamma^0 V_{\gamma_1}'. \tag{20}$$

This equation states that the aid is allocated in a such a way that the 'corrected' marginal utilities of the poor in the two countries are equalized.

Equations (18)-(20) give three equations in three unknowns: μ_β, μ_γ, and θ.

Having described the basic framework of our analysis,[11] we shall now examine how the equilibrium allocation variables are affected when some of the parameters of the model are changed. In the following section, we shall examine the effects of a change in the total amount of aid T, and how changes in the corruption parameters affect the equilibrium.

3 Comparative Statics

In this section we shall carry out two comparative static exercises, first with respect to the total amount resources available for disbursement to the two recipient countries, i.e. T, and then with respect to the degree of corruption in one of the two recipient countries, i.e. ρ_β or ρ_γ. However, before doing so using (18) and (19) we rewrite (20) as

$$\lambda_\beta \mu_\beta^0 \rho_\beta = \lambda_\gamma \mu_\gamma^0 \rho_\gamma. \tag{21}$$

Considering the first exercise, i.e. comparative static exercise with respect to T, we differentiate (21) to obtain

---

[10] Strictly speaking, in order to get an interior solution for μ's, given that we assumed that we could not get it when the rich do not lobby, we need to assume that ρ is sufficiently large. This does not seem a very strong assumption given the extent of corruption in many of the recipient countries.

[11] In a recent paper [18] use a similar framework to consider how lobbying by various ethnic groups in a donor country affects the allocation of aid to competing recipient countries. In another paper [18] commitment strategy of a donor country towards a single recipient country affects fungibility of aid.

$$\lambda_\beta \rho_\beta d\mu_\beta^0 = \lambda_\gamma \rho_\gamma d\mu_\gamma^0. \tag{22}$$

The above equation shows that an increase in T will have the same qualitative effects on the allocation of aid within the two recipient countries: the poor will receive either a bigger share of aid in both recipient countries or a lower share.

Differentiating (18) and (19) we get

$$\theta T d\mu_\beta^0 = -\mu_\beta^0 d(\theta T), \tag{23}$$

$$(1 - \theta)T d\mu_\gamma^0 = -\mu_\gamma^0 d((1 - \theta)T). \tag{24}$$

Equations (23) and (24) show that an increase in the total amount of aid flow to either country reduces the proportion of it going to the target groups. The special interest group in each country will have more to lobby for and therefore will make larger political contributions. The government in each country then pays relatively less attention to social welfare and more to its political funds. This will lead to a lower proportion of aid going to the poor.

Solving (22)-(24), we get

$$\frac{d\mu_\beta^0}{dT} = -\frac{\mu_\beta^0}{T} < 0, \tag{25}$$

$$\frac{d\mu_\gamma^0}{dT} = -\frac{\mu_\gamma^0}{T} < 0, \tag{26}$$

$$\frac{d\theta}{dT} = 0. \tag{27}$$

The above three equations show that the shares of total aid going to the two recipients do not change (equation (27)) and therefore the total aid allocated to each country increases. As a result, the share of the poor in each recipient country go down. The net result of a higher T and a smaller share for the poor is such that the per-capita utility of the poor remains the same. These results are stated formally in proposition 1.

Proposition 1. *An increase in the total amount of aid does not affect the proportion of this amount allocated to each country. It also does not affect the equilibrium amount of aid flows to the target groups in the two recipient countries as the recipient governments allocate the whole of the increased amount of aid received to the interest groups.*

We now turn to a comparative static exercise with respect to the corruption parameter (ρ) in one of the two recipient countries. Without loss of any generality, our exercise will consider a change in the degree of corruption in country β, i.e. in ρ_β.

First of all, differentiating (19) we get

$$d((1 - \theta)\mu_\gamma^0) = (1 - \theta)d\mu_\gamma^0 - \mu_\gamma^0 d\theta = 0. \tag{28}$$

This equation tells us that an increase in the degree of corruption in one recipient country will have no effect on the net amount of aid flowing to, and therefore to the welfare level of, the poor in the other recipient country.

As for the recipient country in which the degree of corruption has increased, differentiating (18) we get

$$\frac{L_{\beta_1}}{TV''_{\beta_1}} \cdot d\rho_\beta = d(\theta\mu_\beta^0) = \mu_\beta^0 d\theta + \theta d\mu_\beta^0. \tag{29}$$

From (29) we find that an increase in the degree of corruption in a recipient country will unambiguously reduce the level of aid reaching the poor in that recipient country and therefore the welfare level of that group.

Finally differentiating (21) and then substituting (28) and (29) and using (18) we get

$$\frac{\mu_\beta^0 T}{1-\theta} \cdot \frac{d\theta}{d\rho_\beta} = Y_{\beta_1} L_{\beta_1} \rho_\beta \left[s_{\beta_1} - \frac{1}{\sigma_{\beta_1}} \right], \tag{30}$$

where

$$Y_{\beta_1} = \bar{Y}_{\beta_1} + \frac{\mu_\beta \theta T}{L_{\beta_1}}$$

$$s_{\beta_1} = \frac{\mu_\beta \theta T}{L_{\beta_1} Y_{\beta_1}}$$

$$\sigma_{\beta_1} = -\frac{V''_{\beta_1} Y_{\beta_1}}{V'_{\beta_1}}.$$

From (30) it is clear that an increase in the degree in corruption in a recipient country will result in a decrease in its share of total aid if and only if the share of aid income in total income of a poor person (s_{β_1}) is smaller than the reciprocal of the degree of relative risk aversion of the same group (σ_{β_1}). In other words, if $s_{\beta_1} > 1/\sigma_{\beta_1}$ an increase in ρ_β will in fact increase θ. One implication of this result is that, *ceteris paribus*, a more corrupt recipient country will receive a higher share of total aid if the share of aid income in total income for the poor in that country is sufficiently high. This result can be explained as follows. An increase in ρ_β will initially reduce the share of total foreign aid going to that country. This is the direct effect. However, from (21) we see that for a given μ_γ^0 an increase in ρ_β will reduce μ_β^0. This reduction in the share of aid going to the poor will induce donor country to allocate a higher share of total aid to this country. The magnitude of this second effect depends on the the share of aid income in total income for the poor in that country. Thus, if the share of aid income in total income for the poor in that country is sufficiently high we may obtain the perverse result that a more corrupt country receives a higher share of total aid. These results are stated formally in proposition 2.

Proposition 2. *Other things being the same, a more corrupt recipient government receives a bigger share of foreign aid if the share of aid income in total income is sufficiently large for the target group in that country.*

4 Concluding Remarks

In this paper we have examined the interactions between two types of allocations of foreign aid: (i) allocation of aid by a donor country between recipient countries, and (ii) allocation of received aid by recipient countries between target groups and other parties. For the donor country, the reason for giving aid is altruism towards the poorer sections of the population (the target group) in the recipient countries. However, the non-target group (the rich) lobby the government and diverts part of the aid away from the intended groups.

We model lobbying following the generalized common agency problem as developed in a recent paper by [5]. In this framework, each recipient government accepts political contribution from lobby groups and the level of contribution depends on the policy that the government pursues. The governments, however, also cares about the welfare of their nationals. Thus, the allocation of aid in each recipient country is determined by recipient government's attempts to balance its social welfare objectives and its preference for political contribution, the latter indicating the degree of corruption in the government, which is assumed to be different between the recipient countries.

In the above framework, *inter alia*, we examine if a more corrupt recipient country receives a lower share of foreign aid and surprisingly find that it is not necessarily the case.

References

1. Alesina A, Dollar D (2000) Who gives aid to whom and why?, Journal of Economic Growth 5: 33-63
2. Bernheim B, Whinston M (1986) Menu auction, resource allocation, and economic influence, Quarterly Journal of Economics 101: 1-31
3. Boone P (1996) Politics and the effectiveness of foreign aid, European Economic Review 40: 289-330
4. Burnside C, Dollar D (2000) Aid, policies and growth, American Economic Review 90: 847-868
5. Dixit A, Grossman GM, Helpman E (1997) Common agency and coordination: general theory and application to policy making, Journal of Political Economy 105: 752-769
6. Drazen A (2000) Political economy in macroeconomics, PrincetonUniversity Press
7. Feyzioglu T, Swaroop V, Zhu M (1998) A panel data analysis of the fungibility of foreign aid, The World Bank Economic Review 12: 29-58
8. Findley R and Wellisz S (1982) Endogenous tariffs, the political economy of trade restrictions, and welfare, In: Import competition and response, Bhagwati JN (eds) Chicago University of Chicago Press
9. Grossman GM, Helpman E (1994) Protection for sale, American Economic Review 84: 833-854
10. Hagen RJ (2000) Aspects of the political economy of foreign aid, mimeo

11. Hillman AL (1989) The political economy of protection, Harwood Academic Publishers, Chur
12. Hillman AL, Ursprung H (1993) Multinational firms, political competition, and international trade policy, International Economic Review 34: 347-363
13. Khilji NM, Zampelli EM (1994) The fungibility of U.S. military and non-military assistance and the impacts on major aid recipients, Journal of Development Economics 43: 345-362
14. Krueger AP (1974) The political economy of the rent-seeking society, American Economic Review 64: 291-30
15. Lahiri S, Raimondos-Møller P (2000) Lobbying by ethnic groups and aid allocation, Economic Journal 110: 62-79
16. Lahiri S, Raimondos-Møller P (1997) Competition for aid and trade policy, Journal of International Economics 43: 369-385
17. Lahiri S, Raimondos-Møller P (1998) Altruism and the optimality of foreign aid, In: Gupta K (eds.) Foreign aid: new perspective, Boston, Kluwer Academic Publisher: 21-36
18. Lahiri S, Raimondos-Møller P (1999) Special interest politics and the fungibility of foreign aid, Discussion Paper No.497, Department of Economics, University of Essex
19. Lahiri S, Raimondos-Møller P, Wong KY, Woodland A (2002) Optimal foreign aid and tariffs, Journal of Development Economics 67: 79-99
20. Maizel A, Nissanke MK (1984) Motivation for aid to developing countries, World Development 12: 879-900
21. Magee SP, Brock WA, Young L (1989) Black hole tariffs and endogenous policy theory, Cambridge: Cambridge University Press
22. Mayer W (1984) Endogenous tariff formation, American Economic Review 74: 970-985
23. Mayer W, Raimondos-Møller P (1999) The politics of foreign aid: a median voter perspectives, Review of Development Economics 7: 165-178
24. Pack H, Pack JR (1994) Foreign aid and the question of fungibility, Review of Economic and Statistics 75: 258-265
25. Pedersen KR (2000) The Samaritan's dilemma and the effectiveness of foreign aid, International Tax and Public Finance 8: 693-703
26. Rama M, Tabellini G (1998) Lobbying by capital and labor over trade and labor market policies, European Economic Review 42: 1295-1316
27. Rodrik D (1995) Political economy of trade policy, In: Grossman G, Rogoff K (eds) Handbook of International Economics, vol.3, North-Holland Publishing House, Amsterdam
28. Svensson J (2000) Foreign aid and rent-seeking, Journal of International Economics 51: 437-461
29. Trumbull WN, Wall HJ (1994) Estimating aid allocation criteria with panel data, Economic Journal 104: 876-882
30. World Development Indicators (2000) The World Bank, Washington, D.C.

163-75

Optimal Competition Policy in a Model of Vertical Production Chain[*]

Makoto Yano[1] and Fumio Dei[2]   *L42 F13 F12*

[1] Department of Economics, Keio University, 2-15-45 Mita, Minato-ku, Tokyo 108-8345, Japan myano@econ.keio.ac.jp
[2] Graduate School of Business Administration, Kobe University, 2-1 Rokkodai, Nada-ku, Kobe 657-8501, Japan dei@kobe-u.ac.jp

1 Introduction

The recent work of [6] and [8] has demonstrated that a country can increase its own utility, at a cost of its trading partner, by suppressing competition in that country's market for nontradables. In other words, for a large country, suppression of competition can serve as a beggar-thy-neighbor policy similar to the imposition of a tariff. Since the end of the World War II, as represented by the series of GATT rounds, many countries have made continuous efforts to reduce existing tariff rates. As a result, remaining tariff rates in developed countries have become minimal. At the same time, a focus of international economic issues has shifted to non-tariff trade barriers. In particular, many policy makers have come to realize that the organization of a country's internal markets, or in other words a country's domestic competition policy, can serve as a trade impediment.[1] In order to analyze the effect of such a policy, [6] and [8] develop general equilibrium models of vertical production chain, which can render the terms of trade effect of a change in the non-tradable sector tractable.

While those studies have shown that a country may optimize the degree of competition in a non-tradable market so as to maximize the country's utility, they have provided no characterization for the optimal competition policy. This study intends to provide such a characterization by using the static trade model developed by [8]. In that model, it is assumed that countries trade different middle products, which are transformed into a single non-tradable consumption good. The dynamic model of [6], which is designed to capture the intertemporal terms of trade effect, is not suitable in order to characterize

[*] We gratefully acknowledge financial supports from the Ministry of Education, Science, Sports and Culture and from the Nomura Foundation for Social Science.
[1] This fact is symbolized in the Japan-U.S. trade relationship over the last two decades. See, for example, [5].

the optimal competition policy in relation to the optimal tariff policy because of the complexity of intertemporal terms of trade effect in that model.[2]

The importance of characterizing the optimal competition policy stems from the fact that under the current international economic climates it is almost impossible for a country to adopt the optimal tariff policy. In order for a country to make a significant welfare gain from the optimal tariff policy, tariffs must be imposed on a broad range of imports. Under the WTO agreements, however, tariffs are tolerated only in very limited cases.[3] Under these circumstances, the optimal tariff policy is not an effective policy tool for a country to seek for a welfare gain by influencing the terms of trade. In contrast, no international agreement has yet been developed that aims to align competition policies of various countries. By controlling the way in which antitrust laws are enforced, a country can affect a broad range of its domestic markets, including those for non-tradable services and for labor force. As a result, a country may influence its terms of trade more effectively by competition policy than tariff policy. In such circumstances, the optimal competition policy may be a more effective policy tool than the optimal tariff policy in order to seek for a welfare gain by influencing its terms of trade.[4]

This paper is organized as follows. In section 2, we describe Yano and Dei's model, on which this study is based. In section 3, we set up a two-country case. In section 4, we discuss the objective budget constraint and the foreign offer curve as a preparation for the optimal competition policy. In section 5 we characterize the optimal competition policy. In section 6, we present an alternative approach to the optimal competition policy by using trade indifference curves.

2 Yano and Dei's Model

Yano and Dei's vertical production chain model has the following features.

1. There are two countries, the upstream sector of each of which produces a unique middle product from labor.
2. The downstream sector combines the two middle products produced by the countries with labor to produce a single consumption good.

---

[2] Because Yano's model is of infinite-time horizon, it involves highly complicated intertemporal terms of trade effects, which unnecessarily complicates the characterization of the optimal competition policy. Also see the recent work of [2], which reveals that the intertemporal effect of a change in a downstream sector can be highly complicated even in a small country setting.

[3] The WTO allows tariffs to protect agricultural products, to be imposed against dumping, to offset subsidies, and to safeguard domestic industries.

[4] With such a motivation, the recent work of [4] compares the welfare effects of the tariff policy and the competition policy and demonstrates that the competition policy may in fact be a more effective alternative.

3. The two middle products are tradable, but the consumption good of each country is non-tradable.[5]
4. Consumers consume the final consumption good and leisure.

The home country's preference is represented by its representative consumer's utility function $u = u(x_F, x_L)$, where x_F and x_L, respectively, are the consumption of the final consumption good (good F) and leisure. Let L be the total labor endowment and $\ell = L - x_L$ be the labor supply. Let p_F and w be the price of good F and the wage rate, respectively. The home country's representative consumer maximizes utility $u(x_F, x_L)$ subject to the budget constraint, which we will introduce below. Denote the compensated demand functions for good F and leisure as

$$x_F = x_F(p_F, w, u) \quad \text{and} \quad x_L = x_L(p_F, w, u). \tag{1}$$

There are two middle products A and B, which are, respectively, produced exclusively in the home country and the foreign country under Ricardian technologies. The downstream sector of each country combines products A and B with labor to produce the final consumption good, F, under constant returns to scale. Denote by p_A and p_B the world prices of A and B, respectively. Denote the cost minimizing input coefficient vector as

$$(a_{LF}, a_{AF}, a_{BF}) = (a_{LF}(w, p_A, p_B), a_{AF}(w, p_A, p_B), a_{BF}(w, p_A, p_B)), \tag{2}$$

where a_{iF} is the amount of input i, $i = L, A, B$, that is required to produce one unit of the final consumption good, F. Denote the corresponding unit cost function by[6]

$$c = c(w, p_A, p_B). \tag{3}$$

The downstream sector is imperfectly competitive due to the existence of legal and institutional entrance barriers. All firms in the downstream sector are identical. The government controls the degree of competition in the downstream sector by the number of firms n that it allows to operate in the downstream sector (competition policy, antitrust policy). Producing a homogenous consumption good, the firms in the downstream sector behave in a Cournot-Nash fashion. As in the standard treatment, assume that the perceived marginal revenue of an individual firm can be written as $MR = [1 - 1/(n\varepsilon)]p_F$, where ε is the perceived elasticity of aggregate demand

---

[5] Trade takes place only between middle products. In a different context, one may be interested in trade between middle products and consumption goods in the vertical production chain. For example, see [3].

[6] The unit cost function is defined as

$$c(w, p_A, p_B) = a_{LF}(w, p_A, p_B)w + a_{AF}(w, p_A, p_B)p_A + a_{BF}(w, p_A, p_B)p_B.$$

for good F capturing an individual firm's perception about the aggregate demand function for good F.

The unit cost is equal to the marginal cost, $MC = c$. The optimization behavior of a firm in the downstream sector is described by condition $MR = MC$, i.e.,

$$\left(1 - \frac{\delta}{\varepsilon}\right) p_F = c, \tag{4}$$

where $\delta = 1/n$. Parameter δ may be referred to as the degree of imperfect competition; $\delta = 0$ corresponds to the perfectly competitive case ($n = \infty$) while $0 < \delta \leq 1$ to the imperfectly competitive case ($n < \infty$). If the perceived elasticity, ε, is formed in a rational manner, it depends on various endogenous and exogenous variables. Since the economic activities of agents can be written as a function of prices and exogenous parameters, we write the perceived elasticity simply as a function of prices and δ.

$$\varepsilon = \varepsilon(p_F, w, p_A, p_B, \delta). \tag{5}$$

Since the total profit of the downstream sector is

$$\Pi = \frac{\delta}{\varepsilon} p_F x_F, \tag{6}$$

the budget constraint of the consumer is written as

$$p_F x_F + w x_L = wL + \Pi. \tag{7}$$

The middle products, A and B, are traded in world markets that are perfectly competitive. They are produced by the Ricardian technology. Denote by a_{LA} the input/output ratio of product A in the home country. The zero profit condition in the middle product sector (upstream sector) implies

$$w = p_A / a_{LA}. \tag{8}$$

The labor endowment is partly consumed as leisure and partly used as input by upstream and downstream sectors. Let x_A be the supply of product A. Then, the full employment condition is

$$a_{LA} x_A + a_{LF} x_F = L - x_L. \tag{9}$$

The volume of exports is

$$E = x_A - a_{AF} x_F, \tag{10}$$

whereas the volume of imports is

$$M = a_{BF} x_F. \tag{11}$$

The country's external budget constraint is

$$p_A E = p_B M, \tag{12}$$

which stipulates a country's trade account must be balanced.[7]

---

[7] In order to obtain this expression, use (8), (9), (10), and (11) to obtain

3 The Two-Country Case

In what follows, we normalize the prices by $p_A \equiv 1$. It is useful to define the compensated export supply and import demand functions. To this end, note that x_F and x_L are functions of (p_F, w, u) by (1) and that a_{iF} is a function of $(w, 1, p_B)$ by (2). By eliminating x_A from (10) by (9), therefore, we obtain the compensated export supply and import demand functions, $E = E(w, 1, p_B, p_F, u)$ and $M = M(w, 1, p_B, p_F, u)$, respectively. We can summarize the home country's behavior as follows.

$$E = E(w, 1, p_B, p_F, u); \tag{13}$$

$$M = M(w, 1, p_B, p_F, u); \tag{14}$$

$$E = p_B M; \tag{15}$$

$$1 = w a_{LA}; \tag{16}$$

$$\left(1 - \frac{\delta}{\varepsilon}\right) p_F = c(w, 1, p_B); \tag{17}$$

$$\varepsilon = \varepsilon(p_F, w, 1, p_B, \delta). \tag{18}$$

In order to describe the behavior of the foreign country, denote the foreign country's variables and functions by attaching superscript *. Since the foreign import demand and export supply can be expressed as functions of prices and utility level u^* in a manner parallel to (13) and (14), the foreign country's behavior can be summarized as follows.

$$M^* = M^*(w^*, 1, p_B, p_F^*, u^*); \tag{19}$$

$$E^* = E^*(w^*, 1, p_B, p_F^*, u^*); \tag{20}$$

$$M^* = p_B E^*; \tag{21}$$

$$p_B = w^* a_{LB}^*; \tag{22}$$

$$\left(1 - \frac{\delta^*}{\varepsilon^*}\right) p_F^* = c^*(w^*, 1, p_B); \tag{23}$$

$$\varepsilon^* = \varepsilon^*(p_F^*, w^*, 1, p_B, \delta^*). \tag{24}$$

The market clearing condition in the international market for tradables (middle products) can be expressed as

$$M^* = p_B M. \tag{25}$$

Given the price normalization $p_A \equiv 1$, the equilibrium in the two-country case is characterized by the system of equations (13) through (25).

$$p_A E - p_B M = w(L - x_L - a_{LF} x_F) - p_A a_{AF} x_F - p_B a_{BF} x_F.$$

Equation (12) follows from $[1 - (\delta/\varepsilon)]p_F = c$, the definition of the unit cost function $c(w, p_A, p_B)$ in footnote 6 , $\Pi = (\delta/\varepsilon)p_F x_F$, and the budget constraint (7).

4 The Objective Budget Line and the Foreign Offer Curve

As a preparation for characterizing the optimal competition policy, it is useful to illustrate the objective budget line of the representative consumer and the foreign offer curve.

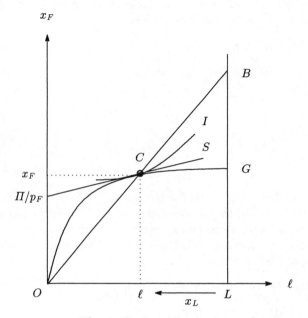

Fig. 1. Optimum in the space of consumption.

From (4), (6), (7) and (16), we have

$$x_F = \frac{1/a_{LA}}{c(1/a_{LA}, 1, p_B)} \ell, \tag{26}$$

where ℓ is the labor supply; $\ell = L - x_L$. When p_B is given, this constraint is drawn as the ray from the origin with its slope equal to the ratio between the wage rate and the marginal cost of good F, w/c. In Figure 1, this is shown by ray OB, which we call the objective budget line of the representative consumer. This line constitutes the "consumption possibility frontier," *i.e.*, captures all possible combinations of good F and leisure that a country's representative consumer can consume. If the market for good F is perfectly competitive, the objective budget line is the budget line that the representative consumer faces in choosing his consumption vector. If the market for good F is imperfectly competitive, the representative consumer's consumption point must lie on the objective budget constraint. However, he chooses his consumption vector subject to the budget line (subjective), which has a slope equal to the relative price between leisure and good F, w/p_F. In equilibrium, his consumption vector must be at the intersection between the objective budget line and the subjective budget line.

Next, solve the system of equations (19) through (24) with respect to $(M^*, E^*, w^*, p_F^*, u^*, \varepsilon^*)$ for (p_B, δ^*), we have

$$M^* = \widetilde{M^*}(p_B, \delta^*). \tag{27}$$

This is the import demand function of the foreign country, with given δ^*. Substitute $p_B = M^*/E^*$ into (27) to obtain

$$Z_{\delta^*}^*(M^*, E^*) = 0.$$

This function, $Z_{\delta^*}^*$, captures the foreign country's offer curve for a given degree of competition, δ^*; in Figure 2, curve Z_F^* depicts the foreign offer curve for the case of $\delta^* = 0$.

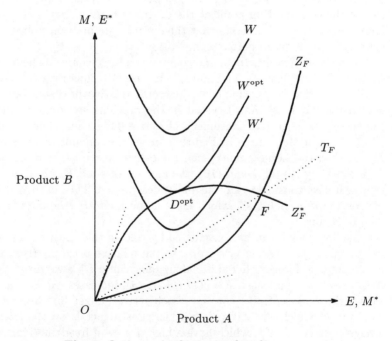

Fig. 2. Optimum in the space of trade.

5 Optimal Competition Policy

This section illustrates the determination of the optimal competition policy in the space of consumption. Before doing so, it is important to note that the optimal competition policy is not the first best but a "second best" policy. If a country's policy variable is confined to the degree of competition in the downstream sector, the optimal competition policy provides the maximum utility that the country can achieve. However, this utility is in general not as high as that which can be achieved by the optimal tariff policy.

As shown below, the optimal competition policy is characterized by the tangency between the "home consumption possibility frontier" (CPF) and a home indifference curve. In the case in which the home country is a small country, this fact is obvious from the discussion in the previous section. In that case, in the space of trade, the home country faces a foreign offer curve that is a straight line, like line T_F in Figure 2. Because the slope of this offer curve determines the terms of trade that the country faces, $1/p_B$, equation (26) captures the relationship between good F and leisure that the home representative consumer can consume. In the space of consumption, this relationship is illustrated by a ray from the origin, like OB in Figure 1, which is what we call the home CPF. In this case, it is optimal for the country to choose the consumption point at the tangency between ray OB and a home indifference curve (this shows that the optimal competition policy of a small country is to maintain perfect competition).

In the case in which the home country is a large country, the foreign offer curve is a curve like Z_F^* in Figure 2. In order to illustrate the home CPF in this case, fix for the moment the world relative price of tradables, p_B, at a particular level. As discussed in the previous section, this determines the home representative consumer's objective budget line, line OB in Figure 1. The foreign offer curve in Figure 2 shows the amount of middle product B, M, that the home country can import at this relative price, p_B. Once M is fixed, by (2), (11) and (16), the amount of good F, x_F, that the home representative consumer can consume is determined. This, in turn, determines his consumption point, C, which must lie on line OB (the objective budget line) in Figure 1.

The home CPF can be constructed by tracing this consumption point, C, by changing the relative price, p_B. As the relative price p_B rises, in Figure 2, the point of foreign offer shifts along offer curve Z_F^* away from the origin. As p_B rises, the unit cost, $c = c(1/a_{LA}, 1, p_B)$, increases. As a result, as (26) shows, the representative consumer's objective budget line becomes flatter. The way in which x_F shifts, as p_B increases, depends on the shape of the foreign offer curve, Z_F^*, which have a high degree of freedom. Thus, the CPF can have various shapes.

How does the CPF behave as the foreign offer point on offer curve Z_F^* shifts towards the origin? Let $\bar{p}_B$ be the slope of the foreign offer curve Z_F^* at the origin. As p_B approaches $\bar{p}_B$, the home country's import of good B, M, approaches $M = 0$. Since $a_{BF} = a_{BF}(w, p_A, p_B) = a_{BF}(1/a_{LA}, 1, p_B)$, a_{BF} increases as p_B falls due to the substitution effect. Thus, as p_B falls to $\bar{p}_B$, a_{BF} approaches a positive value. Thus, by (11), x_F approaches zero, as p_B

falls to $\bar{p}_B$. This demonstrates that the CPF starts from the origin, as shown in Figure 1.

The optimal consumption point is the point at which a home indifference curve, curve I, is tangent to the CPF, *i.e.*, point $C = (\ell, x_F)$ in Figure 1. The slope of the indifference curve, I, determines the relative price between labor and good F, w/p_F, because the representative consumer's subjective budget line, line S, must have a slope equal to w/p_F, as (7) shows. The subjective budget line's vertical intercept is at Π/p_F, which shows the profit income of the consumer. The slope of the objective budget line, line OB, which has a slope equal to $w/c(w, 1, p_B)$, determines the price of good B, p_B, that the home country must induce in the market for good B in order to maximize its welfare by suppressing competition in the market for good F. The gap between the slope of the subjective budget line, S, and the objective budget line, OB, determines what may be called the optimal Lerner index, *i.e.*, the optimal rate of distortion that the home country must induce in the market for good F.[8]

It is important to note that the government can determine the optimal Lerner index without information on the downstream firms' perception with respect to the elasticity of demand $\varepsilon = \varepsilon(p_F, w, 1, p_B, \delta)$. This information becomes necessary in translating the index to the optimal degree of competition, δ^{opt}; in general, the Lerner index can be expressed as $\rho = \delta/\varepsilon$.

In order to characterize the optimal Lerner index, ρ^{opt}, we denote the elasticity of the foreign import demand by $\eta^* = \frac{p_B}{M^*}\frac{\partial \widetilde{M^*}(p_B, \delta^*)}{\partial p_B}$. Then, we may prove the following result.

Theorem 1. *The home country's optimal Lerner index in its downstream sector is given by*

$$\rho^{\mathrm{opt}} = \frac{\theta}{e + \theta + \eta^* - 1}, \tag{28}$$

where $e = -\frac{p_B}{a_{BF}}\frac{\partial a_{BF}}{\partial p_B}$, *and* $\theta = \frac{p_B a_{BF}}{c}$.

Proof. We obtain $\widetilde{M^*}(p_B, \delta^*)/p_B = a_{BF}(w, 1, p_B)x_F$ from (27), (25), (11), and (2). Noting that δ^* is taken as given, totally differentiate this and (26) to obtain $\hat{x}_F = (e + \eta^* - 1)\hat{p}_B$ and $\hat{\ell} = (e + \eta^* - 1 + \theta)\hat{p}_B$, where we denote a relative change in a variable by using $\hat{\ }$; *i.e.*, $\hat{x} = dx/x$. Tangency condition implies $\frac{dx_F}{d\ell} = \frac{w}{p_F} = \frac{w}{c}(1 - \rho^{\mathrm{opt}})$. This can be rewritten as $\frac{\hat{x}_F}{\hat{\ell}} = \frac{w\ell}{cx_F}(1 - \rho^{\mathrm{opt}}) = 1 - \rho^{\mathrm{opt}}$, which leads to (28). $\square$

The optimal Lerner index formula (28) makes an interesting contrast with the well-known formula for the optimal tariff (*ad valorem*), which is

---

[8] The Lerner index, ρ, is a standard index capturing the extent of imperfect competition in a market. This index is defined as (price - marginal cost)/price. Because of constant returns to scale, marginal cost is identical with unit cost in the downstream sector. Therefore this index is defined as $\rho = 1 - c/p_F$ $(= \delta/\varepsilon)$.

$$t^{\text{opt}} = \frac{1}{\eta^* - 1} \tag{29}$$

(see [1], Supplements).[9] As (29) shows, the optimal tariff rate depends only on the shape of the foreign offer curve or, more specifically, the elasticity of the foreign import demand, η^*. In contrast, as (28) shows, the optimal Lerner index depends not only on the same foreign factor but also several domestic factors, i.e., the share of the cost of the imported middle product (B) in the total cost of the downstream sector, $\theta = p_B a_{BF}/c$, and the elasticity of that sector's input demand for the imported middle product, $e = -\frac{p_B}{a_{BF}} \frac{\partial a_{BF}}{\partial p_B}$. This difference between the optimal competition policy and the optimal tariff policy is a natural consequence of the fact that the competition policy targets a country's non-tradables sector while the tariff policy targets the world market for tradables.

The optimal Lerner index formula, (28), does not depend on the parameters concerning the representative consumer's utility function. This fact parallels to the fact that the optimal tariff formula, (29), is independent of the parameters governing the home country's trade utility function (or, in the standard trade model, the utility function itself).

Since the optimal competition policy and the optimal tariff policy give rise to different equilibria, the optimal Lerner index, ρ^{opt}, and the optimal tariff rate, t^{opt}, cannot be compared directly. We may, however, make a direct comparison if the elasticity of the foreign import demand, η^*, is constant. In this case, although the equilibria under the two regimes are different, by (28) and (29), we may conclude that the optimal Lerner index is smaller than the optimal tariff rate; $\rho^{\text{opt}} < t^{\text{opt}}$ since $0 < \theta < 1$ and $e > 0$. In particular, the smaller the foreign content of the final consumption good (i.e., $\theta = p_B a_{BF}/c$), the smaller the optimal Lerner index relative to the optimal tariff rate.

6 Trade Indifference Curves and Optimal Competition Policy

In the previous section, we have characterized the optimal competition policy in the space of consumption. In this section, we characterize this policy in the space of trade.

For this purpose, it is necessary to describe the relationship between the home country's utility and its trade vector in the case in which the home

---

[9] From (13), (14), (16) and (17) with δ held at zero, we obtain the trade indifference curves under tariffs. At the optimal trade vector, a trade indifference curve is tangent to the foreign offer curve. The slope of the trade indifference curve is given by $dM/dE = 1/p_B$ from (37) in the Appendix together with $p_F = c$ and $du = 0$. In the case of tariffs, we distinguish the domestic price p_B and the international price p_B^*. Using $p_B^* E^* = M^*$, $p_B = (1 + t) p_B^*$ and (31), we obtain formula (29).

country allows imperfect competition in the good F market, while maintaining free trade in the markets for middle products A and B. This relationship can be illustrated by a "trade indifference map," as shown in Figure 2. This indifference map is different from a standard trade indifference map, which is drawn for the case in which the home country maintains perfect competition in the good F market. The optimal trade vector is given by the point, D^{opt}, at which the trade indifference curve of W^{opt} is tangent to the foreign offer curve, Z_F^*.

The trade indifference curve under imperfect competition is derived as follows. Solve the system of equations (13) through (16) with respect to (w, p_B, p_F, u) for given (E, M). Denote by $u = W(E, M)$ the relationship between u and (E, M) in this solution and by $p_F = p_F(E, M)$ that between p_F and (E, M).

Note that the derivation of $W(E, M)$ requires the balanced trade condition (15), while that of the standard trade utility function does not. Furthermore, the latter function is based on the assumption that domestic good markets are perfectly competitive, implying $p_F = c$ in our model. In deriving W, in contrast, it is assumed that marginal cost c and price p_F can be freely separated. In consequence, a typical indifference map of W may not have the standard shape; this fact is reflected in the indifference map of Figure 2.

Denote by $(E^{\mathrm{opt}}, M^{\mathrm{opt}})$ the optimal trade vector. Then, the price of the final consumption good is determined as $p_F^{\mathrm{opt}} = p_F(E^{\mathrm{opt}}, M^{\mathrm{opt}})$. The price of good B is determined as $p_B^{\mathrm{opt}} = E^{\mathrm{opt}}/M^{\mathrm{opt}}$. The wage rate is $w = 1/a_{LA}$. By these facts, the Lerner index under the optimal competition policy (optimal Lerner index) can be described as

$$\rho^{\mathrm{opt}} = 1 - \frac{c(1/a_{LA}, 1, E^{\mathrm{opt}}/M^{\mathrm{opt}})}{p_F(E^{\mathrm{opt}}, M^{\mathrm{opt}})}.$$

We can prove Theorem 1 in the space of trade. It suffices to show that the slope of an indifference curve of $W(E, M)$ is characterized by

$$\frac{\mathrm{d}M}{\mathrm{d}E} = \frac{(1-\rho)\theta - \rho e}{(1-\rho)\theta + \rho(1-e)} \frac{M}{E}. \tag{30}$$

This is because the slope of the foreign offer curve can be expressed as

$$\frac{\mathrm{d}E^*}{\mathrm{d}M^*} = \frac{\eta^* - 1}{\eta^*} \frac{E^*}{M^*}. \tag{31}$$

Since, at optimum, the slope of this foreign offer curve must be equated to that of an indifference curve of W and since $M = E^*$ and $E^* = M$ in equilibrium, (28) follows from (30) and (31).

In order to complete the proof, we will derive (30). To this end, recall that $W(E, M)$ is derived from the system of equations (13) through (16). Since $\hat{E} = \hat{p}_B + \hat{M}$ by (15), given $\mathrm{d}u = 0$, we may use Corollary 1 in the Appendix to obtain

$$-\frac{(p_F - c)s}{p_B a_{BF}}\widehat{p}_F = \widehat{p}_B, \tag{32}$$

where $s = -\frac{p_F}{x_F}\frac{\partial x_F}{\partial p_F}$.

Suppose $p_F \neq c$. Then, we have

$$-s\widehat{p}_F = \frac{\theta(1-\rho)}{\rho}\widehat{p}_B,$$

since $\frac{\rho}{\theta(1-\rho)} = \frac{p_F - c}{p_B a_{BF}}$ holds by the definitions of θ and ρ. Substitute this expression and $du = 0$ into (34) in the Appendix, and obtain

$$\hat{M} = -\left\{e - \frac{\theta(1-\rho)}{\rho}\right\}\widehat{p}_B.$$

Since $\widehat{p}_B = \hat{E} - \hat{M}$, this implies (30), given $p_F \neq c$.

If $p_F = c$, (32) implies $\widehat{p}_B = 0$, which implies $\hat{E} - \hat{M} = \widehat{p}_B = 0$. Thus, $\frac{dM}{dE} = \frac{M}{E}$. Since $p_F = c$ implies $\rho = 0$, (30) captures the slope of the indifference curve for the case of $p_F = c$.

Appendix

Lemma 1. *Given $p_A \equiv 1$ and (16), (13) and (14) can be expanded as follows.*

$$\hat{E} = \frac{p_B M}{E}\left\{\frac{p_B}{a_{BF}}\frac{\partial a_{BF}}{\partial p_B}\widehat{p}_B + \frac{1}{p_B a_{BF}}(p_F - c + p_B a_{BF})\frac{p_F}{x_F}\frac{\partial x_F}{\partial p_F}\widehat{p}_F \right. \tag{33}$$

$$\left. -\frac{1}{p_B a_{BF} x_F}\left[w\frac{\partial x_L}{\partial u} + (c - p_B a_{BF})\frac{\partial x_F}{\partial u}\right]du\right\};$$

$$\hat{M} = \frac{p_B}{a_{BF}}\frac{\partial a_{BF}}{\partial p_B}\widehat{p}_B + \frac{p_F}{x_F}\frac{\partial x_F}{\partial p_F}\widehat{p}_F + \frac{1}{x_F}\frac{\partial x_F}{\partial u}du. \tag{34}$$

Proof. To prove the lemma, first obtain the following expressions.

$$\widehat{a}_{iF} = \frac{p_B}{a_{iF}}\frac{\partial a_{iF}}{\partial p_B}\widehat{p}_B, \quad i = L, A, B; \tag{35}$$

$$\widehat{x}_j = \frac{p_F}{x_j}\frac{\partial x_j}{\partial p_F}\widehat{p}_F + \frac{1}{x_j}\frac{\partial x_j}{\partial u}du, \quad j = F, L. \tag{36}$$

(These equations follows from (1) and (2), since w and p_A are fixed.) Since $E = \frac{1}{a_{LA}}\{L - x_L - (a_{LF} + a_{LA}a_{AF})x_F\}$ by (9) and (10), we have

$$\hat{E} = -\frac{x_F(a_{LF}\widehat{a}_{LF} + a_{LA}a_{AF}\widehat{a}_{AF})}{Ea_{LA}} - \frac{x_L\widehat{x}_L}{Ea_{LA}} - \frac{(a_{LF} + a_{LA}a_{AF})x_F\widehat{x}_F}{Ea_{LA}}.$$

Thus, (33) follows from (35) and (36) together with

$$w\frac{\partial a_{LF}}{\partial p_B} + \frac{\partial a_{AF}}{\partial p_B} = -p_B\frac{\partial a_{BF}}{\partial p_B} \quad \text{and} \quad w\frac{\partial x_L}{\partial p_F} = -p_F\frac{\partial x_F}{\partial p_F}.$$

Since $\hat{M} = \widehat{a}_{BF} + \widehat{x}_F$, (34) readily follows from (35) and (36). □

The next corollary follows immediately from (33) and (34).

Corollary 1. *Given $p_A \equiv 1$ and (16), the following holds:*

$$\frac{E}{p_B M}\hat{E} - \hat{M} = \frac{p_F - c}{p_B a_{BF}} \frac{p_F}{x_F} \frac{\partial x_F}{\partial p_F}\hat{p}_F - \frac{1}{p_B M}\left(w\frac{\partial x_L}{\partial u} + c\frac{\partial x_F}{\partial u}\right) du. \qquad (37)$$

References

1. Caves RE, Frankel JA, Jones RW (2002), World Trade and Payments: An Introduction, 9th ed., New York: Addison Wesley
2. Ohta R (2002) Adjustability in Production and Dynamic Effects of Domestic Competition Policy, mimeo
3. Schmid M (2002) Make or Buy: Exploiting the Value-Added Chain for a Gainful Division of Labor between North and South, mimeo
4. Takahashi R (2002) A Comparison of Domestic Competition Policy and Tariff Policy, mimeo
5. U.S.-Japan Working Group on the Structural Impediments Initiative (1990) Final Report
6. Yano M (2001) Trade Imbalance and Domestic Market CompetitionPolicy, International Economic Review, 42: 729-750
7. Yano M, Dei F (2003) Trade, Vertical Production Chain, and Competition Policy, Review of International Economics, 11: 237-252

Some Economics of
Parallel Imports and Trade Policy

Martin Richardson

F13 F14 F12

School of Economics, Faculty of Economics and Commerce, Australian National University, Canberra ACT 0200, Australia martin.richardson@anu.edu.au

1 Introduction

In the late 1990s a number of countries such as Australia, New Zealand and Singapore relaxed restrictions on parallel imports (PIs) – the importation of genuine goods into a country without the authorisation of the intellectual property right (IPR) holder in that country. The US has reacted to these reforms and induced New Zealand, for instance, to weaken its liberalisations in the context of certain goods. The question of how to deal with PIs has also been much discussed recently in the context of pharmaceuticals trade, where developing countries seek access to branded drugs at much lower prices than they are currently supplied, and one of the arguments made against this by drug firms is that supplying some countries at low prices will erode margins in other countries through the flow of PIs.

While PIs might arise for a number of reasons[1] we focus on international price discrimination by a monopolist.[2] If the monopolist is able to segment markets on the basis of geographical location then it will maximise profits by charging a higher price in markets with lower demand elasticity. Permitting PIs then allows entrepreneurs to purchase the product in the high-elasticity low-price market and sell it in the low-elasticity high-price market which leads to the monopolist charging a uniform price and thus arbitrages away price discrimination.[3] This chapter presents the results of two recent papers that have

2 articles combined

new

---

[1] See [1], [5] and [6] as well as [8].

[2] The firm that holds the IPR is by definition a monopolist, since it has control over production of the unique good. [5] (p.171) note that parallel imported products are usually differentiated products, with high fixed costs (such as R&D, advertising and marketing costs) which indicates an imperfectly competitive market.

[3] [6] provide an insightful model in which PI goods may flow from high- to low-price countries: they note that the relevant margin for PI goods arbitraged by retailers is the difference between retail price in the destination country and wholesale price in the source.

looked at the economics of PIs.[4] The first, [8], offers a model in which all countries permit PIs and, from that perspective, one would anticipate that any high-price country in a world without PIs would wish to liberalise its PI regime. From a global perspective, the welfare analysis of [5] (MS henceforth) suggests that the likely losers from a global regime of uniform pricing (a consequence of global PI liberalisation) are small low-price markets that are likely to be dropped.[5] This characterisation might seem to describe pretty well the liberalising countries identified above, and the second paper we summarise, [3] (KR henceforth), noting that the countries we have mentioned above have all liberalised their international trade regimes in recent years, develops a model to look at the joint choice of both trade policy (tariffs) and PI regime. They show that allowing PIs is always attractive to a country with no trade barriers and that, if the country is setting a tariff, the optimal tariff is lower in the presence of PIs than in its absence. Nevertheless, the intuition that high-price countries would wish to permit PIs still holds in the tariff–setting context. So a country facing a higher price, net of its optimal tariff, in a segmented market can always do better still by permitting PIs and adjusting its optimal tariff appropriately. While facing a high price under price discrimination is sufficient for a country to favour uniform pricing, it is not necessary. However, if a country faces a lower price then its PI regime is irrelevant in determining whether or not the monopolist will segment the two markets, whether or not the country favours uniform pricing.

Further, KR show in the context of welfare-maximising governments that the reduction in the optimal tariff following the legalisation of PIs is sufficiently beneficial to the monopolist that overall profitability might be higher in the presence of PIs than in their absence. These findings, however, may be sensitive to political economy complications. In particular, a government that would otherwise choose to permit PIs might prohibit them if it is sufficiently concerned with the profitability of a domestic distributor or if it is subject to lobbying by the monopoly. The latter is more likely in exactly the case where permitting PIs is most attractive to the country – when discrimination is more profitable to the monopolist.

2 A Black and White Result Concerning Grey Markets

2.1 A Multi-Country Model Without Tariffs

Consider a world of $n + 1$ countries indexed by $i = 0, 1, \cdots, n$. A monopolist firm in country 0 produces a homogeneous good sold, potentially, in all $n + 1$ countries under the canonical conditions of international trade theory:

---

[4] As this chapter draws extensively from these two papers, we have not cluttered the paper by crediting all excerpts exactly in what follows. Suffice to say, the material is reprinted from [8] and [3], with permission from Elsevier.

[5] In their model small countries are also low-price countries.

zero transport costs, non-decreasing production costs and full information on (well-behaved) demand conditions. Demand for the product in country $i = 0, 1, \cdots, n$ is given by $x_i(p_i)$ where p_i is the price charged in country i. The firm's costs are given by $C(X)$ where $X_i \equiv \sum_{i=0}^{n} x_i$, $C'(X) > 0$ and $C''(X) \geq 0$. Welfare in country $i = 1, 2, \cdots, n$ is simply consumers' surplus whereas in country 0 welfare includes the global profits of the monopolist. If we denote by a_i the "choke price" in country i (the price at which demand just falls to zero, so $a_i = x^{i-1}(0)$) then $W_0 = CS_0 + \pi = \int_{p_0}^{a_0} x_0(s)ds + \sum_{i=0}^{n} p_i x_i - C(X)$ and $W_i = CS_i = \int_{p_i}^{a_i} x_i(s)ds$ for $i = 1, 2, \cdots, n$. Thus $\partial W_i / \partial p_i = -x_i(p_i) < 0$, $i = 1, \cdots, n$ and $\partial W_0 / \partial p_0 = [p_0 - C'(X)] x_0' < 0$ when p_0 is chosen to maximise profits. Note, too, that $\partial W_0 / \partial p_i = x_i + (p_i - C'(X))x_i'$ for $i > 0$. This last expression is zero, either because the country is not served, or by the firm's FOC. We assume that the firm's problem has an interior solution for at least some markets: $a_i > C(0)$ for some i.

Suppose the monopolist can price discriminate across all markets. Let $S \equiv \{i : x_i(p_i^*) > 0\}$ denote the set of countries that are served in this case where p_i^* is the price charged to country i under price discrimination. Then S is the set of countries in which there are strictly positive sales under global price discrimination. Denote its complement by N so that $N \equiv \{i : x_i(p_i^*) = 0\}$ Suppose further that, under global uniform pricing in $i = 0, \cdots, n$ (that is, when the monopolist must charge the same price in every market) it maximises profit by setting $p_i = \underline{p}$ and sells $\underline{x}_i(\underline{p})$ in country i for total sales of $\underline{X} \equiv \sum_{i=0}^{n} \underline{x}_i(\underline{p})$. Let $\underline{S} \equiv \{i : \underline{x}_i(\underline{p}) > 0\}$ denote the set of countries that are served in this case and denote its complement by $\underline{N}$ so that $\underline{N} \equiv \{i : \underline{x}_i(\underline{p}) = 0\}$. Finally, we consider first only two policy extremes for countries: either parallel imports are permitted with no restrictions or they are prohibited outright. Let I_i be an indicator variable, which takes the value 1 for countries that permit parallel imports and 0 for countries that do not.

Our conclusions depend on the following:

Key assumption 1 *Consider any two countries, i and j, which are both served under price discrimination and face prices $p_i^* > p_j^*$ respectively. Under our maintained assumptions, if these two were to be treated as a single market they would face a common price $p \in [p_j^*, p_i^*]$ and welfare in country i (j) would be weakly higher (lower) than with price discrimination.*[6]

We assume henceforth that $x_i' < 0$ and $x_i'' \leq 0$. This is assumed simply to give a unique global maximum to the firm's problem. In fact, our propositions will apply in any world where our Key Assumption holds (for which these restrictions are sufficient).

We consider a simple two-stage game with the following structure: first, all governments simultaneously choose whether to permit or prohibit parallel imports; second, the monopolist sets a price in each country. If this involves a higher price in a country that permits parallel imports than in some other

---

[6] See [9] pp137-138.

country then arbitrage will occur from the latter to the former (parallel imports) and the monopolist's profits will be lower than if it were to set a uniform price that "groups" the two countries together in the sense of treating them as a single market. Suppose, initially, that either $0 \in \underline{S}$ and $p^{0*} < \underline{p}$ or $0 \in \underline{N}$. We can now state our central result.

Proposition 1. *Consider the one-shot policy game involving the simultaneous and non-cooperative choice of parallel import policy by all countries. In any Nash equilibrium to this game, only countries $i \in \underline{S}$ are served and $p_i = \underline{p}$ $\forall i > 0,\ i \in \underline{S}$.*

Proof. Suppose not. Consider some country $i \neq 0$, $i \in M$ where M denotes the set of countries other than the monopolist's home country facing the highest price in a discriminating equilibrium: $M \equiv \{k : p_k^* = \max\{p_1^*, \cdots, p_n^*\}\}$. Similarly, let J denote the set of countries facing the lowest price in a discriminating equilibrium: $J \equiv \{k : p_k^* = \min\{p_1, \cdots, p^{*_n}\}\}$. While J and M may be singletons, they are clearly non-empty. So no country (other than possibly the monopolist's home country) faces a higher price than country i or a lower price than any country $j \in J$. This can only occur if $I_i = 0$. Suppose country i were instead to set $I_i = 1$ i.e. it were to permit parallel imports. It would then be grouped by the supplier with some country $j \in J$ and be treated as a single market. By our Key Assumption, welfare in country i would be higher than with price discrimination i.e. $I_i = 0$ could not be a Nash equilibrium. Accordingly, all countries $i > 0$ that are served must face the same price and $p_i = p_j$, $\forall i, j \in \underline{S}$, as claimed.[7] Furthermore, $I_i = 1$ $\forall i \in \underline{S}$ such that $p_i^* > p_i$.

This result says that we effectively observe global uniform pricing[8] and the intuition behind it is very simple. The countries that would like to permit parallel importing are those that are discriminated against in its absence. So "high-price" countries can "undo" price discrimination. While high-elasticity

---

[7] Allowing parallel imports is, in fact, a weakly dominant strategy for every country in that a country can do no worse allowing parallel imports than prohibiting them regardless of the policy choices of other countries.

[8] Technically there are multiple equilibria here depending on the policy choices of both the countries in N and those in $\underline{S}$ that would face $p_i^* < \underline{p}$ in the absence of parallel imports (these latter might prohibit parallel imports but with no effect on the equilibrium price). Clearly these equilibria are all equivalent to global uniform pricing. The only exception that might arise is if $0 \in \underline{S}$ and $p_0^* > p_E$ where $p_E < \underline{p}$ is the uniform price that would be charged to all export markets if $0 \in \underline{S}$ but country 0 prohibits parallel imports. If country 0 then permits parallel imports it will lead to a uniform price of $\underline{p}$ – lower at home but higher in the rest of the served markets than p_E. While the sum of consumers' surplus and profits in its own market must increase with this, if the decrease in profits from the served export markets is substantial it could more than offset this. In that case the source country would prohibit parallel imports. Nevertheless, all foreign markets will still face a uniform price, as in Proposition One.

demand countries might favour discrimination, in this set-up they cannot enforce it globally when high-price countries permit grey markets.[9]

We close this section with a final observation. As noted earlier, MS show that world welfare may be higher than with either complete price discrimination or uniform pricing in a "mixed" system in which countries are grouped. The monopolist can then discriminate between the groups but charges a uniform price within a group. Clearly this does not affect the world of Proposition 1.

2.2 An Extension: Re-Export Restrictions

Proposition One suggests that one set of beneficiaries of parallel import restrictions – countries that face low prices in a discriminatory outcome – cannot do anything to prevent global uniform pricing in equilibrium. As MS note, however, there is one way that countries that are favoured by international price discrimination can encourage it, even when others permit grey markets, and that is by prohibiting the re-export of licensed sales. Thus a prohibition on re-exports could retain international price discrimination. So consider the one-shot policy game involving the simultaneous and non-cooperative choice of I_i by all countries along with the choice of whether or not to prohibit re-exports. In this case we get the following result:

Proposition 2. *Consider the one-shot policy game involving the simultaneous and non-cooperative choice of parallel import and re-export policy by all countries. In any Nash equilibrium to this game, only countries $i \in S$ are served and are charged prices p_i^*.*

Proof. If any served countries are grouped together and charged a uniform price then, by our Key Assumption, any country in the group which would receive a lower price if discrimination were permitted can obtain that price by prohibiting parallel imports and re-exports. So no dissimilar countries can be grouped in equilibrium.

□

---

[9] This result seems robust to repeated game complications. The usual complication repetition adds to a one-shot full information game is that, while repetition of any Nash equilibrium to the one-shot game is still a Nash equilibrium in the repeated game, there is a much richer variety of strategies agents can play and this can sustain other mutually-beneficial outcomes through appropriately chosen punishment strategies. However, in the simple setting of this section in which the strategic players are governments only, repetition changes nothing. The reason is that no combination of actions by the countries can raise the welfare of the country facing the highest price in any discrimination equilibrium compared to the equilibrium of Proposition One. Hence, as in Proposition One, any other outcome 'unravels' iteratively.

So now it is "low-price" countries that "undo" uniform pricing and we effectively observe global price discrimination.[10]

While this is a theoretical possibility, the prohibition of re-exports is not a policy one sees enacted in practice, perhaps for reasons of policing difficulties, latent mercantilism and a perception that this is a policy that serves private rather than national interests. Our analysis has taken the behaviour of the monopolist as essentially passive. And yet one might anticipate that the monopoly manufacturer would desire to take steps to prohibit parallel trade, perhaps through closer integration into or control over distribution channels (as has been suggested in the case of Japan where government policies might permit parallel imports *de jure* while private practices prohibit them *de facto*[11]) or through explicit controls on re-exports. Indeed, there is evidence that some manufacturers do attempt to control this behaviour (see [7] [12]). Interestingly, however, a recent decision in Spain has questioned such steps – a pharmaceutical company (Glaxo Wellcome) employed a dual pricing system with one price for products sold through Spanish pharmacies and a higher price for those sold to Spanish wholesalers who were deemed to be the source of re-exports into the rest of Europe. Spanish legal authorities ordered in December 1998 that this dual pricing scheme be suspended pending a further ruling; since then the European Commission's competition directorate, DGIV, has notified the company that it perceives this pricing system to be a restriction of competition in violation of European competition rules.

3 A Two Country Model with Tariffs

Consider a country that is facing a high price under a system of international price discrimination. This country has two broad tools available to reduce the effects of price discrimination by the IPR holder. One option is to tax imports of the good in question. This allows the government to capture some of the monopoly rent as tariff revenue. Alternatively, it can remove restrictions on parallel imports so that the monopolist is "constrained by the threat of arbitrage to set a uniform price" ([5], p.171): entrepreneurs can import the good from a low-price country. A third option is both to allow parallel importing

---

[10] Again there are multiple equilibria here depending on the policy choices of the countries in N but now they are all equivalent to global price discrimination. Note, too, that the choice of parallel import regime in this setting is redundant: whether or not countries permit parallel imports, re-export restrictions ensure that they do not occur.

[11] See also the analysis of [6].

[12] However, only 18% of respondents in [7] survey of U.S. manufacturers reported that they would prohibit parallel exports of their products under all circumstances, indicating that it can serve international marketing purposes other than simply arbitraging third degree price discrimination.

and to use tariffs. Thus there is interaction of parallel import and tariff policy. The model developed in this section examines the optimal parallel import and trade policy for a high-price country in a two-country framework.[13] To obtain closed-form solutions for the optimal tariff a linear model is used but the intuition for the results does not hinge significantly on this linearity.

Consider a monopolist, based in the foreign market, which produces a final good at a constant marginal cost, c, for sale in both the domestic and foreign markets. It faces the following inverse demand curves in the domestic and foreign markets respectively:

$$p = a - bq$$
$$p^* = a^* - b^*q^*$$ (1)

where a represents the domestic country's choke price – the price where demand in that market goes to zero – and p and q denote domestic price and quantity respectively. Foreign market values are denoted with an asterisk. Henceforth, without loss of generality, normalise the value of b^* to unity. The restriction required for the domestic market to face the higher free trade price when markets are segmented is simply:

$$a > a^*$$ (2)

The authorised channel into the domestic market can be characterised by either the monopolist granting a domestic firm the exclusive right to import the good or the right to produce it under licence, or the monopolist selling the good directly itself. Either way, in this full-information setting in equilibrium the monopolist can appropriate any producer surplus created in the domestic market.[14] Therefore, welfare in the domestic market can be thought of as the sum of consumers' surplus (CS) and government revenue (GR).[15] The timing of moves is as follows: first, the domestic government sets its PI policy and any tariff; then the monopolist sets its prices to each or both markets (if PIs are prohibited or allowed, respectively) and finally markets clear. Assume throughout the analysis that tariff policy in the foreign country is fixed – in that case one can normalise the foreign tariff to zero (alternatively, one can

---

[13] The market of interest is the country facing high free trade prices under a system of international price discrimination. This market will be referred to as the home, or domestic, market. The other market will be referred to as the foreign market.

[14] The monopolist is able to appropriate all producer surplus in the domestic market, since the maximum amount a rational domestic firm would be willing to pay for the right to distribute/produce the good would be the total amount of surplus it could derive from the market.

[15] As discussed below, allowing parallel imports may have a one-off wealth effect on the domestic IPR holder if the contractual arrangement between that firm and the foreign IPR owner was based on producer surplus under the parallel import restrictions. This would reduce the benefit to the domestic country of removing parallel import restrictions and may change the optimal policy choice.

think of a^* as being the foreign choke price minus the foreign tariff). Suppose also that the foreign country – the home country of the monopolist – prohibits PIs throughout. This is only relevant if the domestic country sets a tariff such that it faces a net-of-tariff price below p^*, of course, as no arbitrage from the domestic to the foreign country would otherwise be attempted. As PIs are still legal trade they, too, are subject to any tariff levied by the home country.

3.1 No Parallel Imports

Consider first the case in which the domestic country levies no tariff and prohibits all PIs. The discriminating monopolist will maximise profits by equating marginal revenue and marginal cost in each market and it is straightforward to calculate closed-form expressions [16] for the variables of interest: p_{ft}, q_{ft}, CS_{ft}, GR_{ft}, W_{ft}, π_{ft} and Π_{ft} where π denotes the profits earned by the monopolist in the domestic market, Π denotes its aggregate profits and the ft subscript denotes free trade, no PIs.

If the government can levy a specific tariff of t, welfare can be rewritten in terms of the tariff, maximised to find an optimal tariff of $t = \frac{(a-c)}{3}$ and solved out once more for the variables of interest. These are subscripted with a t to denote values under the optimal tariff and p_t denotes the price to domestic consumers ('world' price plus the tariff). It can be shown that, compared to free trade, there is a positive tariff, domestic price is higher and quantity less but the tariff revenue more than offsets the decreased consumers' surplus. Thus welfare increases. This is simply the well-known observation that a country facing a monopolist can gain from a tariff by extracting some of the monopoly profit: the domestic price increases by less than the tariff.

Parallel Imports Permitted

By construction, the domestic market benefits from allowing PIs, absent trade policy, as it faces the higher price in the segmented markets case. If PIs are allowed then the monopolist treats the two countries as one aggregate market and maximises profits off the (horizontal) summation of their individual demand curves. It now faces the inverse demand curve given below:

$$
\begin{aligned}
p &= a - bq - t & \text{if } p \geq a^* \\
p &= \frac{(a+b(a^*-Q)-t)}{(1+b)} & \text{otherwise}
\end{aligned}
\tag{3}
$$

---

[16] The basic linear model used here is a very familiar one and the results hinge on sometimes messy and tedious but always simple algebraic manipulations. As there are no technical innovations here, in order to leave the paper as uncluttered as possible all of the analytics are summarised in the KR Appendix and complete calculations are in a further Technical Appendix available from the author on request.

where $Q \equiv q + q^*$. From this one can find the profit-maximising price, the quantities sold in each market and the other variables of interest. First suppose there are no tariffs so $t = 0$. Again one can solve for the values of the variables of interest, where a pi subscript alone denotes free trade but with PIs allowed. But when the domestic government can levy a tariff, it transpires that the uniform price is decreasing in t and that, again, the domestic price increases by less than the tariff. Indeed, denoting the domestic consumer price with parallel imports and a tariff by $p_{\text{pi},t}$:

$$\frac{\partial p_{\text{pi},t}}{\partial t} = \frac{1 + 2b}{2(1 + b)} \in \left(\frac{1}{2}, 1\right) \tag{4}$$

Finding the optimal tariff is somewhat messier here than in the absence of PIs but doing so demonstrates the following:

Result 1 *The optimal tariff is lower when PIs are permitted than when they are prohibited.*

Note, first, that this result applies far more generally than to just the linear model studied here — see the KR Appendix. The intuition for the result is simply that under the threat of PIs a given tariff has less of an effect on the monopolist's price ($\partial(p_{\text{pi},t} - t)/\partial t < 1/2$ in the linear model) than when markets are segmented ($\partial p_t/\partial t = 1/2$) as a given price cut must be extended to both markets under uniform pricing. As the only source of gain from the tariff is this "terms of trade" effect, the optimal tariff is lower as this effect is lessened.

Model Implications

The domestic country's welfare in each policy regime is summarised in Table 1.

Table 1. Welfare comparisons of policy regimes.

PI policy	Trade policy	Welfare
Prohibited	No tariffs	$W_{\text{ft}} = (a - c)^2/8b$
	Tariffs	$W_t = (a - c)^2/6b$
Unrestricted	No tariffs	$W_{\text{pi}} = [(1 + b)(a - c) + b(a - a^*)]^2/8b(1 + b)^2$
	Tariffs	$W_{\text{pi},t} = [(1 + b)(a - c) + b(a - a^*)]^2/[2b(1 + 2b)(3 + 2b)]$

The next two conclusions follow from this.

Result 2 *A tariff is welfare-improving for the domestic country given its PI regime – $W_t > W_{\text{ft}}$ and $W_{\text{pi},t} > W_{\text{pi}}$.*

This is as it must be, of course: setting the tariff optimally can be no worse than setting it to zero (free trade). More interestingly, however, permitting PIs is (weakly) welfare-improving whatever the tariff regime:

Result 3 *While allowing PIs is always attractive for a free trading country – $W_{pi} > W_{ft}$ – uniform pricing will only be attractive for a country setting the optimal tariff when the following condition holds: $6(1 + b)(a - c)(a - a^*) + 3b(a - a^*)^2 < (b + 2)(a - c)^2$. However, this condition implies that $p_t - t < p^*$ so the domestic country cannot induce global uniform pricing by permitting PIs in such a case.*

So prohibiting PIs can never be attractive for a country that faces the higher price from the monopolist in the segmented markets case under an optimal tariff. The KR Appendix demonstrates that $p_t - t > p^*$ is sufficient for $W_{pi,t} > W_t$ where p_t is the domestic price cum tariff, p^* the foreign price and t the domestic country's optimal tariff. The reason is that PIs must still then be attractive – even with an unchanged tariff, PIs would further reduce the price charged by the monopolist and thus raise domestic welfare. And while uniform pricing (and therefore, so it might seem, permitting PIs) is less likely to be attractive for a tariff-setting country the lower is a and the higher is a^*,[17] in fact there is nothing the country can do to induce uniform pricing when it is desirable: in such a case it is the low-price country and PIs, were they to flow at all, would be from the domestic country, not to it. Under the maintained assumption of a PI prohibition in the foreign country, domestic liberalisation has no effect.[18][19]

Note that a higher domestic price in segmented markets with an optimal tariff is sufficient but not necessary for global uniform pricing to be attractive

---

[17] The intuition being that the beneficial consequences of PIs on the price charged by the monopolist are greater the greater the choke price (as it leads to a greater difference between the prices charged to the two countries when the markets are segmented). This price fall from uniform pricing more than offsets the increased monopolist price due to the reduction in the domestic tariff.

[18] If, instead, the foreign country were to permit PIs, then we would observe global uniform pricing in this case regardless of the home country's PI regime. The result still holds: liberalising PIs is never worse than prohibiting them.

[19] It is also the case that a quantitative restriction on PIs can never be attractive to a country. While PIs lead to uniform pricing by the monopolist, a quota on PIs will not, generically: it will reduce the price discrimination margin but, if the quota is quite tight, the monopolist may prefer not to undercut PI arbitrage entirely. Now, totally prohibiting PIs can only be attractive when a country can set a tariff and, by the discussion of Result 3, when the country faces a lower price from the monopolist, absent PIs, than does the foreign market. PIs are not then attractive because they lead to worse terms of trade, after the tariff is adjusted optimally. This is still the case even if the volume of PIs is restricted so PIs under a quota cannot raise welfare in a case where prohibition is preferred to unrestricted PIs. If, on the other hand, PIs are attractive then a quantitative restriction will again not be used as it leads to only a partial price reduction.

to the home country – it's just that such pricing cannot be induced through PI liberalisation unless the home country is the high-price country. So uniform pricing can still be welfare improving for a "low-price" country as, even though it yields a worsening in the terms of trade (the function of the optimal tariff), it permits a smaller tariff, which lessens the latter's consumption loss.

I have stressed that these results do not depend on country size (which, in this setting, is inversely related to b). Nevertheless, permitting PIs is likely to be more attractive for a small country than a large one, ceteris paribus, when it can set a tariff optimally. The reason is a general one: the uniform price set by a monopolist serving two markets will be closer to the discriminatory price faced by a particular country the larger that country is. This is still the case here (the gain from liberalising PIs is increasing in b) even though the home country's optimal tariff under PIs is increasing in its size ($dt/db < 0$). Thus, given the size of the other country, a high-price country that liberalises PIs will experience a greater reduction in price – and so a greater welfare gain – the smaller it is. Another interesting conclusion concerns the effects of PIs on the monopolist:

Result 4 *When a country sets its tariff optimally, allowing PIs may benefit the foreign monopolist.*

So permitting PIs can benefit the monopolist – while the restriction of uniform pricing alone reduces its profits, the decrease in the domestic tariff raises them by even more.[20] This might seem counter-intuitive: if uniform pricing yields higher profits, why does the profit-maximising monopolist not simply charge each country the same price even when discrimination is feasible? The answer lies in the timing of the game: the firm acts when the PI regime and tariff have been chosen. So if the domestic government prohibits PIs and levies a tariff then, given this, the best the firm can do is price discriminate. Even if the firm were somehow to commit to not discriminating against the home country, it would still face a tariff and, in a sense, a regime of allowing PIs can be thought of as a commitment by the country to a lower tariff.

4 Political Economy Considerations

The previous section argues that a welfare-maximising country will choose to permit PIs whether or not it is free to set its own tariffs. This section considers two objectives a government might pursue and investigates whether these might constrain a country to prohibit PIs.

---

[20] The comparison of total profits under an optimal tariff with and without PIs is a messy one that yields few clear-cut comparative static results. While the firm is more likely to benefit from allowing PIs the lower is c, its marginal cost, little else can be shown, as the gain in profits from allowing PIs is non-monotonic in a and a^*.

In the analysis above it was assumed that the legitimate domestic license-holder had no interest in prohibiting PIs: while the possibility of PIs affects profits earned in the domestic market, these can be entirely appropriated by the parent company through its licensing fee. While an unanticipated change of PI regime would have an impact on the subsidiary, in a fully-specified equilibrium the optimal PI regime would be fully anticipated. The trigger for a regime change could be, as noted, a liberalisation of a country's trade policy (perhaps through bilateral or multilateral agreement).

The New Zealand experience following PIs liberalisation was that considerable opposition was expressed by domestic holders of foreign IPRs. This suggests (correctly, as it turns out) that the liberalisation was not anticipated. In such a setting, where licence fees have been paid in anticipation of PI prohibitions, there will be a once-off wealth loss to domestic IPR holders when PIs are permitted. If the domestic government has agreed not to impose tariffs but is motivated by a concern for the profitability of the domestic IPR holder, it is a simple matter (see KR Appendix) to see that PIs might not be attractive. As in Result 3 above, a free-trade government that cares only about consumers will permit PIs. But a government that cares only for domestic profits will prohibit PIs. Furthermore, some manipulations show that the gain from prohibiting PIs is monotonically increasing in the weight placed on domestic profits so there is a range of such weights under which PIs would be prohibited.

A second political economy scenario to consider is one based on the common agency model exposited in [2]. In this model the domestic government chooses its PI regime and its tariff subject to lobbying by industry interests. To make the problem tractable suppose that it is the foreign monopolist who lobbies the domestic government directly, rather than through the medium of a domestic licensee.[21] While this structure differs somewhat from that of [2] in that it allows for foreign lobbying, it is similar to − if somewhat simpler than − [4].

The home country government seeks to maximise $U = \lambda + \gamma[\text{CS} + \text{GR}]$ where CS denotes consumers' surplus, GR denotes government revenue, λ is a lobbying payment and γ is the weight placed by the government on economic welfare. The timing is as follows: the monopoly producer first determines its lobby contribution, λ; second, the government sets a tariff and decides whether or not to permit parallel imports and finally the market clears.[22] By Proposition One of [4], an equilibrium to this game will involve a trade policy

---

[21] Little is changed through this simplification, as a domestic licensee would be susceptible to the international IPR holder extracting the former's entire surplus through the license fee.

[22] Technically, the lobbying contribution is a schedule of offers $C(\alpha, t)$ dependent on the subsequent trade policy actions, α and t, of the government where $\alpha \in$ {allow PI, prohibitPI} and $t \in [\underline{t}(\alpha), t^{\text{p}}]$ where $\underline{t}(\alpha)$ is the (negative) tariff that yields a zero price to consumers and t^{p} is the prohibitive tariff. The government then selects α and t and the firm contributes the corresponding λ. So apparent

choice that maximises the joint welfare of the IPR holder and the government and the lobby payment is simply a transfer that affects the distribution of that joint surplus across the two players. The monopolist's payoff here is its joint profits in both the home and foreign countries ($\Pi = \pi + \pi^*$) as profits in the foreign market are affected by domestic tariff policy when PIs are permitted. The home country government's payoff is the value of consumers' surplus plus revenues: $\gamma[CS + GR]$.

Unsurprisingly, in light of Results 3 and 4 above, maximising the sum of total profits and government welfare may or may not favour PIs. We know from [5] that PIs would maximise global surplus in this setting: with low demand dispersion all markets are still served and with linear demands total output is unchanged. But in the current exercise foreign consumer surplus is ignored and prohibition of PIs may be attractive if the weight on domestic surplus (γ) is sufficiently low. It may also be attractive if aggregate profits from price discrimination are sufficiently great. Whether PIs are prohibited or allowed, the structure of this problem is such that the entire surplus from the lobbying relationship is extracted by the firm – it will set its lobbying payment such that the government's surplus is reduced to its reservation level in each case.

The case of greatest interest here is where, in the absence of lobbying, PIs would be permitted but they are prohibited in the political equilibrium. If it is optimal for the government to permit PIs in the absence of lobbying then setting the optimal tariff as in Section 2 allows one to solve for government welfare (see KR Appendix). But when PIs are prohibited, the optimal tariff with lobbying is given by:

$$t = \frac{\gamma - 2}{3\gamma - 2}(a - c) \tag{5}$$

which varies from a large subsidy at low γ[23] through free trade at $\gamma = 2$ up to the optimal no-lobbying tariff in the limit as γ goes to infinity. One can then calculate the surplus achieved by the government in the presence of lobbying and thus derive the level of lobby payments from the monopoly that drives government surplus down to that which prevails absent lobbying.

Turning to the firm and calculating its profits in the absence (and facing PIs) and in the presence of lobbying (with PIs excluded, the optimal tariff given in (5) and the lobbying payment just calculated), it can be shown that solutions in which $\lambda > 0$ and the firm is, indeed, better off in the lobbying outcome, do exist; i.e. where

---

issues of time consistency (that the government would renege, given λ) do not arise.

[23] Second-order conditions for the government's problem hold unambiguously at the tariff specified only if attention is confined to the case of $\gamma > 2/3$, as is done henceforth. Further, at $\gamma = 1$ the optimal tariff is $-(a-c)$ which yields a domestic price of $p = c$.

$$\Pi|_{\text{lobbying, no PIs}} - \Pi|_{\text{PIs, no lobbying}} - \lambda > 0 \qquad (6)$$

In such a case PIs would be permitted in the absence of lobbying but are excluded in the political equilibrium. The monopoly captures the entire surplus from this arrangement, however, although it transfers a lobby payment to the domestic government.

When is this more likely? A government allowing PIs *sans* lobbying is more likely the smaller is a^* relative to a (as the fall in price following PIs is then greater) but the prohibition of PIs in the lobbying equilibrium is then also more likely as the relative profitability of price discrimination is greater. Similarly, prohibition of PIs in the lobbying equilibrium is more likely the lower the weight placed on consumer welfare, γ, as lobby payments are then relatively more significant and the effective weight placed on aggregate profits is increased.

5 Conclusion

This chapter started by noting that recent policy reforms by a number of countries have involved relaxing restrictions on parallel imports and that it has frequently been small countries that have liberalised in this fashion. We then summarised the argument from [8] that, in a simple price discrimination model where countries choose their parallel importing regime simultaneously and non-co-operatively, any Nash equilibrium is effectively one of global parallel importing. This perhaps renders less surprising the observation that policy-makers globally are sympathetic to grey markets, despite their ambiguous consequences for global welfare.

Still, that result begs the question of why we do not then observe all countries permitting parallel imports. One explanation, of course, is that parallel imports may be driven by more than arbitrage across a discriminating monopolist's markets. Even in the latter setting, however, a number of other qualifications and extensions, which would temper this stark and rather stylised result, suggest themselves. We argued that allowing prohibitions on re-exports renders PI policy redundant, for instance. While the ability to set tariff policy might also seem to be an extension that could undermine this result, we presented the results of [3] which show, in a model in which a country chooses both its PI regime and its trade policy, that allowing PIs is still always (weakly) attractive to a country whether or not it is also setting a tariff. Considering political economy arguments, however, demonstrates that the attractions of allowing PIs can be overcome by other considerations, notably a sufficient concern for (i) the profits of domestic license holders, or (ii) the political contributions of the global monopolist.

Finally, while these final arguments have been made in the context of a simple linear model, the intuition for them does not seem to depend on that linearity. The most significant feature of the KR model is that allowing PIs leads to a lower optimal tariff against the monopolist and this is a consequence of the fact that a price reduction induced by a tariff under PIs must be extended to all markets, not just the domestic market. This is a very general property.

References

1. Gallini N, Hollis A (1999) A contractual approach to the gray market, International Review of Law and Economics 19: 1-21
2. Grossman G, Helpman E (1994) Protection for sale, American Economic Review 84: 833-850
3. Knox D, Richardson M (2003) Trade policy and parallel imports. European Journal of Political Economy 19 (1): 133-151
4. Konishi H, Saggi K, Weber S (1999) Endogenous trade policy under foreign direct investment, Journal of International Economics 49; 289-308
5. Malueg D, Schwartz M (1994) Parallel imports, demand dispersion and international price discrimination, Journal of International Economics 37: 167-195
6. Maskus K, Chen Y (1999) Vertical price control and parallel imports. World Bank, Policy Research Working Paper 0-2035. Also, Review of International Economics, forthcoming
7. Michael J (1988) A supplemental distributive channel? The case of US parallel export channels, Multinational Business Review 6: 24-35
8. Richardson M (2002) An elementary proposition concerning parallel imports, Journal of International Economics 56: 233-245
9. Tirole J (1988) The theory of industrial organisation, MIT Press: Cambridge, MA

Contributing Authors

Scott Bradford   Brigham Young University, UT, U.S.A.
Kong P. Chen   Academia Sinica, Taipei, Taiwan
Satya Das   Indian Statistical Institute, New Delhi, India
Fumio Dei   Kobe University, Kobe, Japan
Gil S. Epstein   Bar-Ilan University, Tel Aviv, Israel
Arye Hillman   Bar-Ilan University, Tel Aviv, Israel
Jota Ishikawa   Hitotsubashi University, Tokyo, Japan
Seiichi Katayama   Kobe University, Kobe, Japan
Kazuharu Kiyono   Waseda University, Tokyo, Japan
Sajal Lahiri   University of Southern Illinois, Carbondale, U.S.A.
Ngo Van Long   McGill University, Montreal, Canada
Cheng Z. Qin   University of California, Santa Barbara, U.S.A.
Larry D. Qiu   Hong Kong University of Science and Technology, Hong Kong
Martin Richardson   Australian National University, Canberra, Australia
Heinrich Ursprung   University of Konstanz, Konstanz, Germany
Makoto Yano   Keio University, Tokyo, Japan

Index

Druck: betz-druck GmbH, D-64291 Darmstadt
Verarbeitung: Buchbinderei Schäffer, D-67269 Grünstadt